Triumphs, Trophies and Troubles

Peter Bills is a former rugby columnist for both the *Irish Independent* and *Belfast Telegraph* and the author of 22 books, including *Passion in Exile: 100 years of London Irish RFC*. He is also the author of the 2018 worldwide best-selling book on the New Zealand All Blacks *The Jersey*, which reached No. 1 in New Zealand's bestseller lists and No. 2 in Ireland. His most recent book is *Le Coq: A Journey to the Heart of French Rugby*.

Triumphs, Trophies and Troubles

In Search of the Soul of Irish Rugby

PETER BILLS

ALLEN&UNWIN

First published in hardback in Great Britain in 2025
by Allen & Unwin, an imprint of Atlantic Books Ltd.

Photography credits: Endpaper photo of Westport RFC, Carrowholly by
Conor McKeown; all other featured images courtesy of the author.

10 9 8 7 6 5 4 3 2 1

A CIP catalogue record for this book is available from the British Library.

Hardback ISBN: 978 1 80546 138 8
E-book ISBN: 978 1 80546 139 5

Printed and bound by CPI (UK) Ltd, Croydon CR0 4YY

Allen & Unwin
An imprint of Atlantic Books Ltd
Ormond House
26–27 Boswell Street
London
WC1N 3JZ

www.atlantic-books.co.uk

MIX
Paper | Supporting
responsible forestry
FSC
www.fsc.org   FSC® C171272

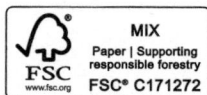

In Memory of Tony O'Reilly
7 May 1936 to 18 May 2024

A commentator wrote…

*'He was a hero from a time when Ireland
was short of heroes.'*

Contents

CONTENTS

Foreword by
Ollie Campbell

> It is here that patience and humility course through the veins; this is where character is demanded; these are the people for whom honesty of effort is valued above all else; here is the spirit, the determination to succeed; and here you will find the camaraderie that sets us apart; this is our land and it is all of this that we are proud to represent. This is rugby country.

These are the inspiring words of the Guinness advert that first appeared on our TV screens promoting Irish rugby about a decade or so ago.

For over 150 years, rugby has been an integral part of the sporting life of this country. When I began playing rugby in Belvedere College in Dublin (when a try was worth just 3 points!) rugby in Ireland was viewed as elitist and largely restricted to fee paying schools. Limerick was, of course, an honourable exception to this. It has always been said that rugby there was played by all classes – from dockers to doctors.

Back then who could have imagined that rugby would have the profile or the popularity it has in Ireland today, where it is passionately played, watched and followed by so many boys and girls and men and women throughout the whole island.

It is said that winning solves everything, and the fact that in the past 25 years or so Ireland has enjoyed unprecedented success has been a major driving force in making the game so popular, with the men's team winning three Grand Slams and the women's team one in that period, not to forget the two recent consecutive men's U20 Grand Slams and their World Cup final appearance in South Africa last year, too. In addition, Ulster, Munster and Leinster have each tasted European glory with Connacht also winning the Pro12.

Michael Cusack, the legendary founder of the GAA, actually founded a rugby club in Dublin called Cusack's Academy five years before he founded the GAA. But even a visionary like him could hardly have ever imagined that one day over 80,000 people would fill the hallowed Croke Park for a rugby match, as happened when Leinster recently hosted Munster in the URC, at a time when Ireland was also ranked No. 1 in the World.

So, how did all this happen?

In what I am sure was a labour of love, this is what Peter Bills addresses in this revealing book. In his search for the soul of Irish rugby he travels the highways and byways of Ireland to meet a great cross section of male and female rugby people in many rugby clubs, big and small, as well as explores the crucial role of the schools and the provinces.

He has also interviewed some of the great and the good of Irish rugby to help throw even more light on this twenty-first-century Irish rugby revolution.

I hope you will find it as informative, as interesting and as entertaining as I did and will especially enjoy discovering how it is that Ireland can now so publicly and comfortably be referred to as 'rugby country'.

Introduction

The trophies have lain strewn at their feet, just like the conquered in times of war. In recent years, they have come in all shapes and sizes for Ireland's rugby players. The Six Nations Championship Trophy, The Triple Crown plate, the Millennium Trophy, the Centenary Quaich Trophy. And that's just for the Irish national team. What of the provinces, the likes of Leinster, Munster and Ulster, all of whom have won the European Rugby Champions Cup?

Alexander Pope's memorable quote stirs images of Ireland's rugby participants in future retirement:

> Our generals now, retired to their estates,
> hang their old trophies o'er the garden gates.
> In life's cool evening, satiate of applause.

As the year 2024 unfolded, Ireland's international rugby players could reflect upon an astonishing era of success. 'Satiate of applause', for sure.

They had won nothing in almost twenty years from 1986 to 2004. As for a Grand Slam, those Irishmen who achieved the unique feat for them for the first time back in 1948 were

1

almost all long gone when a new Ireland finally laid the bogey, winning the Six Nations Grand Slam in 2009.

But since 2004, the trophies have fairly tumbled into the grasp of eager Irishmen. There were more Grand Slams, in 2018 and 2023, with the nation also finishing as Six Nations champions (without a Grand Slam) in 2014, 2015 and 2024.

As for the ultimate cherry on the cake, Ireland sat proudly as the number one side in the world rankings from 2022 to the start of the tenth Rugby World Cup in September 2023. Not least because, in 2022, they went to New Zealand and beat the mighty All Blacks 2-1 in the three-match Test series. Then, in July 2024, they went to South Africa and beat the reigning world champions in Durban to tie the two-match series.

These remarkable, record-breaking achievements catapulted Ireland into rarefied air at the top of the world game. Yet in the late 1980s, Ireland had languished in an anonymous eighth place in the world rankings, with New Zealand in their customary first place.

Go further back than that, to 1984, and Ireland were in an undistinguished tenth position in an unofficial ranking of the world's top ten countries. Even a nation like Romania was listed above them.

This was intriguing. For decades, the country with a minuscule population sitting at the top of world rugby was New Zealand. They might have had a population of only 5.12 million even early in the twenty-first century, yet they dominated the sport throughout the twentieth century with the consistent excellence of their teams.

Until, that is, a country with an equally small population nudged them off the world rankings top spot. Ireland, north and south, could muster a combined population of just 7.1 million at the time of the 2023 Rugby World Cup.

INTRODUCTION

For many long years, New Zealand seemed to hold a mesmerising control over the men in green. From 1905 when they first met to 2016, New Zealand enjoyed an overwhelming supremacy. At one stage, Ireland had played twenty-eight Tests against them and lost twenty-seven. One match was drawn.

But from 2016 onwards, suddenly the tables were reversed. Then, with characteristic unpredictability, Ireland beat the All Blacks five times in their next eight encounters. The tormentor had been toppled; the era of tumbling trophies was nigh.

Whatever had caused this seismic change, this shifting of the rugby tectonic plates that run across the world? For it had occurred at a time when many were forecasting doom for the game in whichever land, at whatever level. With excessive physicality at times bordering on violence and legal cases mounting against some of the governing bodies concerning alleged cases of dementia, rugby had acquired an unwanted reputation for danger.

As you will read later in this book, one former Leinster CEO, asked to identify the biggest problem confronting the game of the future, replied with a single word.

Concussion.

Furthermore, the truth was that Ireland's greatest era was taking place against a backdrop of growing calamity and concern at the state of the game at club level. Indeed, financial problems in countries the world over were threatening the traditional core elements of the sport.

In England, for example, three professional Premiership clubs – Worcester, Wasps and London Irish – went to the wall in a single season, 2022/23. That left just ten clubs in English rugby's number one club competition. Then, the Jersey Reds club, Championship winners in May 2023, likewise collapsed five months later.

INTRODUCTION

In August 2024, England announced they were selling the naming rights for Twickenham Stadium, an act long refused, for about £100 million. These and other subsequent events confirmed no one could make the sums add up. Thus, images came to mind of flogging the family silver, just for survival.

In Wales, too, dwindling support, financial shortcomings and the presence of an unwanted franchise system threatened seismic change. Nor were things much better across the world in Australia where rugby increasingly struggled for a foothold on the national sporting ladder.

Then, in August 2024, came news that Ulster were facing a deficit of between £2.5 and £3 million, according to their chief executive Hugh McCaughey. Optimistically, McCaughey boldly said he expected the province 'to break even within two to three seasons'.

Fact is, if you or I ran a business and announced a deficit of up to £3 million, it's highly unlikely we would be allowed to continue trading. And as for banks owed money and asked for time to reschedule payments, forget it. As Tony O'Reilly found out to his cost.

Yet in other parts of Ireland and especially on the international scene, the game was roaring. Fuelled by the achievements of the national team and pride in their nation, Irish men, women and children flocked to the game, as players and spectators. Yet rugby was still only rated as the fourth most popular sport in the land, behind Gaelic football in first place, soccer in second and hurling third.

That rugby, with a playing population of around 160,000 in Ireland (compared to 2.2 million in England) should have seized the nation's attention, was extraordinary. Not least of the triumphs was the emergence and growing strength of women's and girls' rugby, an issue which will be dealt with in some depth later in the book.

INTRODUCTION

Successful Irish players, a champagne glass at their lips, luxury sponsored cars outside their doors and the constant target of adulatory supporters, stumbled into this new world like novices on the stage, blinded by the lights. Yet they hardly missed a beat.

True, dreams of World Cup glory in 2023 would ultimately disappear, an agonising four-point defeat to New Zealand in the quarter-finals sending Ireland home after they had beaten the eventual champions South Africa 13-8 in an earlier pool match.

A few months later, they retreated to Dublin in more disappointment, a Grand Slam campaign in the Six Nations unexpectedly derailed by England at Twickenham. Yet just a week later, Ireland beat Scotland to land another Six Nations Championship title.

By now, wherever they played, Ireland's top players took with them the best wishes and undying support of an entire nation. For they were competing vigorously and often highly successfully at rugby's top table.

Sure, you win some, you lose some. But the margins defining victory or defeat at this level were wafer-thin. Beaten by four points by the All Blacks in the World Cup. Defeated by one point by England in the 2024 Six Nations. Victors over South Africa in July 2024 by a single point.

But as the former Ulster, Ireland and British & Irish Lions wing Tommy Bowe said after Ireland's narrow defeat to New Zealand in that 2023 Rugby World Cup quarter-final: 'When I played, if we had lost the scrum battle, the battle in the air and the line-outs against New Zealand we would have lost by forty points. That all happened this time round, and they only lost by four points. They were very unfortunate.'

Quite deliberately, at around the same time as Ireland flew to France for that 2023 World Cup, I began a journey in the opposite direction. I spent time researching in Dublin, visiting renowned clubs like Monkstown, Clontarf and Trinity College, where the game had first begun in 1854.

Then, to begin my circumnavigation of Ireland, I headed up the east coast, stopping off at towns like Skerries, Balbriggan and Drogheda before going further north, past Carlingford and into Northern Ireland.

For rugby is unique in one sense alone in Ireland. It is a leading sport that is unified, played by and against teams from all over the land. Good rugby devotees of the time clung to that moniker during the Troubles that engulfed the north from the late 1960s to the late 1990s.

As I journeyed on, across the north, then to County Donegal, down the beautiful Wild Atlantic Way on the west coast to visit clubs in areas such as Sligo and the Dingle Peninsula, I stopped to take the pulse of the game at all levels. I wanted to ascertain whether there was still a future for so many clubs or whether rugby will increasingly focus only really on the top echelon with little interest beneath.

This is not a journey in search only of those with dozens of caps for Ireland or a Lions jersey, now under attack from the moths in some musty old cupboard. By no means did I seek to talk only with the biggest and the best of traditional clubs, the likes of Ballymena, Dungannon, Garryowen, Cork Constitution and Blackrock College.

There are renowned internationals included. Their views offer a variety of analyses.

But I also wanted to hear the voice of little clubs, like Oughterard beyond Galway, Inishowen, the most northerly club in Ireland, little Rugbaí Chorca Dhuibhne (Dingle) in the far west and Boyne, the product of two amalgamated Drogheda clubs in the 1990s.

I talked to the great and the good but essentially, the largely anonymous yet loyal, quietly determined hard-working rugby people, some of whom have spent decades in the service of their local clubs; simply to ensure that when their time comes to depart, they will pass on a secure, vibrant club that continues to serve its community with zeal and care.

Their stories, whether it be Nigel Carr in Belfast recounting the day he almost died (and his rugby career ended) at the hands of terrorists, or the dynamic, rugby-loving club president Anne Scott at Inishowen telling of how this game and the exceptional people it unearths helped get her through the tragic loss of her husband, comprise a potpourri of examples of how rugby changed lives. For good and bad.

On this journey, I try to answer some of the most intriguing questions of the time: how could Ireland, so small a nation and traditionally always opposed to professionalism, have masterminded so effectively the eventual road to success in a professional era?

How have they unearthed such a production line of young talent? But is there a future role for junior clubs, the long-neglected grassroots element of the sport without which there can be no serious long-term future for the game? In any country...

A final thought. Please permit this Englishman to delve deep into the annals of Irish rugby. He comes with no baggage, no prejudices or political points to enforce. My remit was to question, debate and listen. I did plenty of all three.

There is, I believe, a great value in the outsider assessing another's nation and sport. The concept worked well in *The Jersey*, my 2018 published bestseller on New Zealand rugby.

It is my hope this approach in the Emerald Isle proves equally revealing to the reader.

CHAPTER 1

The Military Men

Summer 2023. They come to meet me on a typical Belfast day. Early sunshine and its promise; scudding low clouds and rain by noon.

No matter. This is a special occasion. James Joseph McCoy, J. J. or Jimmy to one and all, and Brian McCall, once warrior brothers in the famous green jersey, have not met for twenty years. Today, at my behest, they come to Belfast to share memories of their times, days when rugby's entire future as a unified sport on this island, seemed imperilled.

They greet each other with a warm, powerful embrace. McCall has journeyed here from the country on his Harley-Davidson – 'his over-sixties, crisis time of life vehicle' – as McCoy jokes. McCall, shaven-headed, rather bulkier than in his playing days, admits it.

'It's true. Most men of my age who buy a Harley are going through a midlife crisis. You'll find the dealerships full of balding, middle-aged men.'

In his playing days for Ireland from 1985 to 1986, Brian McCall stood 6ft 3ins tall and weighed in at 17st 10lbs. But such statistics would impress few today looking for an international second row forward. He jokingly describes himself as the last of the 6ft 3in locks. At best, he'd be a No. 6, a blind side flanker. If he had the pace.

Even men once regarded as physically intimidating, like the great Willie John McBride, just don't match up in height or weight with their modern-day counterparts.

Yet height and weight alone can never override the warrior spirit. Without the latter, the former is an irrelevance. My guests this day epitomised that in their time. Listen to McCall on McCoy, his old prop forward pal.

'It was great meeting him again. I have always had a huge amount of respect for him. He was a player who never took a backward step. He was the sort of guy you go to war with. He was always a physical specimen. He was that size when he was seventeen, playing for Portora Royal School at Enniskillen. He was a beast in schoolboy rugby. After all, he's a County Fermanagh man. Tough as hell.

'Unlike me, who was flying in and out to play matches in Ireland from my UK base, Jimmy was there the whole time.' That, he added, put a unique strain and pressure on a man from the services in those days.

Likewise, tight head prop McCoy clearly has a deep respect for his old mucker. Squat, steely and wiry, with a good shock of hair, he still bears the unmistakable frame of an old prop forward.

'We shook hands and then gave each other a big hug. It was probably more like two bears hugging as we are two big men. Even though we hadn't seen each other for about twenty years it was just normal and natural, as if we had never been apart at all.'

Over lunch, they chatted about their families, health, careers, pensions. They discussed past Ulster and Irish teammates, plus the current Ulster set-up. It has to be said, the reviews of the latter were not especially complimentary.

They talked together and then to me. Then they made a firm pledge. It wouldn't be another twenty years before they met again!

For they have great memories to share. McCoy, a steely, strong prop forward made his debut for Ireland, against Wales, in 1984. He went on to win sixteen caps, his last in 1989 against New Zealand.

McCall, a moustachioed, industrious second row forward afraid of no one and nothing, won his first cap in 1985 in what would be Ireland's Triple Crown-winning team. He was strong, in body and mind.

They played alongside each other just three times, against France, England and Scotland, and featured in Ireland's 1985 Five Nations Championship and Triple Crown successes. In the 1986 match against England at Twickenham, McCall scored a try, a rare moment for lock forwards in those times.

But both players had nudged the Irish selectors by their performances for Ulster in their 1984 victory over the touring Australians at Ravenhill. An Australian team of Lynagh, Burke, Hawker, Lawton and Campese could not quell Ulster's fire and fell to a 15-13 defeat. As the Wallabies cleaned up the Grand Slam with wins over England, Scotland, Wales and Ireland – the first Australians ever to do it – the magnitude of Ulster's triumph became clearer. A commentator described McCall's performance that day as 'majestic'. They called the team the 'Ulster immortals'.

The Troubles in Northern Ireland, which began in the late 1960s and ground on until 1998 and the signing of the Good Friday Agreement, affected these two men in special ways. Even so, one, an officer in the British Army, and the other, an officer in the Royal Ulster Constabulary (RUC) came together to play international rugby for Ireland.

For each man, never mind their greatly differing backgrounds, it was the culmination of a lifelong dream. Yet the era the gods had chosen for them to climb on to the ultimate sporting stage was notorious.

Explosions of social unrest presaged explosions of a more lethal kind. Good men, women and children from all communities were dying cruel, vicious deaths. Bombs destroyed bodies, families, lives.

Yet critically, rugby ploughed on in search of its dream. What is more, its adherents mingled and forged friendships with the boys from the south, some of them from families who had long ago fought the British Army for independence. Collectively, rugby offered the nation, north and south, a template of how the different communities could come together, even amidst terrible adversity, to join forces on Ireland's behalf. To wear the famous green jersey. As McCall reflected, rugby was and still is the game that unites the nation.

From the comfort of our armchairs in a Belfast hotel room, those dark times may seem long ago. In the minds of some of today's youngsters, it is a scenario they can barely understand.

But the memories and realities, the agonising personal experiences, remain tangible for these two men. Strong they are and have always remained, even in the face of tragedy. But they struggle to forget a time when the entire pattern of their lives was dictated by events.

McCoy was a tough, nuggety prop forward for Dungannon (until 1985) and then Bangor. Lock forward McCall, later to rise to the rank of brigadier in the British Army, was taller but likewise as tough as teak. They needed to be.

McCall was based in the UK, hence his connections with the London Irish club. But whenever he flew home, to play for Ulster or, on three occasions, Ireland's national team, he was always escorted by a Garda Síochána close protection detail.

McCall is quick to pay tribute to the Garda Síochána Special Branch, without whom he says he would never have been able to play for Ireland.

'The security situation was such that the Army couldn't have agreed to the whole enterprise unless the Garda were willing to provide the security on the ground.'

But the routine was demanding. Every Saturday evening, he was flying to Dublin for Sunday training. Wherever London Irish were playing, he would find the nearest airport and book a flight to Dublin.

It sounds like great fun, but eventually it just became exhausting. So he applied for a job that was coming up at Army HQ at Lisburn. He was keen to do it. His travelling would have been cut to the minimum. But the Army turned him down, not for reasons of proficiency but security.

'They told me, "We are happy for you to fly into Dublin each weekend but we're not happy with you crossing the border in a car each weekend." So they put a stop to the job for me.'

But, as McCall acknowledges, it was the right call. Just a couple of seasons later, three of his Ulster and Irish teammates were caught up in a border bomb attack on the eve of the inaugural Rugby World Cup in 1987.

'My circumstances were unusual because after my time at university (Queen's, Belfast) I went to Sandhurst and was commissioned into the Army. When I was at university, like a lot of young men in the province, we were wild and reckless, much more so than our English counterparts. I have always felt that was the influence of the Troubles.

'We were devil-may-care because there were bombs going off and people getting shot. When you live in a society like that, it affects you.'

By the time he went to Sandhurst, McCall had played for Ireland B and was an Irish trialist. It had been many years

13

since the Army had had an international rugby player within their ranks and the likes of former Scotland international Mike Campbell-Lamerton (then still serving as a colonel) pulled him aside and promised that the Army would give him every support possible to become a full Irish international.

McCall recounted how the former Lions captain told him that his regimental side, the Duke of Wellington's Regiment, used to turn out a Regimental 1st XV during the days of National Service that was comprised entirely of internationals and British & Irish Lions.

In fact, when Campbell-Lamerton, the Lions captain in New Zealand in 1966, first joined the regiment, he couldn't get into the side. McCall remembered the honours board at the Army Stadium clubhouse in Aldershot listing all the players who had gained international honours whilst serving in the Army and how the names ceased in the early 1970s.

'But what struck me most was the Ireland board – there were huge numbers of players who had gained their Irish caps post the 1920s. Most of them were from southern Ireland. I thought to myself, *If I am going to make it, I would be the exception, an Ulsterman!*

When the moment came, when the door became open to a full Irish cap, McCall understood the debt he owed to the Garda, once he was over the border.

He knew that was crucial. 'They could easily have turned round and said to the RUC and British Army, "No, we can't provide close protection details for these guys coming down from the north." That would have been the end of it for me.'

Mind you, the Garda boys came to see the job as one to be coveted. They suddenly found themselves in the heart of the Irish rugby team.

McCall describes the close bonds that were formed with his Garda Close Protection detail. 'I'm sure that they initially

14

Brian McCall, who won three caps for Ireland in 1985 and 1986. He was a member of their 1985 Triple Crown winning side.

thought, *what on earth are we doing babysitting this Brit*, but once they realised that they were living cheek by jowl with the Irish rugby team, it soon became a much sought-after duty.'

Jimmy McCoy was invited to the wedding of one of the Garda plain clothes guys. Even to the players in those tense circumstances, there was something to smile at. 'The minders stuck out a mile in their jackets and ties. The Irish team was wearing shell suits. It couldn't have been more obvious they were police officers,' said McCoy.

'When we went down to Dublin for a training weekend, there might have been four of them there. But when it was an international weekend and the game was on, there might be twenty minders because they got in to watch the game for free.

15

'They got to go to the dinner afterwards, too. They were fighting each other for that duty. We couldn't even go for a walk without a minder.'

The protection continued when McCoy was playing a club rugby match south of the border, somewhere in the Republic like Galway. He had to notify his people at HQ in the north he was going to play rugby in the south that weekend. They would make arrangements with the Garda.

'You would arrive at the hotel and they would be there waiting.'

But familiarity with the Garda threw up a problem. McCall remembered one particular night before an England international in Dublin that summed up the relationship players had with the Garda by then. In those days, before professionalism, the six replacements on the Irish bench were allowed to go out on Friday night for a drink, if they wanted.

On this occasion, the Garda officers announced they would like to invite the guys on the bench for a wee drink. McCall thought that was fine. They had a couple of beers in a city pub and then, with the clock ticking past 11 p.m., McCall said, 'Time to go now, boys.'

But the Garda officers had other ideas. 'No, no. We want to take you to our social club for a last beer,' they said. McCall agreed but admitted later, 'As soon as we walked into that clubhouse, I realised I had made a strategic mistake. They had told everyone they were going to bring the bench guys to the club and the place was packed.'

A 'last beer' multiplied. They finally left the club at 3 o'clock on the morning of the match. Much the worse for wear.

Later that day, sitting on the bench with his pals, McCall asked, 'Do you fancy getting on today?'

'Absolutely not, I feel bloody awful,' someone replied.

Such a philosophy epitomised the era. McCall remembered his first Irish trial when he was still at university and rooming with back row forward Willie Duggan at the hotel in Dublin. Duggan was a hell of a fine player, probably the best No. 8 in the northern hemisphere at that time. But quintessentially, he was a glorious throwback to the times of fun in the game.

Born in 1950, he won forty-one caps for Ireland from 1975 to 1984, including a spell as captain. He went to New Zealand with the 1977 Lions. In Irish club rugby, he played for the Cork club Sundays Well and also Blackrock College.

He was respected by players all around the world for his fearlessness, ball handling, quality and strength.

But he was a heavy smoker and absolutely hated training.

Once, he ran on to the ground for a match against France smoking a cigarette. He passed it to the Scottish referee, a bemused Alan Hosie, as he ambled past him on to the pitch.

One of his coaches once suggested that if he gave up smoking he would be faster around the field, to which Duggan replied, 'Ah yes, but then I would spend most of the match offside.'

In January 1977, together with the Welsh lock Geoff Wheel with whom he enjoyed a lively 'how's your father' type of punch-up, he became the first player to be sent off in a Five Nations international. But according to his fellow Irish forward Moss Keane, Duggan did not consider himself to have been sent off, simply being asked by the referee, 'Would he mind leaving the field.' He is said to have replied, 'Sure, not at all. I was buggered anyway.'

Apocryphal or not, the tale tells everything of Duggan. Brian McCall said, 'What an experience that night was in the Dublin hotel. He was smoking in the room, smoking everywhere. They said he was getting through sixty a day.'

But his faith in Duggan as a player was confirmed when he watched Ireland's first match of the Five Nations Championship a week or two later. 'Duggan was the standout player. Some people just had the talent. Duggan was a wonderful guy and a great character.'

But the stark reality of everyday life in the north, especially for McCoy as a serving officer in the RUC, washed away the smiles, like the tide on sand. They travelled around the province in unmarked cars as well as Army vehicles. Sometimes, they had to do searches, route clearances in conjunction with the Army. Occasionally, they would be flown into a dangerous area by helicopters, alleviating the risks of approaching the border on foot, by road or field.

'You would be walking up a road looking for trip wires. You knew the terrorists could be watching you. So the thought was always there. Sometimes, you had to search a house at four or five in the morning. A light would go on when we banged on the door and someone inside would say, "Oh, they have brought the big feckin' rugby player." They knew me through the game.'

At the end of the day, back in RUC barracks or HQ, McCoy would ponder a short time and reflect on his day. 'You always had one overriding thought: *There's another shift over.*

'Perhaps it is only now that I realise I was quite lucky. A lot of people did lose their lives. You knew that people were always watching. It could have happened. It didn't happen to me, but it did to a lot of other people.'

Not least when a barrage of mortars rained down on an RUC base at Newry, near the border, in February 1985. The attack killed nine RUC officers and injured another forty. McCall remembered, 'I know for a fact, that day of the Newry bombing what J. J. went through.

'I saw him that morning in the Shelbourne Hotel in Dublin and emotionally, he was completely in bits. The guys that died weren't necessarily his best mates. But he would have known all of them. And he could easily have been there himself.'

McCoy nodded, sadly. 'I was not personal friends with any of the victims. But I knew a lot of those guys who were killed.'

It was the closest he ever came to standing down from a game. He wrestled with his decision for some while. But his love for rugby and firm conviction that it had to continue as a sport of unity, made his decision for him.

He said later, 'People forget so many police officers were playing club rugby through all this. They were crossing the border every weekend to play the game. We had no problem with opposition players and that worked both ways. We would slag each other off and call one another names. But there wasn't any bother; it was good-natured craic.'

McCall concurred. 'We played with a lot of the guys from down south at underage levels for Ireland. Those guys from the south were great friends and we got to know them very well. We came through the age groups together. So it wasn't a case of the rest of the Irish team suddenly having to get to know an RUC man or a British Army officer – we had all known each other from schoolboy rugby.'

Thus, somehow, rugby carried on. North and south of the border. By doing so, by mixing freely and sharing fun with their pals whatever their background, wherever they lived and whichever school they had attended, they were demonstrating rugby's age-old creed: this is a game for all people, all sizes and classes, whatever their background or circumstances. It is a game that unites, not divides, people.

McCall said, 'It is a truism that men who have shared physical hardship together form closer bonds than those that haven't. Any successful rugby team that endures physical (and mental) hardship and has to show courage and bravery, comes together. It's the classic 'Band of Brothers' thing.

When you see these guys again, you just pick up where you left off.'

McCall insists there was never a danger that rugby would split, that cross-border journeys and relationships would fracture. 'If the bad boys had targeted rugby, it would have been a massive own goal because rugby is the one true sport in Ireland that unites a nation. Cricket is a united Ireland sport, but it doesn't have the gravitas rugby enjoys.

'They have talked for years about the football teams being united. But that will never happen.

'Every time the Irish rugby team plays, it unites the nation. It brings everyone together from all over Ireland; north and south. There is no other sport that does it to that extent.'

Ironically, the violence aimed at Belfast city centre offered rugby clubs in other towns a paramount opportunity to do what rugby clubs have always done. Bring people together.

'Clubs in places like Malone and Armagh were places of safety to go for a drink, certainly compared to the pubs of Belfast. People wouldn't go into the centre of Belfast; it wasn't safe. So they stayed out at the clubs,' said McCoy.

McCall highlighted the mixing of the communities. 'When you were outside Belfast, particularly at small clubs near the border, quite often you had a little bit of cross community. There might have been half a dozen players in the club who were Catholics, GAA guys. That was wonderful. Otherwise, it was absolute opposites. There was nothing in the middle.

'In Armagh, and at clubs like Enniskillen, you would have some guys from a GAA background and you were able to socialise with them. That was a godsend. It wasn't going on anywhere else in society.'

You can hardly expect men like Jimmy McCoy to forget those times. Especially his own near miss, in terms of proximity to a violent death. The prop forward who still has a handshake more like a mincer than a human hold, had been a serving officer in the RUC based at Dungannon on the tough west side of the town. 'I was in Dungannon for a number of years. It was fairly hairy at times, and you had to be careful where you trod.'

Mixing rugby with work was hard enough. Add on the mental toll of knowing your life was constantly on the line and you have the potential for serious exhaustion, mental and physical. He would go and do a training session with Ulster and afterwards clock in around 11 p.m. for a night shift with the RUC that didn't end until 7 a.m.

Some nights, if he was lucky, he'd start at 11 p.m. and finish early at 3 a.m. so he could go and get some sleep before a big game the next day.

He was in Dungannon one day, out on the beat, when he got a call on his radio and a curt message. 'A car is coming. It will pick you up.' The line went dead.

'The car came almost instantly and I got inside. The chief inspector was sitting there and said, 'A threat has come in and you're no longer working in Dungannon.'

A credible threat had been uncovered targeting the big rugby man's life. He wasn't married at the time and admits he was somewhat gung-ho. 'I didn't worry about it and I never went into the details of the threat. But apparently it was for real.

'With hindsight, it was probably always going to happen. They couldn't stand by and let me walk around in a police uniform when I was known through my rugby.'

McCoy had a sister living in North Down, almost 50 miles away, and he was whisked away to stay there. He arrived on St Patrick's Day, 17 March 1985. He found a new life in more ways than one.

'I found a huge difference in terms of policing when I moved from Dungannon. It was like night and day. People in

Bangor would call into the station and say, "A seagull has just pooped on my washing."

'When you got a call at Dungannon maybe reporting an accident, we would have to check and make sure it was safe to go out there and there were no booby traps.'

McCoy served twenty-two years in Bangor and admitted that when he retired, he thought the threat was over. After all, Ireland is like a different country now in so many ways, compared to the 1970s and 1980s. Likewise, Belfast is a transformed city.

Yet he concedes, even at Bangor, there were still threats. 'Out in the country, people notice things. There's a stranger in town – what car is he driving? Take Brian. People would know he is Army-trained from the way he walks. People note these things. So if you've no need to go to these places, why would you?

'As for Belfast, there are still places I wouldn't go there.'

McCall echoed his old friend's sentiments. 'Life now is immeasurably better in the province, but if you want to be totally accurate, there still is a threat. It's not a very big one but there still is that threat. They haven't all gone away. The bad people are still there, lurking in the shadows. It would be foolish of me not to acknowledge that.

'In 2023, a police officer in Omagh thought he was safe coaching kids at football. You think you are safe, but you never know.'

This is what they live with, the everyday reality of their lives.

On the evening of 23 February 2023, Detective Chief Inspector John Caldwell was loading up footballs into his car, with his young son, after taking a training session for local youngsters. Caldwell was shot multiple times by three gunmen and suffered 'life-changing' injuries.

'It brings back hard memories for the people of this town,' said a local woman.

McCall remembered the time back in 1972 when he was just a wee lad. He'd bought an old motorcycle for use on the family farm and needed to get some parts for it.

'The motorcycle shop in Armagh was on the other side of town, if you understand what I mean by that phrase.'

McCall went to the Royal School, Armagh and after school one day, he set off to the shop for the parts. 'A man was standing outside. He would have been about thirty-five years old. He said, "Where are you going?"

'I said, "I'm going to Danny McShane's motorcycle shop."

'He said, "No you're not. Fuck off back to your side of the town."

'I have never forgotten that. I was twelve years old and shit-scared. I didn't even know there were different sides of the town.'

Is that hatred still there, on both sides? McCoy admitted, 'In certain areas, there are still families entrenched in their views. But overall, not as much.'

McCall shrugged. 'There are hard-core elements that will never change on both sides.'

McCoy conceded it was still there. But he said, 'It is a triumph that rugby stayed united. There were lots of rugby guys killed from both sides of the communities.'

McCall remembers especially Henry Livingstone of Armagh, a man he called a big bachelor farmer, a prop forward and a real gentleman. 'When you joined the club straight from school, he always kept an eye out for the youngsters.'

He was a farmer in what McCall termed 'a very nationalist area' and was in a barn feeding the cattle one morning. 'Gunmen came on to the farm and shot him dead. His death was pure ethnic cleansing. He was a lovely gentle giant of

23

a man, only about thirty-eight or forty. He was just an easy target.'

It happened on both sides. Such acts devastated and broke hearts in both communities. Of course, rugby clubs suffered, just like anywhere else.

Yet somehow life went on. It had to, even against such a background. Rugby clubs, for example, worked harder on their cross-border relationships, determined to retain the unity they enjoyed with clubs from the north or south. As McCall said, 'There might have been rioting on the Falls Road but people in Stormont were having cocktail parties the same night. Life went on. It had to.'

McCoy grimaced at some of his memories from those times. 'I attended a couple of horror scenes after explosions, picking up and putting parts of bodies in bags. It was your job, you had to do it. Once, a senior officer was leading the recovery of body parts but we could not find the head. We had to look everywhere to find it. We did, in the end.

'Luckily, I had rugby as a release. I had to go and train and play. It didn't blanket your mind completely, but it dulled the senses a bit.'

Just a bit.

But now, today, around fifty years after those times, Ireland and rugby union have taken quantum leaps forward.

They put up the 'Sold out' signs for the big games at the RDS in Dublin, at Thomond Park and in Ulster. There is always a lively crowd at The Sportsground in Connacht.

Yet what is the true legacy of those men of the 1960s, 1970s and 1980s? Can we say they left Ireland's rugby team in a better place than when they first encountered it? Or were other events and powerful voices critical to steering Irish rugby on to sunlit uplands it had scarcely dared to dream of all those years ago?

In assessing the health of this unified sport in a land where at times unity seemed to be hanging on by little more than a thread, we must examine each level, whichever part of this island we are considering. Only by talking to rugby people of all backgrounds from both communities, those charged with ensuring the ongoing progress and prosperity of the game overall, can we glean a true picture of the state of the sport in Ireland.

CHAPTER 2

Monkstown: Proudly Contributing

In the mid-1850s, Irishmen were achieving some extra-ordinary things all around the world.

Take Charles Davis Lucas, a native of Poyntzpass, County Armagh. On 21 June 1854, during the Crimean War, Lucas was on board HMS *Hecla* as she fired at the shore defences of Bomarsund, a fort off the Finnish coast in the Baltic Sea.

Guns in the fort returned fire and a live shell landed on the deck of the ship, its fuse still fizzing. Immediately, every man flung himself flat in an attempt to minimise the effects of the inevitable explosion.

But Lucas, just twenty years of age and a Master's mate, had other ideas. Dashing forward, he picked up the shell and hurled it overboard. It had barely hit the water when a mighty explosion shook all the ships close by.

It might have given any passing fish a bit of a headache. But on HMS *Hecla*, not a man was killed or seriously wounded. For his act, the young Royal Navy officer was instantly promoted to lieutenant. More importantly, he became the first recipient of the Victoria Cross, the highest award for gallantry in the face of the enemy that can be awarded. Fewer than 1400 recipients worldwide have since won the medal.

Lucas would go on to become a rear admiral and live until he was eighty.

By 1854, Irishmen made up around 35 per cent of the British Army. They came from towns and villages all over Ireland to sign up. More than 30,000 served in the Crimean War and in all, Irish-born soldiers and seamen won twenty-eight Victoria Crosses in that conflict, a remarkable testimony to their courage and bravery.

Meanwhile, 1854 was proving a memorable year in other ways, too. At 21 Westland Row, Dublin on 16 October that year, a son was born to Sir William Wilde and his wife, Jane. The new baby was named Oscar.

But the background to these times was distressing. The Great Famine that raged from 1845 to 1852 had cost the lives of around 1 million people. Another million fled. In fact, between 1845 and 1855, at least 2.1 million people left Ireland. A report of the time stated: 'Dublin has the worst living conditions in Europe.' Poverty and disease were omnipresent.

A strange time, then, you might think for a group of young men to come together and make the first attempts to introduce a new game into Ireland. It was called rugby football and it was brought into the country at the start of the 1850s by students returning home from public schools and universities in England.

The first organised club was Dublin University, formed in 1854, followed just a few years later by a new club in the north, North of Ireland Football Club (NIFC) in 1868. Queen's University Belfast followed a year later and back in Dublin, the Wanderers club was founded the same year.

Early enthusiasm for the game was such that clubs began to shoot up like mushrooms in the night. Another Dublin club, Lansdowne, was set up in 1872/73, with Dungannon established the same year. Others, like County Carlow,

University College Cork and Ballinasloe all quickly followed.

The game was taking off all over Ireland.

By the end of 1874, the Irish Football Union had been formed to administer the game. They wasted little time in arranging a first international match. In early February 1875, having boarded a steamer at Dublin docks, a group of intrepid young Irishmen set out for London and a rugby match against England. It was played on 15 February at Kennington Oval in London. England won 7-0 against an Irish side that contained twelve players from Leinster and eight from Ulster.

But the chief curiosity was that each side fielded twenty players. It would be three more years before playing numbers came down to fifteen a side.

In those early times, separate bodies administered the game in different regions: the Irish Football Union with jurisdiction over clubs in Leinster, Munster and parts of Ulster. But the Northern Football Union of Ireland, formed in 1875, was in charge of clubs in the Belfast area.

That was until 1879 when the IRFU was formed as an amalgamation of the two different bodies. The same year, both Leinster and Munster were inaugurated.

England were keen to cement early relationships on the rugby field. They travelled to Dublin in 1876 and 1878, winning both matches. In fact, Ireland would have to wait until 1887 for their first victory over England.

Young Irishmen, like young men in France, Wales, Scotland, England and other nations, took to the game for its physical challenge and commitment. They liked, too, the sense of comradeship and fun once the final whistle had been blown.

Rugby was the new sport in town. Its almost instant popularity ensured it was a game here to stay.

Another Dublin club formed around that time was Monkstown, in 1883. Their golden age was probably from when they were founded until the First World War. Tragically, in that conflict, this one club alone lost eighty members. It is a harrowing statistic.

Their fall from favour, post 1918, was in part due to the huge loss of members, but may also have had something to do with their strong ties with the British Army and the changing political landscape in Ireland with the struggle for independence.

The club has also struggled due to its location which is within a 500-metre radius of six well-established and successful clubs, including Wanderers and Lansdowne.

You couldn't really accuse Monkstown of hogging the headlines. When they became the first club to win the Division 4 title of the All-Ireland League in 1994, it was their first senior trophy since 1902.

By then, others had emerged to make any time in the spotlight desperately short for Monkstown. Belvedere came late to the party; it was a closed, Old Boys club, for a long time. Of course, there were others too, the likes of Blackrock and Wesley, who shared a ground with Bective.

Monkstown also suffered because they had few links to dedicated feeder schools. Yet, here we are, 142 years later, and they're still around, still contributing. What is more, you sense they have found their place at the rugby table. As their 2023/24 president, David O'Brien, said, 'We have always been a club that doesn't take itself too seriously.'

Yet they have a reputation for great hospitality, a point to which many will concur. Now they're an AIL Senior club again.

They will probably never have a powerful rugby-playing school, a Blackrock College, feeding in so much of its talent to the club structure. After all, Blackrock's record in Irish rugby school circles is legendary. They have won by far the most Leinster Schools trophies in their history. And their alumni is to be envied. Brian O'Driscoll might be arguably the most famous but myriad others have progressed from the school's 1st XV to an Ireland international place.

Monkstown won't be at the top of the AIL Division 1 year after year. Nor will there be a cluster of Monkstown men lining up in the national colours.

But does any of that matter? Was it not the wish of the founding members that a great old club such as this should offer its members something beyond the single-minded pursuit of winning trophies over the years? Were not elements such as friendship, comradeship, fun and fitness the values the original club founders treasured more than anything?

I will tell you a short story to illustrate my point. Just around the end of the decade of the noughties, about 2009/10, a young man from England went to Dublin to spend eighteen months working for a company in the oil business.

He didn't know anybody much and he found the guys where he'd rented a room in a house preoccupied with their own friends and contacts. After about six weeks, he rang his home back in England and admitted he wasn't enjoying the experience. He hadn't made any friends, didn't know anyone and felt pretty homesick.

'Isn't there a rugby club quite near where you're staying?' his father asked him.

'Well, yes, Monkstown is very close. I pass it most days,' was the reply.

'Right,' said his father. 'Get yourself along there with a pair of boots, sign up to play and you'll make friends for life.'

Fast-forward to the weekend before he was due to return to England, eighteen months later. His pals at Monkstown knocked on his door after work, told him he had five minutes to pack a bag for an overnighter and they all set off by car for County Donegal. The group of them stayed the weekend at the house of one player's parents. And they sat up all night on the beach, cooking food, downing beers, watching the first streaks of the sunrise and chewing the cud about life and the future.

It was their gift to him to celebrate a quintessential rugby friendship.

Two days later, the young man was, figuratively speaking, dragged kicking and screaming on to the plane back to London. He just didn't want to leave. But he never forgot his Monkstown mates. More than a decade later, when he got married in the UK, he invited a group of his Irish friends over to the wedding. Friendships of this kind endure. Very often, for life.

More than a century earlier, Monkstown had found themselves supporting the family of another young man from their playing ranks. But these were very different circumstances. Jasper Thomas Brett, a member of the Monkstown club, won his first cap for Ireland as a nineteen-year-old wing three-quarter.

He played against Wales in 1914, a match Ireland lost 11-3, at Cardiff Arms Park. Tragically, it would be the last match either nation played before the First World War and the only international cap won by Brett.

When war broke out, he signed up with the British Army, serving as a 2nd Lieutenant in the 7th Battalion of the Royal Dublin Fusiliers. Sadly, he suffered shell shock. On a later trip home on leave, two days before he was due to return to the front line, he committed suicide by gunshot at Dalkey, outside Dublin. When he died in February 1917, he was just twenty-two.

Rugby friends from Monkstown were among those who gathered around to offer what consolation they could. It is what rugby does. This story epitomises the role clubs like Monkstown have always played in their community.

Of course, none of this minimises the task of keeping the club in good order. Season after season. Last year, David O'Brien found himself with a multitude of tasks at the club he has known all his adult life. O'Brien is a Monkstown man through and through. He played in the 3rds and 2nds, and occasionally for the first team, especially the latter when he became captain.

'I had an absolute ball over the years,' he reflected.

But since retirement from playing, his involvement has ramped up significantly.

He has been club welfare officer and then took over the role of club secretary for a while. He then became president, fully understanding the realities of that job. He could anticipate attending twenty-six dinners during the course of the season, at various rugby clubs across Leinster.

'We all get to meet the other suckers nominated as presidents,' he laughed.

'I am just the same as a lot of other officials at our club and a host of other clubs. You do all sorts of things for your club when you get involved. I wrote some stuff for the club programme, got involved with fundraising and a host of other things. All the volunteers at these clubs do this kind of work behind the scenes.

'People put in monumental shifts over the years at unknown numbers of junior clubs. Then, with all those dinners, it gets busier and busier. In all, I would estimate during my peak time contribution, spending approximately three to four days a week collectively working for the club. Over the whole season, it would average out at two days a week.

'But most of that is spent socialising which is one of the reasons you put yourself forward to be president!!'

That is some commitment which begs a question. Who is coming through from the recently retired playing ranks at clubs like Monkstown to fill those roles in the years to come?

The club has around 250 non-playing members and perhaps another 250 members in their minis section. Then there would be forty-five to fifty squad players for their two senior sides. The minis are thriving, but they don't yet have a women's section, although it is something they're working on.

Yet the extent of David O'Brien's involvement indicates the shortage of one-time club members willing to get involved in administrative roles, years later. It is a problem widely encountered in modern-day sports clubs. There are fewer numbers offering their services, either on or off the field. Many clubs are in the same boat. That is partly due to other distractions in modern life, like watching sport on TV, or greater access to all manner of events and interests.

But O'Brien also points the finger at some key factors in this scenario.

'At the moment, we have a situation where the rugby-playing schools prevent kids from playing for their local clubs. That applies even if you have had those kids from Under-6s upwards. I have had personal experience of that.

'My son was in the Under-14s but we had to dissolve that group because their school told them they couldn't play for their clubs. It was made clear to them that if they were caught playing club rugby, they would be dropped from their school team.

'To me, that sends a very strange message to kids.'

Perhaps there is an explanation for this. Senior rugby-playing schools have made massive investments in technology and equipment. Their training regime, says O'Brien, is almost on a par with the professional outfits. Every aspect of the player's performance is analysed with match reports and personalised video analysis of their match play provided for them every

Monday morning. As well as a nutrition and gym programme, they are given weekly updates on the aspects of the game that they have to work on.

It doesn't get much more professional than this, is O'Brien's view.

'But it is of concern because these schools are excluding from clubs a lot of youngsters who would otherwise be playing for us at various age levels. But the sport is not a sport if people are not participating. Where will all the alickadoos of the future come from if kids are not allowed to participate and become involved?

'It is certainly my view, despite our failure to progress beyond the quarter-finals of the 2023 Rugby World Cup (again), that the IRFU is doing an amazing job in managing the professional game. We are punching well above our weight given rugby in Ireland is ranked fourth in terms of team sports, well behind football, Gaelic football and hurling/camogie.

'What is of concern is that adult participation at a club level has declined considerably, from our club fielding five to six adult teams when I joined after school in 1986 to a point where we were struggling to field two in 2023. The population has grown substantially, the sport is gaining considerable exposure and spectators flock to see Ireland, Leinster, Munster, Connacht and Ulster. But it does not translate to participation.

'The IRFU may want to reflect upon this if, in a few years' time, there is a large reduction in the number of clubs. But the IRFU is unlikely to have too many concerns while they have such success at international and provincial level. As a measure of success, it cannot be disputed, but on other metrics, the picture is not so positive.

'Whilst the relative health and vibrancy of an individual club is down to the endeavours of its members, nonetheless the overall decline in participation levels of adults should be a cause of concern to the IRFU.'

It leads a lot of those involved in the amateur side of the sport to wonder whether amateur rugby would not be better served if it were regulated and run by a body separate from the IRFU, the national union.

All over Ireland, these men of rugby have thought long and hard about this. Does it serve the best interests of the amateur game to have the IRFU running both the amateur and professional games? At what cost to the game in general is the amateur part being sidelined?

O'Brien goes on: 'If Ireland keep winning, at some point the question will have to be asked. There are tensions already between the clubs and the union. Frankly, I am surprised it is not debated more hotly.'

In a sense, the recent success of the Irish national team has been something of a mask, covering up the true picture regarding the overall health of the game. There is the national team, the Leinster Schools programme and production line plus the achievements of provincial sides like Leinster and, a few years ago, Munster. These are glittering examples of success.

But the decline of so many junior clubs cannot be masked forever. For at this moment in time, the numbers do not add up in a variety of ways.

Yet amateur clubs build the base for the whole game to thrive. As my son discovered back in 2009 when, boots in hand, he walked through Monkstown Rugby Club's doors for the first time, not knowing a soul, and made friendships to last a lifetime.

It is only a special kind of sport that offers that.

CHAPTER 3

Clontarf

Getting anywhere out of Dublin by road in any direction nowadays is not one of life's great pleasures.

The traffic is endless, frequently blocked. Not just in the rush hours, either.

But rugby names of some of the great clubs in the nation's history litter the landscape. Lansdowne, Wanderers, Old Belvedere, Monkstown and Blackrock College are just some of the thirty clubs in the Dublin area alone.

Then there's Clontarf. The archetypal rugby club in the archetypal modern-day Dublin suburb.

The train heading up the east coast, to Drogheda, Dundalk and beyond, is barely slipping into another gear as it crawls through Clontarf Road station. The eye spies some pleasant, red-brick properties interspersed among a few roads of trees.

The bad news is, as in most areas around Dublin, contemporary property prices should be viewed only with a defibrillator at hand. In one orthodox Clontarf street, I saw a home, modest semi-detached, with limited proportions of 151 square metres. A snip at €925,000, the sellers would doubtless tell you.

You could get one three square metres less than that for €875,000. A real bargain.

'Viewing advised' said a banner over a picture of a bigger semi-detached, comprising four bedrooms, three bathrooms spanning 221 square metres. The asking price, €1.3 million, invited the thought that 'viewing advised' must have referred to your own bank account before you climbed into these super-exalted prices.

Whoever claimed they had slain the infamous 'Celtic Tiger' was telling us porkies (porky pies = lies, in olde London Cockney rhyming slang).

Clontarf Rugby Club was founded in 1876, the year George Custer was killed at the Battle of Little Bighorn. Back on this side of the Atlantic, just as Custer was about to make his last stand, a bunch of young Irishmen proudly representing the new Clontarf club were preparing to meet their foes in an early game.

Like many clubs early in their foundation, Clontarf swapped one playing field for another in those times. But in 1896 they moved into grounds at Castle Avenue where the Clontarf Cricket Club played. At that time, they were renting the grounds from the Vernon Estate who owned Clontarf Castle. But it wasn't until 1947 that the cricket and rugby clubs finally got to purchase the land.

But something in Clontarf long preceded the founding of the rugby club. Following the Battle of Clontarf in 1014, a castle was built on or near the present site by Hugh de Lacy, Lord of Meath, in 1172. It then became a home to the Knights Templar.

The castle passed through various hands before it was eventually surrendered to the King by Viscount Clontarf in 1541. In later years and different centuries, the castle was associated with a potpourri of names. George Frideric Handel visited several times, most notably for the premiere of his *Messiah* in 1742. The lady of the house at that time was from Hanover.

The English artist J. M. W. Turner painted the castle (although he never visited it) and the Irish rock group Thin Lizzy recorded a song on their debut album in 1971 entitled 'The Friendly Ranger at Clontarf Castle.' Dana was crowned 'Queen of Cabaret' at the castle in 1968 before winning the 1970 Eurovision Song Contest.

The modern-day version of the castle was rebuilt in 1837, the start of Victorian times. Finally, it was turned into a swish hotel in 1997. The handsome prices almost match some of those in the estate agents' windows down the road. I gulp at the cost of bed and breakfast and move on.

Teams bearing the Clontarf name and crest have won a silver mine full of trophies down the years. Yet there is a compelling argument to be made that the rugby club's finest hour came in the 1960s, in a single match. It represented Irish innovation at its best.

The fixtures secretary of the club at that time, Richie Lyons, noticed in his morning paper's sports pages a report of a match played in the UK involving the Athletic Club from Wellington, New Zealand. This was a famous club, rich in history and generous in its supply of All Blacks and Junior All Blacks to a multitude of national sides.

Lyons, no doubt with a mouthful of Clonakilty sausage and tongue firmly in cheek at the breakfast table, dashed off a short note to the New Zealanders, suggesting that they must be afraid to come to Ireland as they had no fixture scheduled there during their tour.

It was certainly true that, up to that time, no New Zealand club side had ever played a match in Ireland. Negotiations began over the cost of the team flying to Dublin, but in the end, Clontarf agreed to pay the air fares and put up the players at a variety of supporters' homes. This was how so much of rugby operated in those times, little more than fifty years ago.

The tough men of Wellington duly arrived, all brawny forearms, noses that veered left and right and a few gaps where teeth ought to have been. In other words, the traditional New Zealand rugby competitors. A few fearful locals took one look and suggested to Clontarf officials that they should invite some well-known leading players of the day from other clubs to bolster their ranks.

'Lads,' one said, 'if you don't, it'll be horrible to witness.'

After all, Athletic Club had five players in their ranks who had played against (and defeated) the touring British & Irish Lions when they met Wellington on their 1966 tour. There were a few junior All Blacks to boot.

Clontarf's finest did what the great rugby communities of Ireland had always done. Scoffed at the doom merchants and their warnings. They chose their normal 1st XV.

But then, defying the odds was their go-to position. Besides, like Baldrick in the *Blackadder* TV series, they had a cunning plan up their sleeves.

The rugby doyens of New Zealand were feted and royally entertained wherever they went. The highlight of a traditionally warm Irish welcome was scheduled for the eve of the match. A visit to the renowned Guinness brewery.

The Kiwis enjoyed their tour of the premises, the climax to which was a convivial downing of a few pints at the end. Alas, a few became a lot, a lot became too many. As Clontarf's finest clambered into their beds for an early night, some of the New Zealanders hardly saw their beds that night.

Next day, the ground at Castle Avenue trembled with excitement as Clontarf beat the mighty Athletic Club 19-16. History had been made.

Athletic captain Nev MacEwan, himself an All Black, famously remarked, 'I thought we played it hard in New Zealand. But these Clontarf boys really put it up to us.'

Undeniably, the New Zealanders had been brought down partly by too much of the original black stuff. Which, when you come to consider it, has been the all too frequent demise of visitors down the centuries. Ever since Arthur Guinness first introduced his noble brew in 1759.

CHAPTER 4

Skerries

So, on a calm, quiet Friday morning, I am heading for a town in Fingal which an early tourist reached in AD 432. Saint Patrick. The town's name is Skerries, 'Na Sceirí' in Gaelic (meaning rocky islands) and home to a grand old Irish rugby club.

Skerries was always a fishing port. The Vikings used it when they arrived and no wonder. It is an enticing, curving, horseshoe-shaped bay with small fishing boats bobbing on the water. Much, much later, the town became a centre for hand embroidery.

Just over 100 years ago, a British destroyer landed 200 troops at Skerries, following the 1916 Rising. They were intending to march to Dublin. But enterprising rebels heard of their arrival and blew up the railway bridge at Donabate, hugely impeding their progress.

But that was back in the day. Today, the man I have come to see lives quietly at the back of the town, close to Skerries railway station.

Bill Mulcahy played forty games for Leinster between 1955 and 1969, won thirty-five caps for Ireland between 1958 and 1965 and then played six Test matches for the British & Irish

Lions on their tours of New Zealand in 1959 and South Africa in 1962. What is more, he captained his country, for the first time, against England in 1962, played for Skerries for some years and later became president of the club.

He is one of THE great rugby legends of Ireland.

Like Brian McCall of later vintage, Mulcahy might have lacked a little in sheer statistics, by modern-day standards. Even as a lock forward, he stood only 6 foot and half an inch and weighed 16 stone. But he lacked for nothing as a tough, combative, ball-handling and line-out jumping second row forward.

In February 2024, he was eighty-nine years of age and the same twinkle that was in his eyes when he and his pals had so much fun on all those grand rugby occasions remained as vibrant.

Mulcahy was paired in the second row, for the first time, in 1962 against England at Twickenham with a strong, young Turk of a player from a farming background at Ballymena. Willie John McBride. Wonder what happened to him...?

Between them, the pair won ninety-eight caps for Ireland and twenty-three Test caps for the Lions. Mulcahy, the man who spent his entire working life in the medical world when he wasn't enjoying rugby, had not a single regret.

The eyes may be weaker, weeping a little at times. The hands, once powerful, muscly and intimidating on the field, are now bony and wrinkled, the skin softer. But still the impish expression comes to life as we talk of those times.

Playing for Ireland? He smiled. You would have a bit of a run-out on a Friday afternoon with a few mocked-up line-outs. Harmless stuff, he scoffed. Today, countries with millions to spend and waste on the professional game, have a run-out every afternoon. But many of them are still hopeless. At least Ireland in the professional era have progressed significantly.

What about tactics in those times? 'No, you would just play off the cuff. Other countries like Wales were better organised than we were. What we were playing in Ireland was social football. The attitude was, let's get the match over and have a good weekend.'

Ah, the innocence of it all. Fun meeting up again with pals the night before the international. Endless japes on the Saturday night after the match. No one ever took it seriously. Life wasn't like that.

He made his debut for Ireland in 1958 against Australia. He was working in Dublin at the time, so it was convenient. After the Friday afternoon run-out, they went back to the hotel and had dinner. Then, he slipped back to the hospital for a couple of hours' late work.

He went back there again on the Saturday morning for another two hours before joining the boys in the Shelbourne hotel.

The senior house doctor had his priority in life. It wasn't rugby football.

He remembers 1962 well, his first experience of captaining the Ireland team. They went to Twickenham to meet an experienced England side. Ireland chose an incredible nine new caps that day. It was the sort of thing people did in those days.

I hand Mulcahy the programme from that match. How did I have it? I saw the game, a 16-0 win for England. It was one of the first matches I ever attended at the old Twickenham.

'Hunter... L'Estrange... Gilpin... Quirke... Dick... McLoughlin... McBride... Turley... Hipwell.'

He exhaled a little air. 'Mmmmmmmm... Some of them didn't surface again after that match. I tried to forget that game. But I recall trotting back to the halfway line after one England try, for another kick-off. The guys' heads were down.

'"Where is your f***ing pride," I said?

'1962. Willie John's first cap. He was always a character. There was a bit of devilment in him, all right. He certainly had that. He was very big and athletic. We had four years together, 1962 to 1965.'

He remembered, too, the game two years later when they went back to Twickenham.

Ireland chose another new cap for that match in 1964. His name was C. M. H. Gibson and his genius, already apparent as a schoolboy at Campbell College, Belfast and then at Cambridge University, helped Ireland to an 18-5 win that famous day.

Then, a year later, came the Ireland v New Zealand match at Lansdowne Road. McBride remembered Mulcahy, his fellow lock, saying before the game, '"Look, I don't know what we are going to do today. But let's just make their lives a bloody misery. Let's just throw everything at them. Get in among them and mess them up." So that's what we did. It nearly worked. We lost 6-5 in the last minute at Lansdowne Road.'

Of course, they thought it was tough then. But compared to today? 'It doesn't compare at all,' Mulcahy cheerfully conceded. 'Mind you, the exchanges could be robust and many "digs" (punches) were given and taken.'

He realised life was rather different when he found himself trapped at the bottom of a ruck during the 1959 Lions tour of New Zealand. They met a provincial side, Horowhenua, whom the Lions were expected to beat comfortably. But they didn't do comfortable in New Zealand. Certainly not in those days.

'The boots came at me from all over. It was very aggressive, a terrible match. I identified one guy who had put his boots into me and told the referee. "Serves you right for lying on the ball," came the reply.' Mulcahy never complained again.

He was witness to one astonishing moment on that tour. The Lions were awarded a penalty and Bev Risman, their outside half, had it teed up for a shot at goal.

Just then, a policeman walked up the side of the pitch and tapped the referee on the shoulder. 'The touch judge on the far side has his flag up,' he said.

Risman went ahead and slotted the kick. After it had sailed over, the referee went over to the touch judge, had a conversation and gave the line-out.

What happened off the field, just as much as what occurred on it, was most important. Especially on a Lions tour when no one wanted to upset the locals.

The Lions tour manager to South Africa in 1962 was Naval Commander Brian Vaughan, a serviceman from England. Vaughan readily espoused the creed: mingle at every cocktail party and charm the natives. Whatever the circumstances.

After one tough, bloodied game, Vaughan approached Mulcahy back at the Lions' hotel in the town. He told him one of their opponents that day, a tough, gnarly forward who had dished it out liberally, was still back at the ground with a cut head oozing blood.

'I say, Billy,' said Vaughan. 'Would you be so good as to pop back to the ground and put a few stitches in his head?'

Mulcahy was incredulous. 'I am here to play rugby,' he replied. Even so, Vaughan's wishes prevailed. Mulcahy was taken in a taxi back to the stadium. His opponent's head was duly stitched up. 'I wasn't even licensed to practise in South Africa,' he complained, the small matter of sixty-one years later.

Even to make the tour, Mulcahy had been forced to resign his post at the hospital. When he got home, he had to find another job. 'No one would give you the time off.'

Professionalism? He is no dinosaur, lost and thrashing around in its own domain. 'Nowadays, it's hard to imagine the top levels of the game without it. Ireland were slow to agree to it. But if we didn't partake, we would have been left behind. But there was a certain amount of reluctance to be part of it.'

He believes one of the greatest highlights of his rugby days came very early on. He played his first three internationals for Ireland with his boyhood hero, fly half Jack Kyle. 'It was such a thrill for me. I had always admired him so much. He was always very humble. I called him a saintly figure; he was so nice.'

What made Kyle so special? 'He was always a great stepper, an elusive runner. He hardly ever kicked. Except that he did sometimes. Before I was chosen for Ireland, I happened to be at an international at Lansdowne Road against Wales. They had come over expecting to win the Triple Crown.

'They didn't make it, in part because Kyle dropped a goal on the West Stand side 10-yard line with his left foot. I gather it was the only drop goal he ever kicked in international rugby. We beat Wales.'

It might even have been the game before which Kyle astonished his opposite number, Cliff Morgan. As the teams lined up to go on to the field, Kyle called across, 'Have a good game today, Cliff. Enjoy it.'

I am not entirely sure, but I somehow doubt England captain Martin Johnson made it his business to pass on similarly warm greetings to his opponents before matches. Nor any members of the New Zealand sides.

Mulcahy thought the All Blacks were more physical than the South Africans in those days. He had plenty of time to study them because he arrived in New Zealand injured in 1959 after wrecking his shoulder on a concrete-hard pitch in a provincial game in Australia. That was how tours operated in those days. They took six weeks to get from the UK to Australia by boat, via the Panama Canal.

'What an experience,' Kyle told me, years later.

Mulcahy didn't aid his recovery from the injury by slipping on the washroom floor whilst wearing his steel-studded boots before an early match in New Zealand. He missed about seven weeks, yet surprisingly was asked to stay on and recovered in time to play in the fourth Test.

His fellow Irish Lions Mick English and Niall Brophy were not so fortunate. Both picked up long-term injuries and were told they had to return home. The sweetener was, they could choose their preferred method of travel. Steamer or a long, convoluted journey by air with dozens of stops.

They chose the boat and apparently had a ball of a time. Big dinners every night, plenty of female company. All expenses paid. What's not to like for a couple of healthy young sportsmen?

It was a different time. Decorum was expected, decent behaviour a given. Players could have fun but it was a pretty innocent variety. Sensitivities were to be adhered to. Which was why Mulcahy was so upset when his good friend, the 1966 Lions captain Michael Campbell-Lamerton was excoriated in an English daily newspaper.

Campbell-Lamerton was a Scotland international player and a British Army man, perfect qualifications for a Lions captain in those straight-laced times. Whether the man was good enough to be a first-choice player for the Lions' Tests was another matter. But the selectors rarely considered that. Being 'a good chap' was key to most appointments in those days.

In fact, the Scottish lock forward had become close enough to the Irishman to ask him to become godfather to his last son. 'I was very friendly with him,' said Mulcahy.

Campbell-Lamerton's extraordinary life story is worthy of a book on its own. He served for thirty-three years in the British Army, during which time he saw action in Korea, Cyprus and Northern Ireland.

In Korea, he and a friend led two platoons of the Duke of Wellington's Regiment (West Riding) during the Battle of the Hook. They were tasked with recovering positions overrun by the Chinese offensive.

By then, Campbell-Lamerton had already escaped a life-threatening injury at school when, at the age of fifteen, he was hit on the chest by a javelin in flight.

Then, during the Korean campaign, out on a foot patrol, he trod on a mine. Two things saved him – firstly, he heard the faint click and remained still, not lifting his foot. The second factor was, by chance, a corporal alongside him had worked in bomb disposal and managed to make the mine safe.

Then, three years later serving during the EOKA campaign in Cyprus, he fell 60 feet out of a helicopter in full combat gear, suffering severe back, leg and hip injuries. Eventually, he reached the rank of colonel in his military career, leading him to command a battalion in Northern Ireland.

No wonder he wasn't that bothered about any physicality he might run into on the rugby fields of the world.

But Mulcahy reveals the big 6ft 5in, 17st Scot was shaken by the comments of a journalist after the 1966 tour in New Zealand which the Lions lost 4-0 in the Test series. 'Mike sent me the cuttings; he always read the newspapers. I remember one banner headline. It said, "The lamentable Lamerton. A giant too small for the task".

'It was very hurtful for an amateur player. I know he was very upset, and I felt for him.'

The author of the piece was Terry O'Connor of the *Daily Mail*, a notoriously insensitive soul when it came to others' feelings.

Mulcahy enjoyed the 1962 South African tour most. Even though the 1959 Lions ended up with ten Irishmen in their ranks. But what Mulcahy loved primarily was the fun and fellowship of a Saturday night at a club somewhere back in Ireland.

'The post-match craic in the clubhouse, the singing. I got to love it,' he said softly. 'We had a laissez-faire attitude to the game in those days. Whichever team you were playing for you never took it very seriously. We would have a good win but the next match we would be terrible. There was no consistency.'

He played for clubs all over Ireland: Bohemians, UCD, Bective and Skerries. As well as assorted hospital sides.

Today, he says, Irish rugby is so much better. He greatly enjoys watching it. 'Even though we were reluctant to embrace professionalism, I think it suited us. Their fitness levels are very good and under this management they seem to be encouraged more to take a chance.

'In those early days when I played, other countries had coaches that we didn't have. They had a more professional attitude to the game, even then. We just weren't serious about it.'

But it did change, even in Ireland. He knew the tide was turning when Ireland appointed prop forward Ray McLoughlin as captain for the first time in succession to Mulcahy. McLoughlin was a County Galway man; tough, nuggety, intense. He certainly never suffered fools gladly.

Ireland teams always stayed at the Shelbourne Hotel for international matches. Even now, Mulcahy can remember the crowded foyer of the Shelbourne on matchday mornings, with players scrambling around trying to find some tickets for friends.

'This was just a few hours before kick-off. It wasn't any sort of preparation for a Test match. I found it difficult enough captaining Ireland. Frankly, I would rather not have had the onus. I wasn't forceful enough; I was too quiet with my own guys. I could have done without it and wouldn't have been in the least bit sorry if someone else had been captain.'

But when McLoughlin took over, he put a stop to it all. He insisted teams he was leading would relocate to the Royal Marina hotel in Dun Laoghaire, well out of Dublin and beyond the gaze and fuss of fans. What helped trigger the move was an event prior to the previous match when the team was still at the Shelbourne in 1965.

'We were down the end of a great big dining area, eating a light lunch before the game. We were talking and thinking about the game. At the other end of this long table were the alickadoos, guffawing and laughing. It was Ray's first match as captain and he wasn't happy with the noise they were making. So he stood up and said, "We are trying to get our minds set on this match. You fellas shut up."'

The committee men were humbled. '"Certainly, Ray; sorry, Ray," they mumbled. Maybe that was the start of getting our minds more fixed on the situation.'

We've roamed far and wide, meandered through the pages and several years of Irish rugby history. I am aware Mulcahy no longer has the strength of his youth. But I ask him about the greatest characters he ever knew in the Irish game.

He thought Willie John McBride would have to be right up there. Then there was Mick Doyle, an abrasive wing forward who played for Cambridge University and Ireland, then went on to become national coach in the 1980s. He was into all sorts of devilment, he thought. 'He didn't drink for a number of years. But he more than made up for it later on.'

The conversation alighted on a name probably not familiar to the modern generation. But strong, powerful men doffed their cap in respect when they met back row forward Ronnie Kavanagh.

The Dubliner, one of three brothers, won thirty-five caps for Ireland between 1953 and 1962. He was a rough, tough competitor on the field. The kind of man who never took a backward step. It is said he was once introduced to 'Monty', Sir Bernard Law Montgomery, in an Irish dressing room before a match. 'Monty' got more than he bargained for.

'You're not a real Irishman,' Kavanagh scoffed at him.

'I certainly am,' protested Monty.

'No you're not. You come from the north.'

In fact, Montgomery was the fourth child of a Church of Ireland minister whose family came from County Donegal. But he was born in Kennington, in the London suburbs.

The point was, Kavanagh was as hard as nails as a rugby player and a man. Few took on the hero of the Battle of El Alamein. Ireland and Lions scrum half Andy Mulligan once penned some poignant comments as to Kavanagh's value.

'If his virtues had been recognised throughout his career, he might have been the most capped player in any position of all time. Kavanagh's attitude to rugby was years ahead of its time and thousands of miles away from its spiritual source – the crucible of winning thinking in New Zealand. He was one of the few people who, pound for pound, was quite as physically hard as the hardest New Zealander.'

Mulligan called him 'a dedicated kind of man'. He explained, 'Dedication made him Irish amateur boxing champ, Ireland's champion high diver, and dedication won him a place on Ireland's water polo team. In all he did, perfection was the keynote.

'He went to Blackrock College in Dublin, perhaps Ireland's most reliable mass production line for players. His arrival on the rugby scene at nineteen was merely the culmination of an outstanding schoolboy career and some outstanding performances in the Blackrock senior cup team in the Leinster Schools Cup.

'Apart from his phenomenal physical attributes, he was always a great thinker about the game. He believed that rugby is a game which must be played ruthlessly hard and with total commitment.'

Mulcahy remembered: 'Ronnie could give it out on the rugby field. But he could certainly take it, too. He was a good boxer when he wasn't playing rugby.'

Maybe sometimes when he was, too...

Mulcahy recalled a story when Kavanagh's name cropped up amid a Lions tour selection meeting in the 1950s. In those days, each of the Home Unions had two representatives on the Lions selection committee.

A dispute arose over a back row position because England wanted Peter Robbins to go, Wales wanted Clem Thomas. Someone proposed Kavanagh as a compromise but, Mulcahy alleged, one of the Irish representatives said of his own man, 'No, he is too dirty. He will give us a bad name.'

Kavanagh, who died in Dublin in 2021 at the age of ninety, never went on a Lions tour. Yet he was exactly the kind of hardened player who would have been invaluable to the tourists in the southern hemisphere. 'He was certainly hard and tough,' said Mulcahy. 'But for his own man to say he would give the Lions a bad reputation, well...'

Mulligan added, 'It was a scandal that he was never a British Lion. Was he omitted from two and possibly three tours because he was privately considered by the powers that be to be too tough? It's unthinkable.'

But it would seem so.

CHAPTER 5

Balbriggan

Just a few short years in the early twentieth century represented tumultuous times in Ireland's history.

Firstly, 24 April 1916 saw the start of the Easter Rising. Nine weeks later, 1 July, the first Battle of the Somme began. Over 3500 Irish soldiers would be killed.

In November 1918, a general election would bring sweeping political change in Ireland. Also that year, the first signs of Spanish flu, the pandemic that followed the First World War, emerged. Around 800,000 people would catch it across the country out of a population of around 4.3 million, and 23,000 died.

Between 1919 and 1921 came the War of Independence. Then 1921 to 1923 saw the Civil War. Towns and cities throughout Ireland became convulsed in violence.

Yet in the midst of all this, a strange thing occurred. More rugby clubs in towns and cities all over the country began to be founded around this time. One of them, in 1925, was in the small town of Balbriggan on Ireland's east coast, just 4.4 miles north of Skerries.

Balbriggan had seen wild, tragic events in those years. In April 1920, a Royal Ulster Constabulary (RIC) sergeant was shot dead as he walked behind a procession on Clonard Street in Balbriggan. Not long after, a district inspector of the RIC, Peter Burke, was shot dead at Smyth's pub on Dublin Street in the town. His brother Michael was injured.

Violence begat violence. On 20 September 1920, the entire town was sacked by the 'Black and Tans' who were based at Gormanston, a little over three miles away. Named because of the colour of their uniforms, they were a force of temporary constables recruited to assist the RIC in trying to keep control of the IRA during the War of Independence. In truth, they were largely out of control themselves.

They were recruited from Britain at the start of 1920 and approximately 10,000 men signed up to join. But they quickly gained a brutal reputation for their violence against the Irish people.

Amid the chaos that September night, two local men, Seamus Lawless and Sean Gibbons, were killed and many injured. Suffering was widespread. Houses and businesses were looted and burned. Balbriggan was a factory town but the damage meant it was subsequently cut off from most of its UK markets.

One of those affected by the violence was Joseph McGowan, a keen rugby man who was involved with the club from its first days. McGowan and his wife Teresa, together with their young family, had to flee their home and business. They were burned to the ground by the 'Black and Tans'.

McGowan's premises were later rebuilt and he became a vice president of the rugby club before being voted president for the 1931/32 season. Four sons, Matt, Patrick, Gerry and Francis all went on to represent the Balbriggan club.

Another strong, future supporter of the club, local publican John Derham, also found himself caught up in the violence.

At the height of the chaos that infamous September night, Derham was dragged out of his bed and badly beaten by the

'Black and Tans'. His premises were then ransacked and looted before being burned.

Derham was a town commissioner at the time. So when a group of politicians and their advisers was set up afterwards in Washington DC to look at the Irish question, Derham was invited to America to appear before the committee.

It is said that his evidence had a significant effect upon American opinion at the time.

Derham later became president of the Balbriggan Rugby Club for their 1935/36 season.

Back in 1925, a group of local men like Derham had come together to propose that 'a rugby club should be founded which would help heal divisions'.

Laudable ambitions.

After all, there was a rich seam of talent to be mined in the local area. By then, due to Balbriggan's prominence as a town with increasing job prospects, many young men who had played rugby either at school or for a Dublin club relocated to the Balbriggan area. They helped swell the ranks of recruits for the new club.

Not that the Balbriggan club was a big draw initially. They used an open field, Rope Walk, in those early times and facilities were basic. The players had to change for matches at a shop next to the courthouse and then walk through the town in their kit to the field. That part of it wasn't universally popular.

But the opponents queued up for a match. Malahide visited, then Drogheda. Carlow and Skerries, too. By 1926/27 they were mixing in exalted company. The new club even beat Trinity College, Dublin, one of the oldest rugby clubs in continued existence anywhere in the world, by thirteen points to nine.

They then beat Lansdowne's second XV and there was an easy win over Navan. They also played Bective and then Enniscorthy in the final of the Provincial Towns Cup.

To lose so narrowly, 11-6, to Enniscorthy, who won their third successive Cup, confirmed Balbriggan's remarkably rapid progress as a new club. Then in 1928, they won the coveted Provincial Towns Cup themselves, beating Athy 8-0 in a replay at Donnybrook after the first final had ended six-all.

The players and their supporters took over part of the centre of Dublin that night, celebrating the club's first ever trophy. The Dolphin Hotel on the edge of what is now Temple Bar was the chosen watering hole. They supped and sang long into the night.

Their achievement, winning the Cup in only their third season in existence, is a record that stands to this day.

Less than two years later, the good men of Balbriggan were in celebratory mood again. William John McCormick, one of their own, became the first player to play for Balbriggan and go on to represent Ireland in an international match, against England at Lansdowne Road in February 1930.

A big, strong, bustling No. 8 forward, he had been a key player for his club when they won the 1928 Cup.

Alas, McCormick was in the banking business and in late 1928/29, was moved by his employers, the Northern Bank, to a branch in the centre of Dublin. It meant he had to play his rugby at a new abode, and he joined Wanderers.

He was doubly unfortunate in picking up an injury in a club match the week after the England game. It meant he couldn't play again that season and by the time the next season had begun, others had emerged to take his place. McCormick never played for Ireland again.

But clubs would always feel the loss of good players. In those times, they often went an awful lot further than down the coast to Dublin. The youngest member of Balbriggan's 1928 Provincial Towns Cup-winning team was Kevin Heeney who was just eighteen.

Heeney was the son of a Balbriggan builder, Thomas Heeney. His roots ran deep in the local soil. Even so, in 1929, Heeney made the momentous decision to leave, not just Balbriggan or even Dublin. He decided to emigrate to the United States. A letter to Heeney from the club, dated 4 September 1929, spells out their sadness at the news.

'We, the members of Balbriggan Rugby Club, have heard with sincere regret that you are about to leave the country. To mark the esteem and regard that you were held in by all your clubmates, they would ask you to accept the enclosed gold Wristlet Watch as a memento of the happy days you spent with us. You will be greatly missed.'

The message is heartfelt; simple and charming.

Kevin Heeney arrived in New York shortly before the Wall Street Crash. He survived the Great Depression, got himself to Columbia University and eventually worked for several large corporations. He married and had four children.

Eventually, in Atlanta in 1953, he set up his own floral whole-sale business, a company that was still flourishing recently. He had a long, successful life, dying at the age of eighty-six. But he always kept not just the watch but the personal letter from the club to him, marking his departure.

But had Heeney stayed he would have been witness to a sad scene that subsequently unfolded.

As the 1930s developed, Balbriggan RFC began to fall into decline and eventual demise. Some key officials and players passed away while several of the vital players joined Heeney in emigrating to try and escape the financial hardships of those times in Ireland.

Part of the clubhouse was vandalised, and they were shocked when thrown out of the 1931 Provincial Towns Cup after they had reached the final, because they fielded an ineligible player in the quarter-final against Skerries. Meanwhile, retirements also took a toll.

By September 1936, it was clear the club was in trouble and by the late 1930s Balbriggan RFC was no more.

But this was a trend that affected not just Balbriggan. Not just in those days, either.

Clubs throughout Ireland have always been, even to this day, subject to the vicissitudes of society. Young men may be available for some seasons but then drift away to new locations or fresh activities. Talk to rugby people in Ireland today and many express deep concern that youngsters who leave school for university study lose the tradition or perhaps desire to play the game, week in week out.

By the time they have played so much at school over the years, some seem weary of the game. Too many never return to it when they leave university and embark upon a new life.

Rugby would not be seen in Balbriggan again for many years. When it did re-emerge, it was in a very different format to the 1930s example.

CHAPTER 6

Battles by the Boyne (Delvin, Drogheda, Boyne)

Ireland's eastern coastline north of Skerries is a pleasing sight on a sunny day. Streaks of blue sky intermingle with grey, scudding clouds driven, very often, by a stiff coastal breeze. The sea is forever restless; little eddies of water run this way and that close to the shore. The wind whips up the inevitable white caps on the sea.

Already, there is a remoteness that reminds the traveller they have left Dublin and its suburbs far behind.

Little old fishing ports, like Balbriggan, offer a timeless appeal. Sometimes, you can spot seals following the old rusting, battered fishing boats back to port.

Nearby, the sand dunes and open land offer locations where the walker can enjoy the bracing air. There are, too, sports fields up on the cliffs overlooking the sea.

But back in the day, in another time in a sporting sense, Balbriggan rugby club stumbled. Badly. They stopped playing in 1936 and were defunct for a spell. As a result most of the players from that town and area joined Delvin RFC, which was founded in 1953, but more on that below.

It would not be until September 1967 that Balbriggan Rugby Football Club started up again, when they began fielding teams at youth level under Tom Kettle, a former Delvin player. This eventually led to them competing again at adult/senior level in 1975.

Today, they are still going strong with excellent facilities. They also have a very good women's team.

But harsh times in any society invariably bring social change.

So when economic difficulties began to make a significant threat to lifestyles in Ireland after the Second World War and through the 1950s, local ways of life began to fragment. Another Irish diaspora started to unfold. So much so, in fact, that the population, around 4.25 million in the late 1930s, had declined to 2.8 million by the early 1960s.

So many followed the example of Balbriggan rugby man Kevin Heeney, way back in 1929, emigrating to the USA. This time, many went to Britain, as well as America, for work and a future. It left Ireland set back on its heels, unsure of its path to better times.

But bold citizens, people with a vision and energy, emerged. In many fields.

Take rugby. On a bleak February night in 1953, eleven gentlemen met at the Mosney holiday camp to thrash out details for a newly configured club in the area.

The inspiration for a club, which would be named Delvin RFC after a local river, was the genius of Des Scaife, a keen rugby man. He came to this part of the world to manage the Butlin's holiday camp in Mosney, between Julianstown and Gormanston and just up the road from Balbriggan.

But initial progress was slow. In 1954, for example, they played only one game.

But by 1957, Scaife's excellent connections within the rugby world had borne fruit. Irish Grand Slam captain of 1948 Karl Mullen (a good friend of Scaife's) and international wing three-quarter Tony O'Reilly had agreed to hold training sessions once a week. It made a huge difference.

By the time the 1960s arrived, players were coming from everywhere. They stayed in the camp. Irish international back row man Mick Hipwell was another to help.

So the years passed by, slowly for the young, all too quickly for those of more senior status. The club's fortunes ebbed and flowed. There were famous victories, disappointing defeats. Players arrived and departed, some remained far past their retirement to become officials, those hugely undervalued servants of amateur sports clubs the world over.

In this particular story, one of the most dedicated servants, both of his club and the game in general, was Seamie Briscoe.

Today, he is seventy-seven. Still willing to help, still keen to follow the fortunes of club and country.

He comes to meet me at a hotel beside the river at Drogheda. Smartly pressed shirt, blazer and trousers. Club tie proudly knotted at the neck. A suitable location, we might conclude, for Drogheda was to play a significant part in his rugby service from the early 1990s onwards.

Before that, in September 1986, there had been the official opening of Delvin's new clubhouse at Bryanstown. Mosney, their original home, had its advantages and disadvantages. But there was no doubt Bryanstown represented a decisive move forward.

Yet quite quickly, by the start of the 1990s, fresh challenges loomed. Alas, it was becoming increasingly difficult to be optimistic. For a start, there were two rugby clubs, Delvin and Drogheda, feeding from the same trough. As Briscoe said, 'Delvin had been very successful in youth rugby but that didn't

Boyne and Leinster rugby servant Seamie Briscoe.

transfer to adult rugby. There were thirty-five players from the two clubs, and both realised their playing base was diminishing.'

They had tried before to amalgamate without success. But in 1996, Seamus Davis of Drogheda and John Sheridan from Delvin, with the two clubs' agreement, came together to make a final decision on amalgamation. It wasn't easy; remember, rugby had first been played in Drogheda in 1884. Meanwhile, Delvin's history began back in 1952/53.

Such traditions mean a lot to great numbers of people.

But this time, there was an overwhelming feeling in the two clubs in favour of amalgamation. In the old days, Delvin had three teams, Drogheda four. Now there were only the 1sts and 2nds. But two grounds were still being used. Thus, costs were doubled.

Finally, agreement was reached. Drogheda and Delvin would merge and the new club would be known as Boyne RFC, after the famous river beside which the Battle of the Boyne was fought on 12 July 1690.

Today, Shamrock Lodge on the Ballymakenny Road has easy access and is used for all their games. They are in Leinster League Division 1B.

Briscoe can reflect upon half a century of riotous, rollicking involvement with the game in Ireland. What has it all taught him?

'I was born and raised in Termonfeckin and my life has been absolutely entwined in rugby. I was late coming to play the game but the ethics I learned in rugby, things like you had to have discipline on and off the field, have served me all my life. Also, the friendships you made were enduring.

'I have been involved for fifty years. I still am, through the Leinster branch. What has fifty years given me? Something I could never have achieved without it: a reason to respect all people. Also, discipline, friendships, camaraderie and ethics. To meet fantastic people and the enjoyment that offers is out of this world. Rugby has given me so much.'

But don't forget one thing. He has given so much to the game, a fact highlighted by his induction into the Leinster junior clubs 'Hall of Fame' in 2020.

How does he gauge the current strength of rugby in this part of the nation?

'Clubs have sprung up in various areas of the north-east Leinster region. But keeping them going is another thing. They need strong community relations to prosper. For this is GAA country. But the good news is, one is not swamping another. They are both expanding.

'The social element of rugby has diminished off the field. Those followers, players and supporters who stayed in the bar long into an evening were the cash cows. Today, rugby is very much dependent on generous sponsors and patrons. That situation will remain: the rugby-playing fraternity will need to support the clubs.'

Boyne is now one of the leading clubs in the country for developing youth. They have always produced very good players but to Briscoe, the amalgamation has worked superbly. 'Everybody has accepted it. We have won everything at our level apart from one competition, the Harry Gale Cup.

'Had we not amalgamated, I have no doubt those two clubs' playing strength would have greatly diminished. The rugby would not have succeeded to the level and intensity it did. We now have a 1st and 2nd XV and about forty-five players. We also field sides at Under-20s all the way down to minis. The youth section of the club is flourishing.'

Briscoe says himself that rugby has really taken off in recent years. 'The IRFU have managed the professional game well. They got the story right.'

So all is sweetness and light throughout the world of rugby in Ireland? Well, he is a bit reluctant to draw that kind of sweeping conclusion.

'We have a way to go on club rugby. The game at club level has not benefited from the success of the professional era. Some of the famous clubs in Dublin had ten or twelve teams back in the day. Now, some are struggling to fill a second or third team.

'The problem is at eighteen to senior level age groups. Everywhere faces this. It's a job to get the hierarchy to listen to us sometimes. But we want action taken.

'There have been losses with the advent of professionalism. The intensity and volume of the game has diminished. The Dublin senior clubs' 3rd XVs would play us in the old days. But those numbers are not there any more, even among the big clubs.'

But he thinks the spirit of the game is as good as it ever was. 'It has become so popular that at youth level there has been confusion with the rules sometimes. It's important to remember things like you don't abuse referees.

'Clubs like ours have great relationships with some from other countries. We have had a twenty-five-year relationship with Edinburgh Wanderers and Skerries have had one with Dunbar going back fifty-five years. They play fixtures home and away and you can get twenty-five or fifty people, players and supporters, travelling for the game.'

But Ireland's stunning renaissance in recent times on the international stage has been spawned at school level. The Leinster Schools are seriously well organised. Rugby is virtually part of the curriculum. They have coaches for rugby at all levels. People now register their child before it is born. But it all becomes so professional. Some are training six times a week.

To feed the production line?

The trouble is, says Briscoe, if those lads don't reach Academy or Division 1 rugby, they don't go back to the clubs at a lower level. A lot just give up the game and do something else. Fifty years ago, those lads went back to their original clubs and played.

In Munster, he says, there is a different culture of rugby. There, rugby is played in clubs by the working man. In Dublin at the top schools, it is a different story.

'Leinster v Munster matches were always the epitome of rugby in Ireland. Connacht were the poor relations. At the 2023 European Rugby Champions Cup final, they said there were Munster people shouting for La Rochelle rather than Leinster. And not just because of Ronan O'Gara.

'Occasionally, lads from rural areas infiltrate into the Leinster system. Sean O'Brien of Tullow and Shane Horgan from Drogheda did it.

'This is a big GAA area with several clubs not far away. But we don't have a conflict of interest in terms of players. They decide on which game to play. Generally, there is no animosity, and there are good relations between the different codes.'

But whatever the difficulties, the triumphs or just ordinary times, Seamie Briscoe continues to celebrate rugby's intrinsic appeal. The way the game introduces complete strangers and makes them lifelong friends is a quality at which he marvels, even after all these years.

His own example is one of the best. One of rugby's great men of Wales, the Welsh and 1980 British & Irish Lions international Ray Gravell, inhabited a world unknown to Briscoe. They could not have been further apart. Yet when Gravell went to Drogheda, invited over by an Irish friend to do a bit of coaching and see a match, he met Briscoe one night in the pub.

Gravell heard Briscoe singing in the bar and was so taken with his voice, he invited him over to Wales to sing at his wedding.

That chance meeting began a lifetime's friendship, ended only when Gravell died of a heart attack in 2007 at the age of fifty-six.

Meanwhile, Boyne RFC went from strength to strength. What is more, another great friendship was created from those times.

Between 2009/10 and 2014, Briscoe says they found a wonderful coach in New Zealander Craig McGrath. 'John Sheridan had seen him at Treviso and invited him over. He was so keen we even arranged to pick him up at Cherbourg and bring him over.'

Briscoe hesitated. He is not a man given to hyperbole. He sets out his stall by accuracy, facts and discipline in life. His momentary hesitation reflected the importance to him of his imminent statement.

'Perhaps my best years were then. Craig introduced us to professionalism without going over the top. He just brought the best out of players, and we won the League and two Cups under him. I was secretary of the club at that time. Craig spent a few years with us. I think he left about 2014. He was with us about four to five years in all. But that friendship has endured.

'Kiwis are tough men, but when I took him to the airport when he flew home, there were tears in his eyes.'

Rugby union. The game that can reduce strong men to tears.

So what of the future for Irish rugby? His broad smile reveals a strong sense of optimism.

'I have absolutely no doubt, if you have the ability the system will help you to go all the way. Plus the cream of players will keep that high level. Leinster seem to have the pick of Ireland and I cannot see why the future will not be bright.

'Right now, this is the best Irish squad we have ever had.'

CHAPTER 7

Carlingford and Jack Kyle Country

Old John Lackland of England might never have gone down as the most popular visitor to Ireland.

As King John, ruler of England, Lord of Ireland between 1199 and 1216 and captain of the roughest pack of English forwards you ever did see at Lansdowne Road, his relations with Ireland could best be described as fractious. A bit like Martin Johnson's, after those shenanigans in 2003 where the President of Ireland Mary McAleese was forced to walk on grass at Lansdowne Road rather than the laid red carpet because he refused to move his England players for the pre-match ceremonies. All Ireland was scandalised.

Ah, memories, memories. What is more, I can visualise Johnson as a worthy aide-de-camp to old King John. I think it's the same gnarled facial features that make him an ideal candidate.

But you have to hand it to him. King John's Castle, nestling beside the lough at Carlingford, is one mighty impressive building in a simply sensational setting.

On a clear day here, perhaps when a summer sun has warmed

71

The legendary Jack Kyle, pictured (seated, front row) with some of his 1948 Ireland Grand Slam pals. Kyle was revered as a genius of his era and remains one of the country's greatest ever players.

the land on a calm, tranquil morning, you look out past the castle and across the lough to the Mountains of Mourne, the mountain range in County Down in the south-east of Northern Ireland. Here you will see the highest mountain in the province, Slieve Donard at 850 metres (2790 feet).

To recall the rugby theme, the Mountains of Mourne was home for many years to the great Jack Kyle, one of Ireland's rugby legends. I made the journey to see him in his retreat just once. He gave me and my daughter Hannah, the photographer, a warm welcome.

You will find mention of Jack Kyle in other places in this book. There are reasons for that. Kyle was a genius on the rugby field, widely acclaimed by those who saw him. But he brought something even more special to the playing fields of those days.

Humility.

He played forty-six times for Ireland, an immensely large number of caps given that far fewer international matches were played in those days. He also played in all six Test matches on the 1950 British & Irish Lions tour of Australia and New Zealand.

Right across the world, wherever he played, Kyle's pace at outside half and the skilful attacking lines he ran brought a buzz and pizzazz to the scene. To him, kicking was anathema.

He created, fashioned and often scored himself some fantastic tries. 'Made in Ireland' had a resonance far beyond the confines of modern-day commercialism. In 1948, he was a key figure as Ireland at last won a Grand Slam, the first in their history. Mind you, they'd had to wait forty-nine years to achieve it.

Those who were there, among the 30,000 crowd at Ravenhill, Belfast, never forgot it. Given that most of the crowd were from Dublin, eight special trains and hundreds of cars had transported the great throng north. Ravenhill trembled at the waves of excitement pouring down the terraces.

Of course, Kyle hugely enjoyed the day, but not chiefly for himself (he never put himself first) but for the people of Ireland.

For this quiet, self-effacing man was happiest away from the adulation, the attention. Which was one reason why, when he retired from playing in 1963, he became involved in humanitarian work in Indonesia and Sumatra. Then, from 1966 to 2000, the Queen's University, Belfast-trained medic devoted his life to working as a consultant surgeon in Chingola, Zambia.

When he returned to his beloved County Down in 2000, he was to enjoy fourteen years of gentle retirement before his passing.

The photograph taken by my daughter showed a man at peace with his world; calm, unflustered and perhaps a touch reflective. His courtesy and kindness I shall never forget.

*   *   *

Pulling off the main road up to Belfast to take a country road down to the water is always a delight, whatever the season.

But this is strong GAA country which is, perversely, why I am here for a brief visit.

Carlingford Knights rugby club was founded in the early 2000s as an adult tag team. But the real strength of this nascent club is the youngsters who have brought an exuberance and excitement to the place.

From a start of just a few minis playing the game, numbers have expanded significantly. It now has more than 200 registered players in its mini and youth sections. They attract players from the entire Cooley Peninsula and Bellurgan, Lordship, Carlingford and Omeath. There are boys and girls playing at Under-15s level down to minis.

They train on Saturday mornings and the place is a hive of activity on that day of the week.

What Carlingford have done, and done so well, is to tap into the growing market of enthusiasm for involvement in a game that all Ireland now talks about. It is a legacy of Ireland's successes on the international stage in recent years.

Meanwhile, Carlingford are doing something else which is smart and wise if they want a future. They have grown relations with the local GAA side to such an extent that five of the Under-12 GAA league-winning side also now play for Carlingford Knights. That is a significant trend.

And the encouraging results continue to stack up. In past times, their Under-17s and Under-16s beat Newry, the Under-15s beat Dundalk and the Under-13s beat Ardee.

In one sense, the good news is misleading. Carlingford doesn't have a senior men's team so they're not exposed to the difficulties of finding enough players at that level willing to commit to the club every week.

But on the other hand, if the Knights decide to concentrate solely on rugby for youngsters, who is to say they cannot build a modern-day club full of energy and enthusiasm, able to offer an alternative to the GAA in their own backyard?

An appeal to youngsters based on variety can never be a bad thing. You admire the ingenuity and dedication of these rugby people, determinedly drawing in ever greater numbers to their club. Whatever the location.

CHAPTER 8

The Border

The man in the white coat held a clipboard more familiar in an office or research lab than a hospital. But the lines written upon it had nothing to do with office life.

- Lacerations to the head and neck
- Five fractured ribs
- Internal bleeding
- Chipped bones
- Damage to ligaments
- Damage to both knees

But there was no mention of the longer-lasting damage. Even thirty years later, Nigel Carr emits a small sigh as he remembers the worst part of it all.

'The longest-lasting impact was mental. I had considered myself rough and tough. Through my work as a forensic scientist, I had seen bodies in cars. I had seen the effect on bodies of bombs under cars. Doing my work, I was quite insensitive to anything around. It is nice being empathetic, but I preferred being colder.

'But I struggled to get past my own injuries. I became very tearful afterwards. It was the hidden injury, perhaps. I didn't want to be bitter; I didn't want them to have any victory over me. I would rather feel they had not succeeded in getting past me. Still today, I am not sure I fully forgive them.'

Carr's story is widely known. On 25 April 1987, he was in a car with two Ulster teammates, David Irwin and Philip Rainey, driving to Dublin for a national squad training session. Unknown to them, coming in the opposite direction was the second most senior judge in Northern Ireland, Appeal Court judge Lord Justice Sir Maurice Gibson, with his wife Lady Cecily. They had been on holiday and were returning to Belfast.

A Gardaí security unit had escorted the judge close to the border; an RUC police convoy was waiting on its own side, to escort them to their home.

Almost right on the border, on a stretch of road at Killeen, County Armagh, terrorists detonated a massive 500lb bomb as the judge's car drove up to the spot.

A photograph exists of a car totally shattered by the explosion. You think instantly, 'No one could have survived that.' But Carr educates me.

'That was the car we were travelling in. It was a miracle three of us got out of it.'

The judge's car was destroyed, literally torn into pieces, scattered over a huge area. He and his wife were killed instantly.

Thirty-six years offers victims a long time to ponder the what-might-have-beens of a major turning point in their lives. Like it or loathe it, Carr's life has, since that day, always been defined by the atrocity.

So often, he tells me, as we sit together in a Belfast hotel once notorious for being the most bombed in all Europe – The Europa – you are reminded of the smallest details from that day.

THE BORDER

'The explosion? I don't remember it myself. It is more imagined than anything else. But you remember tiny little things. That day, on the journey down, every traffic light we approached (leaving Belfast) turned green. If just one of them had been at red, we would have missed the explosion. That was the way it worked out; such small margins.

'But overall, my chief emotion was a feeling of being lucky to come through it. The three of us were very fortunate. Sometimes I look at the photographs taken, and I realise how fortunate we were to survive.'

He tried to play again; he always wanted to. Just eleven senior caps for Ireland was a meagre return for such a talented back row player. He would, too, certainly have played for Ireland in the 1987 inaugural Rugby World Cup just a couple of months later. But his rugby life was wrecked by the bomb.

What did he feel about the terrorists?

'There was never a prosecution at that time although there is a suggestion that those involved may have succumbed in other incidents. It is not something I look into.'

His health today varies. He has knee problems; he can't do too much.

He has been retired from work for more than three years. That created another gap.

'I miss it a bit. I was a forensic scientist. Science has been my mainstay throughout life. I fall asleep at night thinking of the business of the universe. It is 13 billion years old and I find that amazing. I understand that it is relatively unique.'

Carr gives few in-depth interviews these days. You cannot rewrite history, and no one profits from constantly dragging up painful memories from the past.

'I would much rather be remembered for having been in the British Lions 1986 team rather than the guy whose career ended in a car bombing,' he says, laconically.

1980s Irish flanker Nigel Carr whose playing career was wrecked by a bomb blast on a nearby vehicle.

Unusually, due to the apartheid policies in South Africa and cancellation of any further tours there, a Lions team was chosen in April 1986 for the IRB's Centenary match against 'The Rest of the World'. The team, which included Carr, was organised by the Four Home Unions committee for a one-off game in Cardiff. The players selected were given the status of official British & Irish Lions.

Carr is a softly spoken, calm and patient man. But you can see he wants to move on in terms of this conversation.

'The thing is, I try to look at my situation positively, because 3500 people died in the Troubles and many more were injured. We in that car were very fortunate to survive. Dave Irwin went

80

to talk to the Irish team not long ago about what it means to play for Ireland. After the match, Johnny Sexton referred to it and what Dave had said. I thought Johnny looked very emotional prior to the kick-off that day. But it is nice to think people would still empathise with you.

'I was just lucky that David was a medical student and looked after me that day. At the time, there was a possibility I would not survive it. Their (the judge's) car was on fire, very much close to ours. I would have been at risk of dying if I had stayed in that car. David made sure I got out of it. He may well have saved my life.'

But I have come to Belfast for another reason. I want to hear his views on modern-day rugby, to get his considered thoughts on where the game is going and ascertain the health of club rugby in the north.

Sadly, he confesses his interest in the modern game has waned. 'I don't watch club rugby and I haven't been down to Dublin to any internationals for a couple of seasons. I watch some of the games on TV. I don't really go to matches any more.

'The game would be more attractive if it wasn't just about power. If they could balance that more with playing the ball wide, it would be great for the game. Minimising the number of subs is something else I would advocate.

'But the genie is out of the bottle. With a game like rugby that is a physical contest, there is always going to be that side to it. If you can have a 6ft 5ins wing who can run fast, so much the better. One of the attractions of rugby was always that it catered for the wider range of body sizes.

'Scrums are still important. That's the place where the props can show their unique skills. But there is so much jiggery-pokery going on.

'I find the modern game boring at times. Back lines up flat in defence mean there is very little space to show ball skills. It's just a physical contest much of the time. Forwards rarely commit to rucks... the game has changed. It can be monotonous.

'We have developed the physiques of the players, but we have forgotten about the silken skills. We need to bring them through again. I am thinking of players like the South African Cheslin Kolbe. There are still players like that. It would be nice to see more of them.'

Head contact is a big problem, he fears. 'There is a duty of care to the people we employ. What is happening now (with these impending court cases by those suffering from early onset dementia) must be a major financial concern to the unions and clubs.

'But the problem is, winning has become everything. So if you pick big men to out-power the opposition, your club or region will be delighted. But whether it is good for the worldwide game, I am not sure. My view is, the game needs to move away a bit from that physical battle.'

His perspective on the Troubles and rugby's role in that period contains views that may not be universally applauded. But Carr speaks openly, honestly. His voice, perhaps more than most, deserves to be heard.

'It was the players that wanted to play... through those times. A lot of sporting institutions have worked hard to maintain those connections. Triumph is too strong a word to describe what ultimately happened (rugby remained a united sport on the island of Ireland). But it's great it stayed that way.

'It was just incredibly fortuitous the game did not split like soccer. Of course, there have been tensions. As a guy who came from Newtownards, I remember standing at Lansdowne Road thinking, 'Someone is going to think I am singing the Irish anthem.' I was breathing hard. That is nearly disrespectful to say. But I didn't want to disrespect the anthem. People should be delighted to respect all of Ireland.

'In Northern Ireland, there is more scope for integration. It would be good if kids grow up with people of all colours and creeds. You don't want kids saying, "It's them or us."

'I know that an integrated education system is already under way in Northern Ireland. The first integrated college – opened many decades ago – was Lagan College, and others have taken up the baton since.

'But I think it would be a good thing to roll it out over the whole education system. People get to know each other that way. In Northern Ireland, a lot of rugby is played at the grammar schools. It's more of a class thing. The kids at a place like Limerick are from the estates. There are all sorts of divisions.

'But respect is the key. It is not important what colour and/ or religion you have. When I was young, you wouldn't come into Belfast. There were metal fences around shops, incendiary devices were placed in clubs. You certainly wouldn't come into the city at night. It has made great steps forward from those times and rugby has helped. If we can all have a greater degree of mutual respect, it will help even more.

'Those were sad times, but in a funny way I don't regret living through them. It is a different generation now and I don't think our generation is anything special. Things are not perfect, but they are so much better than they used to be. They were interesting times despite the limitations.'

Ards was Carr's club all those years ago. But he admits, despite the sterling efforts of club officials, interest in the game at that level has waned.

'My club is like a great many others. Back in the day, we had seven teams. Now it is down to three. That has to be a worry. Forty years ago, the counter attractions were starting to come in. Now, there is far more choice but too many youngsters lead sedentary lives.

'Some of the other attractions even included ice hockey which came to Belfast. Whatever, it's a worry because there is a responsibility to try to encourage and develop your young players.'

Yet, he insists, you can still find people who are keen to come and watch and be involved.

'What I call the crossroads has concerned me for some time. Young men reaching seventeen or eighteen don't carry on in the club environment.'

That is a loss that needs urgently addressing, he maintains. Nor is he alone in that view.

But what does he miss about rugby in general? 'I can say two things I miss the most. One is the fun of international games, and the second is being involved in training sessions for my club. Just being part of the team and that camaraderie.'

But Carr refuses to subscribe to the theory, commonplace among many of his time, that the game was so much better in those days. He watches some of the old games now on TV and, he confesses, feels embarrassed. 'They are not that impressive. I thought we were better than that.'

The man demonstrates his fairness in judgement when we discuss Ireland's extraordinary achievements of recent years. Excoriating national rugby unions when things go wrong in individual countries seems to have become a worldwide sport. But Carr refuses to criticise the Irish union. Quite the reverse, in fact.

'One thing the IRFU has done well is manage the provincial teams. Ireland has never had such a sustained period of success. We don't have the clash with wealthy club owners, like in England, forcing players to play just before international matches.

'Every nation has highs and lows, but it's important that everyone is competitive. We had the odd Triple Crown and sniff of a Grand Slam in our day, but to be number one in the world for so long was something else. It is because of the IRFU's management of all the players.

'The majority of our best players are still in Ireland. They feel they are looked after better than they might be in different circumstances. They might earn more money in France, but they will have to work hard for it every time they play.'

Right now in Ireland, he believes, there are talented kids everywhere. And he forecasts we will see the other provinces beyond just Leinster come more to the fore. He doesn't see this era ending any time soon.

A final question. I ask him how he would like to be remembered. He thinks for a moment and forensically toys with the question.

'If people remember me, it is more likely to be because of the bombing. That disappointed me initially but unless you are a McBride or an O'Driscoll, you are lucky if you are remembered at all. I admit, having to stop training and playing rugby was a huge loss to me. But I do look back now and think I was fortunate to have any caps at all. Also, we had some successes. We'll never forget those.'

Nor will we ever forget this brave, humble man who has endured so much.

CHAPTER 9

Trevor Ringland

Close your eyes, just momentarily, and envisage a little scenario that has epitomised the great game of rugby union.

Trevor Ringland made his debut for Ireland in November 1981, against Australia in Dublin. Irish international number 811 and just as proud as all the rest.

But it isn't the intricate details of that game, the passes, the knock-ons or the missed try opportunities that come flooding back into Ringland's mind these forty-four years later. Sure, Australia won 16-12, but it is no longer his overriding memory of that day.

Instead, he recalls a small tradition, a moment of fun and sheer pleasure that has always summed up this game for the former Ulster, Ireland and 1983 British & Irish Lions wing.

'What was lovely in those days was that on your first cap you were dragged across the road from the Shelbourne to O'Donoghue's. If you won, you got free drink, but if you lost you had to buy your own.

'You didn't want to go to O'Donoghue's anyway because you were knackered mentally and physically after the game. The moment you went in, someone shoved a pint of Guinness in your hand. But after two pints you didn't want to leave. You would be having an argument with a guy who said you were rubbish, and you were agreeing with a guy who said you were brilliant.

'Best of all, there were kids standing there talking to players they had watched in the game and to me that was a lovely part of the sport.

'Keith Crossan (his fellow Irish wing) says there should be a rule that you should have to buy your opposite number a drink after every game. Then, he should buy you one back. Thirty or forty years later, you will still have a relationship with those players.'

Ringland espouses the simplest of philosophies.

Sport, he believes, teaches you how to hate without actually hating. It teaches you how to compete without destroying a relationship. These were things that were very important in his day, he says. The older generation should pass down those lessons to the coming generations.

But Ringland has a concern. 'I worry we are not doing that. If we don't, we are losing something from which we have all benefited.'

Ringland was a wing, big (by the standards of those days), strong in his running and hand-offs and mentally determined to prevail. He was never afraid to do what was required to win. Nigel Carr wrote of him: 'He was the "baby-faced assassin" of 1980s international rugby. Those who met him away from the game would have been excused for considering him well mannered and cute.

'He was a public-spirited solicitor who was once late for his law exams after attempting to save the life of a stranger by mouth-to-mouth resuscitation.

'But on the pitch, he rocketed to the top of the game and he loathed losing. He would consider most options to ensure it didn't happen. He had the ability to contemptuously disregard lifelong friendships for a full eighty minutes. But no longer.'

What has rugby given Ringland, this Larne Grammar School, Queen's University, Belfast-educated son of a police chief superintendent? How long have you got, might be the best response.

'It has given me so much. So many friendships. So many good experiences. It has given me confidence in personal development. That is invaluable.

'It has given me an insight into the world because sport plays a very positive role in the world and rugby is a very good example of that in so many ways.

'It has also given me a realisation that sport, when used properly, can do so much that is beneficial to society. In all sorts of ways.'

But, he warned, it must remember that it should not just become focused on making money for individuals or various bodies.

Ringland is involved with the Peace Players International, an organisation that works on the principle that those who play together can live together. It's about community relations using sport.

'We give children the opportunity to play together, with the support of their families. We use a game of three halves with rugby, soccer and Gaelic sports. With the support of the various unions.

'We go into the most difficult areas of Northern Ireland where the Troubles were most intense. We bring the walls down in people's minds. If you can do that and use sport to build relationships between players, then the physical walls may come down at some point in the future.

'We have young people playing in matches like North Belfast v West Belfast. We work with the schools in these areas.

We work intensely with 500 kids a year and it has been going for twenty years.'

It shows, he believes, what is possible in bringing youngsters together.

On 18 May 1996, Ringland helped his fellow Ireland international and 1983 British & Irish Lions colleague, Hugo MacNeill, to put on at Lansdowne Road what was called 'The Peace International'. It was organised after the IRA's bombing of Canary Wharf, as a means of expressing the Irish rugby community's wish for peace.

They invited family members of those killed in recent atrocities to join them at the home of Irish rugby. Their message was, what happened to these poor young people's families should never happen again. As Ringland emphasised, a great number of people contributed to the event and others like it.

Bringing youngsters together. It is a lovely phrase. Just slips off the tongue like liquid honey from a spoon. Alas, reality is seldom so smooth or sweet.

It is next to impossible to have an in-depth discussion about life and rugby with a player from Northern Ireland of that era without the topic of the Troubles looming, iceberg-like, in this Belfast setting. In Ringland's case, it is inevitable. His father worked in the police force throughout his career, rose to become a chief superintendent and somehow survived the entire span of the Troubles in the north.

For some time, Ringland's whole family was conscious of trends and events. After all, back in the day, they lived in police stations. That was the way it was.

The family lived in West Belfast before the Troubles started. Ringland believes society was probably more mixed then compared to now. 'We moved for Dad to be a sergeant in Glenarm where we lived in the police station. Then the

Ireland and Lions wing Trevor Ringland who, together with Hugo MacNeill, has done great work for the peace movement.

Troubles broke out and things intensified to the extent that there was a Sterling sub-machine gun under my parents' bed. It wasn't safe for them to be there any more.'

The whole family moved to a big estate in Larne. But Ringland remembers: 'Around 50,000 people from a Unionist background joined the UDA. There were only 3000 police, and we were living in the middle of an estate. It was like sitting on a powder keg.

'I said to my father sometime later, "Was there any indication society was going to break down in the way that it did?"

'He said, "No. There were issues but nothing that couldn't be resolved."

'"Could you have managed without the Army?"

'"We might have been able to, but once the Loyalist paramilitaries kicked in, we couldn't fight on two fronts. We needed the Army otherwise we would have had a civil war which would have been far worse. It was bad enough as it was," he said.'

That was no exaggeration. Ringland junior can recall several specific occasions when Ringland senior was within an ace of losing his life. 'Every day my dad went to work, he knew exactly who was trying to kill him. But he could only arrest him if he had the evidence. So it was only when they were trying to kill him he could detain them, catch them trying to do something.

'He was injured in a riot situation. He backed up against a wall thinking a petrol bomb had missed him but what he didn't realise was, it shattered against the wall and came down all over him.

'They were wearing those rubberised trench coats and headwear like cycle helmets. He was engulfed in flames and couldn't breathe, but the guys around him managed to put the flames out.

'In the early 1980s, it was the most dangerous place to be, being a police officer in Northern Ireland. People forget how bad it was and some of the things he had to experience were horrendous.

'One day, there was a Loyalist attack on a bar in Belfast where they killed an awful lot of innocent people. My father had to work with the families to help identify the bodies.

'There was another when the IRA set off a bomb and killed a grandfather and his granddaughter. They couldn't find the head of the grandfather, so my father had to keep his men out looking for it. They found it in the end.

'The full effects of a Kalashnikov sub-machine gun being emptied into the head of an individual is appalling. But these were some of the things my father had to deal with.

'Every morning, he had to check his car to see if a bomb had been planted underneath it. As Dad said, "It's the first 100 metres you worry about." Imagine having to do that for thirty years.'

It was, as he conceded, an abnormal situation into which society had got itself. 'It's a conflict I constantly think we should never have got into. Now, we must make sure it never happens again, and I use rugby as a classic example of how to do relationships differently in Ireland.

'As you know, throughout all those times, rugby continued to be played as an all-Ireland team. It was constantly in front of a crowd that wanted all those players to be there.

'There are people that say, we had to use violence, but to me there was always a different way. As someone said, there was nothing achieved through violence that could not have been achieved through peaceful means. That is the tragedy of it all because there is so much hurt that has been caused by the ideologies.

'There was fault on both sides for the violence starting. But there was no logic in trying to unite Ireland by blowing people to bits when rugby was bringing people together on the sports field. Whatever the future is, it's about building relationships.

'I want Northern Ireland to be a place for everybody. I want the whole of Ireland to be a place where people work together. Rugby is one example where we do that on a constant basis. We are happily separate but love getting together. The teams I played on, for Ulster and Ireland, were teams of friends.

'You challenge yourself first then you challenge the others and say, "That's not a basis on which we can operate as a team." There are good sporting examples to use as to how to do things differently.'

But, even from this juncture twenty-seven years after the Good Friday Agreement, the memories won't go away. Perhaps they ease, but never disappear. Ringland recalls two specific incidents.

'One day, my father was part of an Army and police patrol in an area where he would have been under a serious threat. As they were walking on this patrol, some kids began to walk towards them. My father and his colleagues were worried about this.

'As the youths got closer, they taunted the police, saying, "Put us up against the wall and search us."

'So they did, and as they searched them, the youths said, "Don't continue down this street. They are waiting for you at the end. They've got two machine guns. Turn left at the next junction."'

Those words saved the lives of Ringland senior and his colleagues.

As Ringland junior says, those are the sorts of things you build upon. But there was always more sadness to endure.

When Ringland went to Queen's University, he met a police officer named Billy Fulton who was released during term time to study. The pair were both reading law. Just when he was taking his exams, Fulton was shot. Fortunately, he survived.

Edgar Graham was not so lucky. 'He was murdered by the Ulster IRA. He was a law professor, part of the Unionist party,' said Ringland.

'The IRA asked a number of people who would be a future leader of Unionism. Edgar was young, very intelligent, a very respectable guy. He was identified by the IRA and shot because he was good. Because he didn't fit the stereotype of Ian Paisley and the others. Edgar was twenty-nine when he died. He

94

would have been a voice of reason. He showed leadership that our society needed.'

Ringland, like many others, was appalled after an atrocity. But what gave constant hope for a different future was the sympathy for the victims expressed by people right across the community that 'This was not done in our name.'

The Greysteel massacre in October 1993 at the Rising Sun bar was carried out by Loyalist paramilitaries, allegedly in retaliation for the Shankill bomb. Eight people died and nineteen were injured. Someone described the murder scene as 'hell-like'.

Ringland said, 'The same thing happened there; messages appeared saying, "This was not done in our name."

'There were people right across the different societies saying, "We didn't want to go down this road of violence." They were constantly making interventions, saying, "No."

'Rugby was a really good example of people building relationships behind this backdrop of violence. Irish hockey was another.

'You also had people in the GAA working to try and stop the IRA wrapping themselves in what they would see as the cloak of respectability of the GAA. You would never hear those stories, but they did it in subtle ways. That is what we are trying to build on now.

'The Northern Ireland football fans were the same. They looked at themselves and said, "We need to change." The atmosphere was horrible at those matches. But it changed and they started to show how things could be different.'

But rugby needs to solve some of its own issues before it can be considered any paradigm of virtue. Everywhere, the game has become excessively physical, at times bordering on dangerous. Ringland doesn't duck the issue, noting: 'The game is too physical at the moment at every level.'

About eighteen months ago, he watched a 3rd XV club match in Larne and in the first half, six people were injured. There were not many games he played in during his entire career where six people were injured, let alone in the first half alone. There were only a handful of matches where they finished with fourteen men.

But, he says, there is something in the game at the moment. 'In our day, we were trained to avoid contact, to find space. There was space on the pitch in our time. Defence was important, of course, but you didn't drive players backwards the way they do now. Then there's the size of the players.

'It's like American football now, where guys bulk up and might only come on for the last twenty minutes. Because they don't have to play for the whole game.

'Now, they don't let you put your wrist or arm up to protect yourself because that is seen as dangerous. But it means you are exposed to the concussion aspect and that is a real problem for the sport.'

He remembers having only two concussions in his career and they were at school within a week of each other. 'Willie John McBride told me he never had one concussion in his entire career.'

Then there's the problem in the schools, pointed out by others in these pages. Up to the age of fifteen, the general view is that the game is fine. There are lots of minis and kids playing and enjoying the game.

But rugby has become too intense in the schools. That intensity needs to be rolled back, he feels. There is a story on the circuit that one of the major rugby schools in Leinster has used a drone from time to time to track and analyse every movement of individual players. Even in training.

Certainly, the intensity at school level is leading down that road.

'At club level it's not too bad. But the professional level has to find a way to reduce the size of the players and the physicality of the game. The game has to sort out this problem. It is imperative that it does so. It can't not sort it out.'

Ringland reflects for a moment. Then he smiles.

'It was all very different back in the day. One time at Ulster, after a match on a Saturday, they said, "Same team for Tuesday, but could you get your own jerseys washed because we haven't time to do them."

'I asked my girlfriend if there was any chance her mum could wash it. So, she boiled my Ulster jersey all one Sunday afternoon in a saucepan. But the red 'Hand of Ulster' ran into the white of the jersey and so I ran out on a Tuesday night in an alluring pink Ulster jersey!

'The serious point is, I could not envisage all the players in a team in the modern era being able to play another game three days later.'

Of course, professionalism changed everything. The clubs in Ireland were never going to be able to find funds for professionalism so, as the provincial structure was in place, it was an automatic lead in.

It was the foundation to build a structure below international level. Ireland were fortunate in that respect. Now, sometimes 15,000 or 17,000 people turn up to watch Ulster. The same at Munster with Leinster even better supported. Connacht hardly match those numbers but a fantastic atmosphere at The Sportsground is guaranteed.

Countries like Wales and Scotland have struggled to match that loyalty factor.

What you have at the moment, he says, is a provincial structure that works very well. The Academies for younger players, too. It controls players more, so they play for longer.

'People like Best, O'Driscoll and Sexton didn't have such long careers by accident. It was by design.

'That system was put in place twenty years ago. The Leinster Schools system is producing a lot of high-quality players. That challenges the other provinces to do the same. You need three or four players coming through from each province each year and if you get that, there is no reason why we can't sustain this success.

'As long as the structure is right it will continue. Our top guys should not be playing more than twenty to twenty-six matches a season. That is like American football-type level.

'As ever, it's getting the balance right.'

But at levels below that, problems exist.

'We haven't quite got it right yet in relation to club structure because you want to create a level of competition that everybody can enjoy. But not something that tires out the players through aspects like travelling and cost. It is a concern too that many youngsters are moving away from the game.

'Maybe there should be just one division of the AIL with the rest playing in provincial leagues. Maybe there should be a European-style All-Ireland Cup. You still want those connections built across the island. But you maybe only travel two or three times a year. Also, if you travel, you go for the weekend. So it's seen as something to look forward to, not a case of "Oh no, we've got to go to Cork this weekend."'

He believes 90 per cent of players only want to train one night a week with a game on Saturday. 'That's what they want out of the sport. I think the club structure needs to be revamped. This was a proposal twenty years ago when I was on the IRFU committee. They are still talking about it.

'Perhaps just the provincial leagues with an AIL Cup would be better still. Because players tend to retire earlier now at club level. Some even pack up in their mid-twenties. They have had enough of the intensity and part of that is the intensity at schools level. A lot of young people give up the game after school. School sport has traditionally been about the development of the child whereas now it's about the development of the school.

'The big rugby-playing schools of Ulster should really only be playing against the big rugby-playing schools of Leinster and Munster. Ulster also loses a lot of young people who go to university in the UK.

'The professional game and junior game have different interests and needs. But at the end of the day, the club game is about people enjoying themselves. You have to have a balance in rugby. I am happy to see a professional side excel but I want the clubs and the junior clubs to thrive too. That means applying income across the board, not just at pro level, to sustain the game.

'I don't agree with any player being paid at club level because you put too much pressure on your club. But the professional side can't just suck up all the income and think that's OK for the future of the game. It isn't. Both need to succeed.'

Ringland and those of his time were lucky. They played in an era when fun was a component part of the scene. With characters like Willie Duggan and Moss Keane around, there was never a shortage of ribaldry. As J. J. McCoy and Brian McCall told us in the opening chapter.

More of Keane's shenanigans later. But then there was Duggan. Honestly, was there room in any team for two such characters? At Cardiff in 1981, the Barbarians match against Australia was snowed off. So the Irish boys got the last train out of Cardiff, heading for London. BBC commentator Bill McLaren was on board, Ringland remembers.

'It was a lovely experience to have at that age. We stayed at the London Tara hotel that night and they mistook me for Duggan's son! There was good craic between him and my father... like, when was Willie going to start funding some of the cost of me playing rugby?'

Years later, Duggan and Ringland both turned up at RTE studios for an interview and Ringland brought his son, who was eleven.

'Willie was there with his wife and I got stuck into him. I said to my son, "This is the grandfather who hasn't remembered any of your birthdays, nor Christmas gifts. You are eleven years old, and he has totally ignored you all these years."

'My son's birthday was two months later, and on the day, a card arrived from Willie and Ellen and a present through the post.'

Different class.

In 2024, Trevor Ringland's father was eighty-six. He still had lots of stories to tell from his time as a police chief superintendent with the RUC.

But he was only still alive because of a friendship that he had had since before the Troubles started.

Ringland tells the amazing story.

'His friend (who is now deceased) joined the IRA for some reason, and they were targeting my father at one point. This guy had got on well with my dad. A love of motorsport connected them.

'One day, completely out of the blue, he called my father and said, "Don't be driving home that way you take, tonight. They will be waiting for you."'

It saved Ringland senior's life.

It was a friendship that had triumphed over hatred.

His son, himself now sixty-four, said, 'We are constantly talking in our society about things that keep people apart. That was one example of the importance of getting people together and building relationships.

'The biggest injury my father received was probably the trauma he had to experience. He managed it very well, but you should not have to experience those things.

'You don't want to go there again.'

But even amidst the cruelties and intense emotions which became red raw in that time, there was usually some room for humour.

Consider the time when his dad was in charge of policing part of West Belfast in the mid-1970s, where there was a high terrorist threat. Despite that, he formed a strong friendship with the local nationalist politician, Paddy Devlin.

Trevor Ringland takes up the tale. 'Paddy's mother passed away in those times and out of respect, my father and his second in command said they would attend her funeral.

'Paddy warned them it would not be safe as they would be shot. But despite that, they attended and walked with the other mourners and paid their respects at the graveside in the cemetery, which was only across the road from the Andersonstown Police Station. They returned to the station safely.

'A few months later, my father was having a drink with Paddy, who was a strong and colourful character. My dad was suggesting that he had been brave in attending the funeral.

'To which Paddy retorted that he didn't know why my dad was feeling so f...ing brave. After all, he had organised a twenty-four-hour pass to enable them to attend and not be shot...'

CHAPTER 10

City of Derry RFC

In the time when City of Derry Rugby Club played at Branch Road, on the city side of town, the main road led to Buncrana, about twelve miles away.

At the side of that road was a large lay-by overlooking the rugby pitch. There, peering over a hedge on to the pitch, once stood a magnificent rugby man. The collar of his coat would be turned up against the chill autumn wind, and on wet days, a cap defied the frequent squalls that swept down the ground.

In his day, this man was one of Ireland's most promising players. His name was known across Ireland and even South Africa, where he toured in 1968 with the British & Irish Lions.

One day, City of Derry prepared for a home game against Ballymena, club of the famous Willie John McBride. The Ireland international was not playing but decided to go along and watch.

When the Ballymena bus reached the ground and all disembarked, McBride looked down the ground and saw a familiar face. But in a very strange setting.

In the lay-by and all alone stood Ken Goodall, McBride's companion in the Ireland team from 1967 to 1970. McBride was mystified and walked over to see him.

'I couldn't make it out. I said, "What are you doing here?"'
'He said, "I am not allowed in."'

McBride scoffed. 'Then I'll stand here and watch the game with you,' he replied.

The two Lions, among Ireland's finest players of the day, stood together through the match. McBride defined the phrase 'shoulder to shoulder' where his men were concerned. This was no different.

The story of Ken Goodall and his isolation is a sad one. City of Derry RFC were not a very strong club at that time, yet they knew a diamond when it sparkled at their feet. No sooner had Goodall, a local lad who had been born in the city, played a handful of matches for the club than Ulster chose him for an inter-provincial game. No sooner had that happened than Ireland selected him for his international debut, against Australia in Dublin in 1967. He was only nineteen years of age.

Many years later, that late, great Ireland rugby writer Sean Diffley would say in analysing a dire season for his country in the 1984 Five Nations Championship: 'Certainly, and not too surprisingly, the talent among the understudies in Ireland was not very good. In a small rugby-playing population, the Gibsons, Campbells and Goodalls don't come in shoals.'

No. 8 forward Ken Goodall really was that good.

At 6ft 3ins (1.91m) and 14st 2lbs (89.8kgs), he was a significant influence all over the field. McBride remembered him for his prominence at the tail of the line-outs, seizing the ball with his dextrous hands. He had pace, too. He scored a superb try against Wales in Dublin in 1970.

When the Lions called him up to join their party in South Africa in May 1968 as a replacement, it climaxed an extraordinary fast-track rise to the peak of world rugby. Sadly, what was to follow was a crushing, humiliating anti-climax.

During the Lions tour, Goodall broke his wrist and played only one game. When he got home and regained fitness, he would play only another nine times for Ireland. Then, in 1970, came bombshell news.

When he had got back from South Africa, Goodall found himself out of work. The former chemical engineering student had lost his teaching job, a frequent occurrence in those times for those who went on lengthy Lions tours.

Just married, Goodall struggled to find a job and was short of money. So when representatives of an English rugby league club, Workington Town, came calling, Goodall listened. His decision to turn professional, at just twenty-three years of age, dismayed a lot of people. Not least McBride.

'I knew him very well. We lived at Coleraine at that time and I would drive him to Belfast for training sessions with Ulster. He used to come and have tea with us on training nights.

'He never mentioned to me that he was thinking of going professional. I would have told him to stay because he had a lot more to gain. I know that money was short. But I was very disappointed with two of the senior officials in the Ulster rugby administration. They had strong connections with a lot of schools in the north and if they had tried, I'm sure they would have found him a job. Instead, they didn't find a place for him anywhere.'

So Goodall went to Workington, hardly one of the great rugby league clubs in the mould of Wigan or St Helens. He played eighty-two times for the club between 1970 and 1974, scoring twenty-five tries. But when he returned to Northern Ireland and tried to re-enter the world of rugby union, he faced the backlash.

McBride said, 'He was treated dreadfully when he came back. He was a sensitive man, but he had no option but to take it. He never lost his interest in rugby union. But I think he lived to regret turning professional.'

City of Derry club official Gerald McCarter concurred and revealed an incident which had a withering effect on Goodall. 'A while after Ken had returned and early in a new season, we invited him to come along with us to watch an away game. I honestly cannot remember which club it was but when we got there, we started to go into the clubhouse.

'Two officials from this club looked at Ken and said, "We don't want you or your type in here." Ken said very little, but he was clearly hurt.'

Some of the 'blazers' of the time could be like that. Many had souls of darkness; heartless people, hiding behind rugby's intrinsic good nature. When City of Derry club members heard about it, they were outraged.

When they returned to Derry, Goodall told his own club officials he would not embarrass them again. Thereafter, if he wanted to watch a match, he stood alone in the lay-by, just beyond the club's land.

After 1995, when rugby union went professional, the Irish Rugby Football Union 'reinstated' Ken Goodall. But by then, he had only a few short years left to live. On 17 August 2006, Goodall collapsed and died in the shower at his home. He had had heart problems.

He was fifty-nine years old.

* * *

They knew he had a sense of humour from the first time he set foot in the place. He cheerfully conceded he'd never held a rugby ball in his life. But he was willing to give it a go.

He always was. What's more, a smile was never far from his face.

Willie John McBride remembered coaching an Ulster team that included Mark McFeely on a short tour to Romania in 1981. 'He was the life of the party, and we were lucky not to be locked up. We won our three games which did not go down well with the locals.'

McFeely was a solicitor working in Derry. One day, when he'd got back from university in England, at Lancaster, he met a fellow solicitor for a drink.

'He said, "Why don't you come down to the club? There's a game for you."

'I didn't have a clue what to do. But I enjoyed it. It was very entertaining and very good from the socialising point of view. I played GAA on Sundays. I was twenty-one years old.

'For years before that, it was contrary to the GAA regulations to play rugby as well. That was seen as a foreign sport.'

So he played second row. The problem was, being a GAA man, he was used to kicking the ball. Everyone at the club said, 'Don't do that.' But he ended up being the penalty kicker in the side.

He played one season to learn the game and then the following season, went into the 1sts. They played in the Ulster League. 'We also played occasional friendly matches over the border, places like Donegal and Sligo. But you always had to negotiate the big military checkpoints.'

Things weren't too bad in Derry at that time. The club would be fielding six or seven sides each week. It was a friendly, social place.

'We had one policeman from the RUC playing in the team. But he was told he couldn't play in any cross-border friendlies.

'I went to a Catholic grammar school and played GAA for Derry. We were Ulster champions. I played club and county GAA but there was no fraternising after the games. No mixing with the opposition, no having a drink together.

'There was no central point after matches. After a GAA game, it was fairly common for people to get away and just go home. Rugby wasn't like that which was one reason I enjoyed it. You went and had a pint or two and met people. Rugby is great for that.

'When I started with City of Derry rugby club, I found it was a very mixed club. There were a lot of cross-community guys that played, and we didn't have any problems.

'Through rugby, I would meet people from all around the country and I never felt any animosity. No one from the other side of the house would have played GAA or even watched a GAA match. But with a mixed team, it was all good craic.

'You had a drink or two together after the game. It was common knowledge there were five or six Catholics in the City of Derry team.'

Nor was it any sort of difficulty. But even if rugby clubs were continuing to demonstrate the values of tolerance and the mantra that everyone was welcome to walk through their doors, events in society at large were conspiring against that type of moderation.

They awoke one night to urgent messages and calls. Their clubhouse was in flames, set alight and soon burned to the ground by those who didn't want them in that location.

'It was totally destroyed. They wanted the club out of Derry,' said McFeely. 'The city area where the club played was a Catholic area. That was seen as unsuitable. So it was burned down in the middle of one night. They moved to the Waterside which is a more neutral area.'

You might have thought McFeely's profession and job would have tested relationships in some quarters. He explained, 'I am a criminal lawyer. I represented several IRA men, so I had a direct involvement. I was in the defence team. But there was no problem from a Protestant point of view at the rugby club. People knew my job but we all just got on with life.

'That didn't surprise me.'

They even joked about it. Former RUC officer Jimmy McCoy told me, 'I had many great battles against him on the rugby pitch. He was some character. But in the clubhouse afterwards, he would be the first person to buy you a drink and some more.

'He was a well-known and respected solicitor in Londonderry. In the Ulster squad at that time, there were a few police officers or, as Mark would call us "black bastards". He would slag us about him representing people that the then RUC had arrested and him getting them off in court!

'It was all in good fun because he would get slagged back. City of Derry Rugby Club were and still are renowned for their great hospitality.'

McFeely even met his wife in rugby circles, and she is Protestant.

'We just got on with normal day-to-day living. I'd have to say at one or two places I was careful. I didn't hang around after a game at those places.

'In 1994/95, we moved. We got a good price and relocated. But playing numbers today are way down from what we had. The school in the city would have been among the providers of players. But now kids go away and never come back.'

Also, there is an economic issue. A big American company employed a lot of people in Derry. People came from all around the country to work there. But they closed down and were sold off. So the club missed out on a lot of outsiders coming into the city.

Today, he is very involved as a club trustee. It's his role to be upbeat, positive. But he admits: 'Sometimes you get quite depressed about things. We know what we were before.

However, we are still financially quite successful. People come to the games if we are doing well. At a pre-match special lunch which we put on from time to time, we will get around 100 people. It is showing the club to people who wouldn't normally come.'

The realities of everyday life at clubs such as this are laid bare by these loyal servants of the amateur game. McFeely played for the club from 1975 to 1995 and today, twenty-nine years after his retirement from playing, is still involved. Furthermore, he is one of that large band from the north that travel regularly to Dublin to watch the national team.

As McBride said, 'We, as a game, have a lot to offer in the whole island. The number of people that go to Dublin for the international games is extraordinary. It is only good for the country.'

McFeely concurs. 'I am a supporter at international games whenever I can. But the unfortunate aspect now is that the IRFU is really the pro game. The amateur club game has suffered because of that. The whole focus of finance now is on the professional side.

'Back in the day, certainly before professionalism arrived in 1995, we were travelling for fixtures and had a lot of overnight stays. But we got an annual contribution from the IRFU; it wasn't a fortune, but it was enough. But that has disappeared altogether; that doesn't happen now. We can raise some sponsorship money, but it leaves us short. Several clubs have struggled to pay their way.

'We would go to the length and breadth of Ireland. I played for us in places like Waterford and Cork... it was like the far end of the country. We still played AIL until three years ago. Now, we are just in Ulster Junior rugby.

'Some attention should be given to the fact that there has been a major drop-off in numbers involved at clubs like ours. We need to reinvigorate club rugby right across Ireland.

'Of course, there are big crowds at Ulster, Leinster and Munster matches. But some of that money should be redirected to other parts of the game.'

If not? He fears it is a possibility that more clubs in Ireland will just die away.

'I can see it in our club. The hard-core is dwindling. These are the people who do all the 'behind the scenes' work. Without those people, clubs won't exist. Every club in the country is in the same position. For there are a million jobs to do. Always.

'Our base level for players is very low at present. We are trying to attract the kids to our club. We say to them, come and play underage rugby. You just hope they will. But it is a battle.'

What has rugby given men like McFeely? Simple. 'Great times, great friends. You cannot put a price on that.'

*　*　*

Lest we think it is only the older generation who prize their association with Ireland's national team, let me introduce a member of the younger generation.

Richard McCarter is forty and was head coach of the City of Derry club until stepping down in mid-2024.

He suspects his first introduction to the club came when he was born. 'My dad was a player, captain and then head coach for years. We spent a lot of Saturdays and midweek training nights at the club.'

So why would members of this amateur club in the north feel a true association with members of the professional national team who spend most of their time down in Dublin?

Isn't the professional arm of the game all too remote from you, I suggested?

His response was emphatic. 'That is the great thing about rugby. It is different to soccer which is divided. We support Ulster but everyone is fully behind the national team. We have special days on Ireland matchdays with big screens in the clubhouse etc. A lot of our members travel down to Dublin for the internationals.

'Ireland really comes together on those days. Everyone buys into it and their success is ours, no matter which part of the country you are from.'

His words explain precisely why it was so important that rugby stayed united, even amidst its troubled times. Mind you, he doesn't seek to minimise the difficulties confronting rugby people like him at most clubs these days.

They used to have three senior men's teams plus Under-18s, 16s and 14s.

'But now you would be lucky if you got thirty players out training. It's definitely lower than it was. This isn't a great catchment area. It is GAA country really. We have only one rugby-playing school to recruit from, Foyle College.'

But they have worked hard on recruitment in the last few years with rugby development officials. They go into the GAA schools now. That has been quite successful. In fact, one guy they had doing that was a GAA man, but he played both sports.

Founded way back in 1881 on the old Branch Road, City of Derry's heyday was in 1999, the season they won the Ulster League and Cup double. It had never been done before. It was also the first time in the club's history they won two trophies in any season. It was a great team that peaked that year.

McCarter says he was introduced to coaching when still playing, seven years ago. He confesses he has had a love/hate relationship with the role. 'I found it extremely addictive even when things were not going well. You want to try and improve players. The high moments are great, but defeats hit hard.

'We don't struggle to get a team together but numbers at training nights can be frustrating. Yet overall, we have a few hundred members, which represents quite a healthy membership.

'We are fortunate we now have a good clubhouse with a large bar area upstairs. Plus there are three big pitches.'

He shrugs. The floodlights need a few new bulbs. In fact, they have four floodlights probably with no more than ten lights operative in all of them. But he doesn't complain. That is an attribute widely shared by the men and women doing yeoman work at this level of the sport.

'We are quite fortunate. The ground needs a lick of paint, but our playing members would do that to help out. They help with cutting the grass and preparing the pitches, too.

'The spirit is still there but it's up to us to drive it. We are still playing at a reasonable level where we remain competitive. Some older players are very competitive and driven; they really want to do well. Others just want to have a few pints with friends afterwards. It is a mix of all sorts.'

For men like Richard McCarter and his father, Gerald, rugby has been a lifelong passion. The game always stuck with him, he admits.

But what of the future?

'Most clubs are in a similar position. They need to drive up numbers at young age levels, so we have them coming through in ten years. Without them, there won't be a club. It's different if you are in Belfast. Here, there are only three or four clubs (Strabane, Letterkenny, Coleraine) within a one-hour radius. So it is very difficult to attract new players. Which means we always need to develop our own.

'There are a lot of talented players in the city. Remember, too, guys like Tommy Bowe and Rob Kearney played GAA. The more we can get from a GAA background, the better.'

* * *

Gerald McCarter started to play rugby for the 1st XV at City of Derry in 1977. He had been at Loughborough University between 1973 and 1976 and went home to teach. He played for fifteen years before starting to coach. As you did in those times.

Born in 1955, he first saw the game at the local grammar school, Foyle College. He remembers watching Ken Goodall play for the club in his early days. 'He was the star of the team. At that stage, I was about twelve or fourteen.

'It was an enormous shock when Goodall turned professional. He was newly married and teachers were not particularly well paid in those days. My feeling was, someone ought to have helped him.'

When McCarter was at Loughborough, he found it amazing that people didn't understand anything about Northern Ireland. They might profess to but really, they had no idea.

'People would say, "Ian Paisley. Is he the leader of the IRA?" Or... "Northern Ireland. That's near Iceland, isn't it?"

'I felt people in England regarded Northern Ireland as a nuisance. They would ask, "Why don't people get on?"'

Whilst at Loughborough, the Birmingham bombing took place. Very quickly, McCarter sensed people were suspicious of him. He was doing teaching practice in Coventry and would go home every weekend to play rugby. But some people started saying, 'This is suspicious this guy flying home each weekend.'

The date of 30 January 1972 had forever become known as 'Bloody Sunday'. In the heart of Derry, the British Army shot

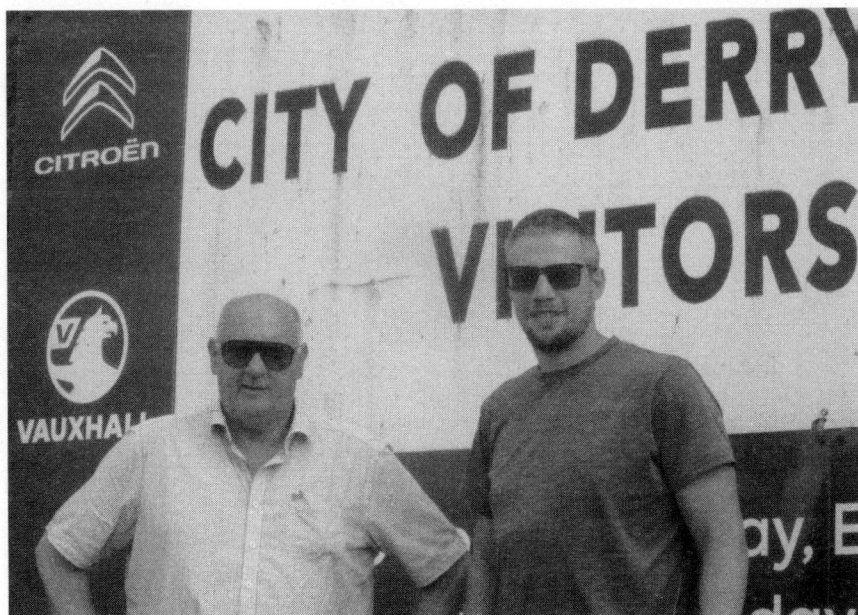

Long term City of Derry RFC club men Gerald and Richard McCarter.

twenty-six people, fourteen of whom died. Most, it was later revealed, had been running away from the troops when they were shot.

McCarter was at home on that Sunday. He remembers: 'It was a normal Sunday afternoon – until that happened. We were two to three miles away from where it occurred. We only heard it for the first time on the local news. Although we were pretty conditioned to trouble by then, it was awful. I remember going to school on Monday morning. It was all the talk.'

What sort of effect did it have on Londonderry/Derry?

'I was from a Unionist background, but we didn't have any involvement in politics. The people mostly affected were from a nationalist background. They said after, it was one of the greatest recruiting drives for extremists.

'Rugby clubs in those areas were generally regarded as safe places to be. There were no restaurants or cafes in Derry open after hours. They brought their shutters down at 5 p.m. So most rugby clubs were regarded as safe in Ulster at that time.'

Mark McFeely was too young to be involved. He was still at his GAA-playing school and had no involvement with the rugby club. But he remembers the shock. 'We lived in the north part of the city. That day, the news gradually came through of what had happened.

'I remember how sad it was and how sombre a city Derry was for a long time.'

In rugby terms, McCarter has seen an inexorable decline in active participation in the game at all levels.

In the late 1980s/early 1990s, he says, they dropped from seven teams to five at the club. Then, when the professional era came, they ended up with three. Now, it's really two and a half sides each week. Where next? Has the slide been stopped?

'Since professionalism, there are fewer school leavers coming into rugby. Some might give it a season or two but after that they walk away. This applies in other provinces, too, like Munster and Connacht. The numbers at grassroots level are in decline.

'Unless the youngsters make it for Ulster, many of them fall out of the game. It is the same in all provinces.

'It's ironic but as long as the provinces continue to be successful in Ireland, the less people play. Then the chances of turning out a good team are reduced in the long run.'

McCarter says, 'City of Derry has been in the doldrums in recent years. It is harder to attract people to your club. We are less well supported than ten to fifteen years ago.

'Our ground is now on the outskirts of Derry at Strathfoyle.

'We have been here since the late 1990s. But we are three kilometres outside town and drink-driving is now a no-no. So that doesn't make it easy.'

What then of the club's future?

116

'The club has a future, but it will be very difficult to really challenge and be consistently successful. We have had ups and downs in the last fifty years. But the coming years will be harder because fewer people are attracted to the club. There are more lifestyle choices.

'When I left school, it was cricket, rugby, tennis depending upon the season. Nowadays, there is always some sport on TV from some part of the world.

'I also think young people want instant success. They want to pick up something and be successful straight away. If they don't, they move on to something else. This also means it gets harder to find people who know and understand the club to fill important positions like chairman or treasurer. As they pass on, getting replacements is very difficult.'

McCarter talks of the lifelong supporters of the club, men like Harry Curtis who is now in his nineties. He has been going to the club forever, he says. They have their own clubhouse, a very substantial one, too. Importantly, the venue finds business in being rented out during the week for events such as wedding receptions.

McCarter thinks city centre teams haven't done so well for a variety of reasons.

'Clubs in Ulster who have been successful in recent times such as Clogher Valley, Ballyclare and Ballynahinch are from smaller towns and are the centre of the community and that community gets behind them.

'City teams (Belfast) such as Malone and Belfast Harlequins have struggled in their leagues but survived. But in my opinion, city people are not so invested or interested in their community.

'If you have a good base of players, you attract others who want to be there. Then crowds come in and people want to be involved in the club. There is a wave of enthusiasm.

117

'But you need success on the pitch in the first place to make all that happen.'

It's a catch-22 situation. He says that Ulster clubs in general have struggled in All-Ireland League rugby with Leinster clubs dominating, but that reflects the professional game also.

McCarter, like McFeely, wants to sound upbeat and positive about the club. But sometimes, all that is needed to put a new spring of optimism into people's steps, is help from others.

As outlined in earlier chapters, no one, the McCarters at City of Derry, the Seamie Briscoes at Boyne or the hard-working club devotees at Skerries, can do it all themselves. Fresh blood, new faces are required.

CHAPTER 11

Willie John McBride

They say the most familiar landmarks in all of Belfast are the rusting old, yellow gantry cranes towering over the Harland and Wolff shipyard. They became such a part of the place they gave them nicknames. Samson and Goliath.

But perhaps the most famous human face in all Northern Ireland belongs to a man who is known only by his pre-names.

Go anywhere across the province and mention the names Willie John. Instantly, you trigger a lengthy conversation about the man and the game he graced.

It is a long while since Willie John needed a surname. But if you never saw rugby and never visited Northern Ireland, let alone the whole of Ireland, here it is. McBride.

One of the great men of the Ballymena club, lock forward McBride earned worldwide respect for his qualities and achievements on a record-breaking five Lions tours from 1962 to 1974. In addition, he made sixty-three appearances for Ireland between 1962 and 1975. In 1971 he was a member of the only British & Irish Lions touring party in history to win a Test series in New Zealand.

Then, in 1974, he captained the Lions on an unbeaten tour to South Africa. These were probably his greatest achievements on a rugby field. But what made him so special?

Brian McCall said of him: 'In my opinion, what made Willie John a legend was the five Lions tours he went on, especially the 1974 tour to South Africa where he was captain.

'From all accounts, his leadership on that tour was quite exceptional. But I have always thought of him as a very modest man. He has never boasted of his accomplishments. In fact, quite the reverse. He downplays them. I often used to stay in his house when I went over to Belfast to train and play for Ulster. He remains a special man. Both on the field and off it. He was so strong as a player and very industrious. A real figurehead to follow.'

And, it should be added, a keen judge of character.

Ireland wing Trevor Ringland had watched McBride on TV when he was a schoolboy, and he saw him playing for Ballymena. Then he remembered playing a match against his hero. Queen's University v Ballymena, McBride's club.

'To start with, I thought, *Here is my hero.* Then I thought, *Why is one of my heroes trying to take my head off my shoulders?*

'But that was the way he played. With formidable strength and commitment. Didn't matter who he was facing.'

Legend is a word tossed liberally into modern-day conversations. But it always seemed highly relevant to me that McBride, one of rugby's great warriors of any era, came into this world two days after the completion of the rescue mission of the British Army from Dunkirk in 1940.

If ever a rugby man could be imagined manning a small boat across the English Channel, creamy white roll-neck woollen sweater up to his chin against the chill breeze and puffing his pipe thoughtfully, to save stranded British and French troops from the Dunkirk beaches, then it would have been McBride.

In all he has ever done, in whatever part of the world, he has been fearless, honest and totally committed.

He was a rugby man prepared to stand by his principles. Whatever the cost. On the rugby fields of the world this earned him huge respect. From Dunedin to Dublin, Cardiff to Cape Town, rugby holds him in an esteem enjoyed by few.

He and his lovely wife Penny are always friendly and welcoming. And he's a splendid man for some of the famous craic.

Like the story of the visit he made one night years ago, with friends, to the La Mon Hotel & Country Club outside Belfast. Friends were round and all sought an evening out, amid the pressures of the Troubles at that time.

But when they came out, they realised six of them wouldn't all get into the car. So McBride offered to go in the boot.

Coming over Queen's Bridge in Belfast, the car slowed. There were soldiers standing at a roadblock. McBride heard the military voices and thought, *Oh my God*.

The soldier asked where they had been, and where they were going.

Then the soldier said, 'Can I have a look in the boot?'

'When they opened the boot, I am looking down the barrel of a weapon held by a young British soldier. The guy nearly died; you should have seen his face. He couldn't believe there was someone lying in the boot. He thought I'd been kidnapped.

'The next thing was, an RUC guy came from around the front passenger side of the car. He started laughing and said to the soldier, "For God's sake, shoot him." He was roaring with laughter.'

Fortunately, the RUC man didn't need a surname to put to the face.

But what of McBride's feelings from when he started out in the game and the values that underpinned rugby union?

'I remember going to Ballymena and about the first or second time I was there, a senior club official called Paddy Owens took me aside. He said, 'Those gates at Eaton Park are open to all. All colours and religions, providing they accept our principles and our standards.

'We train young men here how to be tolerant with each other, how to win and how to be successful. That's very important in life. But probably even more important is, we teach them how to lose, how to handle disappointment. You'll not win all the time, so you have got to remember how to lose and how to accept it.

'This club is about people, about community and it's about family. You never forget that, son.'

That was what club rugby was all about in those days. But, says McBride sadly, 'It's gone now, it's disappeared. It's about different things, today.'

But even then, alas, the so-called lesser standards at some clubs in Britain and Ireland were eroding such noble sentiments. Brian McCall remembered an incident back in 1988, when amateurism was still – well, just about – the modus operandi in the game.

'I was unavailable to play one particular match, a pre-season friendly against Pontypool, and my place was taken by Andy Millar, an old university chum from Queen's Belfast.

'Andy had played a couple of seasons for Ulster and was a good No. 8, but for this match he was asked to play second row. He was up against another No. 8 playing in the second row – one Eddie Butler. At 6ft 6ins, Andy foolishly stole Eddie's line-out call.

'As play drifted across the field, Eddie took a cheap shot at Andy from behind and broke his jaw in two places.' But that was not the end of it.

McCall went on: 'Faced with six weeks of drinking liquids through a straw and a couple of weeks off work, Andy decided to take a private prosecution against Butler which was unheard of.

'The case was settled out of court with a significant award for damages. Years later, when you listened to the poetic commentary of Eddie Butler on TV (he died in September 2022 at sixty-five) you would never have imagined that he would have done such a thing.'

But back to McBride. Has the price for turning professional been too much, for all the trophies Ireland have collected in recent times? His brow furrows.

'To me, there are people earning a lot of money now. But there are a lot of things I would disagree with. However, there are a lot of things that are better. There is better fitness, better aftercare. In some cases, but not all, better coaching. But is the game in general better? No.

'It has become a mixture between American football, rugby league and rugby union. It's very much influenced by rugby league. If you look at the coach or the coaching teams, there is a rugby league guy who is in charge of defence. But to me, the game has nearly become brutal.

'Every tackle is a double tackle low and high which is what rugby league coaches as a game. It is very effective, but I am waiting for a very serious injury one of these days on a rugby field. It's bound to happen because the game has become serious and intense. The fun and enjoyment have gone out of it.

'It has paid a huge price at the level I liked, which was club level, because today, club rugby just doesn't exist as far as the administrators of the professional game are concerned. We have all seen clubs just disappear or amalgamate. NIFC with Collegians, for example.

'You can argue all sorts of things like life has changed. You have husbands and wives now working. You can't expect a husband to disappear every Saturday when both have worked all week. I accept that.

'But the things that are missing are the things that I treasured at that level. Values, enjoyment, friendship, help for others.'

As for the future, he confesses his concerns. Not least, he says, because the professional side picks out the best players. 'They pick them out of the club and take them away. The schools and Academies are doing that regularly.

'I know at least three players from my area who were good school players. They joined the local club and were doing well at Under-19 and Under-20. They caught the eye.

'But then, after a couple of years at the Academy, three of those guys were told, "Sorry, son, you're not going to make it." So they gave up the game because they had no friends any more in the club and they had no club. They have lost all that.

'They are embarrassed, too. "I didn't make it; I wasn't good enough," they tell themselves. So they pack in rugby. This is happening everywhere in Ireland. Ballymena lost six players all in one go. But the people involved with the Academies have done this all over Ireland at all clubs. I find that sad.

'One of the things I said at the very beginning when the game went professional was, leave the clubs alone. They should be totally amateur. Well, they didn't do that. The result was a lot of clubs spent money and tried to pay players to attract guys.

'But most of those have not got anywhere. The trouble is, people get fed up with constantly paying. The game has suffered a lot from all that.'

He suggests the union should pay for developing players if they then take them out of the clubs. But they have never done that. There is an allowance the clubs get but, he says, it's nowhere near enough.

The problem of youngsters missing out in so many ways vexes him. For most will miss out. How many Brian O'Driscolls, Mike Gibsons and Fergus Slatterys emerge to enjoy glittering playing careers? A minuscule number. McBride's concern is for the overwhelming majority who don't make it.

'These kids taken out of the game by the provinces are not playing enough. You get experience by playing with older guys around you. You learn from them.'

He remembers turning out for Ballymena at one stage beside a guy who was a car mechanic. He was strong, used to lifting car engines and such things. One day, they were playing against Monkstown and McBride got a terrible belt. 'I was on the ground and didn't know where I was. He picked me up and said, "Get up, son. Don't let them see you are hurt."'

His point is, you gain experience with mature people like that around you. And the only way you get experience is not by practising but playing.

'These kids need to spend more time with their clubs. But I would say, some of those clubs need better coaches.'

Then there are the laws. The way the game's guardians have mucked around with them, introducing many but just leaving others and allowing players to ignore them, exasperates him.

'I am not happy with the way the game is being refereed. Organised obstruction is now unbelievable, yet it is never blown. The scrum is just a joke. It's a rugby league scrum now.

'What is the point of having laws if they don't carry them out? The scrum feed is a rugby league feed. It goes straight into their own forwards' feet. When did you last see a ball won against the head? It means, you don't need a hooker any more.

'This thing of taking off so many players and having five or six fresh players is a nonsense. It's wrong.

125

'I say, give us our game back. It's a fifteen-man game, not twenty-three. Who voted for that? It is farcical; you should only have replacements if there are injuries.'

But that's about today. What about his time? When he looks back, does he consider it a triumph, a sense of pride that rugby played on through the Troubles?

'Well, one of the things I admire about Irish rugby is that it was always an all-Ireland game. This was long before partition.

'Even before the Troubles and after partition, the IRFU said, "We will still remain the same four provinces." Through the Troubles, there were tremendous efforts made at club level to maintain playing Saturdays north and south of the border. In those days it was difficult because there were all sorts of problems associated with travelling. But very rarely was there a game missed. At Ballymena, our relationship with Galwegians meant we always played them for the Des Dempsey Cup.

'At one particularly bad time, they rang us up and said they were worried about travelling by road. They said, "We have made a club decision and we're going to fly up. Would you give us a bit of help towards the costs?"

'Ballymena agreed to share the costs. It was that important the game went ahead. They flew into Aldergrove airport. Then, when the game had ended, they got stuck into the Guinness until a call came from the airport saying, "You had better come now because this plane is leaving soon."

'It was hilarious, but that's how important it was to the rugby community on both sides. Great efforts were made in many clubs either side of the border to play the games scheduled.'

Someone from the south who greatly anticipated matches in the north was the Irish and 1980 British & Irish Lions outside half Tony Ward, who played soccer in his earlier days.

But when rugby overwhelmed soccer in his active sporting life, Ward found a wonderful welcome whenever he travelled north.

'Rugby has always been the most unifying aspect of sport on this island. It is something in which the game and the IRFU can take immense pride. Because I played for three different clubs, Garryowen, St Mary's and Greystones, they had three very different fixture lists.

'As a consequence of that, I got to play against almost every Ulster club, on both sides of the border. I loved and I mean loved travelling north where the welcome was as sincere as it was consistent. I don't think there's a northern ground that I haven't played in.'

This common accord, what we might term a coming together in the face of great adversity, convinced Willie John McBride that the sport would not splinter.

'There was never a danger rugby would split during this time. There was tremendous effort, tolerance and understanding between the management and administrators of the game to ensure the game stayed together.'

But what of the future of rugby?

'What worries me is that money is going to be a huge problem. The IRFU own the professional players so it's healthy in Ireland, but not England. And Wales has many problems, too.'

Will money destroy rugby as we know it, in the end?

'It could do, because I think some of it is getting nonsensical.

'It could cost billions if those cases (for dementia) are won by the complainants. It could put the game in terrible trouble. It's very worrying because that's not the end of it. There will be more cases.'

I doubt there is a more pressing, more serious issue facing the game today. It leads me to one question, above all others.

Would McBride, knowing what he now does of the potential damage to players' brains, advise a son of his to play the game? He sighs heavily, fully aware of the magnitude of what he may be saying.

'It is one of the saddest things, but I would find it very difficult to encourage a young lad to play rugby now. That is extremely sad.'

Would he let his own son play the game?

'I don't know if I would. I certainly wouldn't want him to become professional. In my day you would have recommended the game to anybody. But not now. The kids are still playing the game. There are hundreds of kids playing at Ballyclare, hundreds at Ballymena. They're enjoying it.

'But the behaviour of their parents is something else to be concerned about. They stand on the touchline and shout, "Kill him."

'That's not right.

'One of the good things about my son is that he never had any inkling of being a professional. I would certainly encourage them to look for a career before rugby. It would be very difficult to encourage a young guy to aim for professionalism. It is because of the very nature of what is happening.'

He insists the first thing the authorities should do to change things is undertake a root and branch study of the game. There should emerge from that, he says, some non-negotiable issues.

Proper scrums, proper line-outs, bring back rucking, change the tackling and the damage that is being done, only have replacements with injuries, police the scrum feed, cut out obstruction.

'But none of this will happen because it has gone too far. There is only one thing that matters now and that is money. The game doesn't matter any more; it's just about money, that's all.

WILLIE JOHN MCBRIDE

Irish legend Willie John McBride, with the author.

'Rugby has never had so many people going to watch. The only trouble is, they are not rugby people; they're not part of a rugby club. I would say at least 50 per cent of the crowds today don't know what the game is about.

'You have the crowd's conduct these days as a major factor at matches. There is all this drinking and then people going in and out to the toilet. I wouldn't go to a rugby match today. I have never been to the Aviva in Dublin. I watch it on TV.

'The last time I was at Lansdowne Road I had to watch the game on TV screens. I couldn't see because of all the people waving flags and walking in and out. They should ban drinking during the match.

'It's the same at Ravenhill. They fill that ground all the time but they are not rugby people; they're not members of Ballymena or Ballynahinch or wherever...

'The vast majority have nothing to do with rugby. It's a place to be seen, it's an evening's entertainment and it's fun. There is a big marquee, and you can have as much drink as you want. At the moment, there is nothing else for them to move on to. But if there is one day... if that changes, rugby will have a big void to fill.'

But, as the legendary Dubliners sang, what of rugby in the 'rare ol' times'? Instantly, there is a warm glow on the old man's face.

'Fun. Great people were involved. There was no hatred whereas nowadays you feel they are on the field to try and injure people. It is really brutal now.'

His Lions career was exceptional, but his Ireland days were mixed. Didn't the players take the game seriously enough before professionalism?

'Yes, it was partly that but also belief. The belief that we could win and were good enough. Having said that, there were guys selected for Ireland who just were not good enough. We had that core of players like Gibson, McLoughlin, Slattery, Kyle... but others were then picked to make up the fifteen and they weren't good enough.'

In his personal view, who was the greatest of Ireland's brilliant outside halves, whom he played with or against? Mike Gibson or Jack Kyle? He blows his cheeks out at that one.

'Everybody has his era and Kyle in his era was brilliant. But he was lucky that the game was different altogether and he had a wing forward who did his tackling. Jack never tackled whereas Gibson did get involved.

'It was a pleasure to have Gibson on the team. He was brilliant and he was tough.

'Gibson didn't have 100 yards of pace, but over 20 yards he could beat three or four men. But he could be caught. However, then there was his vision. Both Gibson and Kyle had tremendous vision. But they played in different eras so it's very difficult to compare. In many ways it was a different game.

'What I will say is, Kyle was a lovely man. I played against him for Ballymena when we met NIFC. At that stage he was playing full-back. But I really got to know him after he retired because he and I were joint presidents of the Wooden Spoon charity in Northern Ireland. I saw a lot of him then. We would have long chats about the game, but he didn't like it at all. He could never understand why players would look for someone to run into rather than running into space. I don't understand this game either.'

What of the greatest Irish player he ever saw?

'There were a few. But I think it would probably have to be Mike Gibson. When you had Gibson in your team you had a confidence. There was no doubt about it. He was always fit, sharp and a very intense player. He was physically tough, too.

'Mind you, there were a lot of good players like Fergus Slattery. He was up at Ballymena in April 2023. We were playing Blackrock. He walked round and round the field. But it was obvious he didn't have a clue where he was. Two guys with him helped him but I doubt he even knew me. He was just smiling but he couldn't have a conversation. It was very sad.

'What is even sadder is that he has now been diagnosed with dementia.'

So, any regrets about his own career, his life?

'Absolutely not. When I think now what I have got out of rugby... I have travelled the world and made a lot of friends. It is fifty years since 1975 when I retired. I am very lucky. For twenty-five years I was president of the Wooden Spoon and by 2024, we had raised £1 million, which is a big thing in Ulster.

'I went on five Lions tours, was captain in 1974 and I managed one, too, in 1983. I also captained the Irish team when we won the Championship in 1974. But the coaching thing didn't work out. I regret that, but it was my own fault. I should never have gone into it. It was too early. I didn't have enough experience. Also, there were guys still playing I had played with and that's wrong. You don't do that. It was a big mistake.

'But there were also a lot of people who were anti me.'

Ireland's great legendary leader is now eighty-four. A stroke two or three years ago tried to knock him over but largely failed. A sudden landslide of stones at the Giant's Causeway up on the tip of the Antrim coast might manage it, I suppose. But I wonder.

For sure, it was in part his mental strength that helped get him through the Troubles.

McBride found himself working at a branch of the Northern Bank based in Belfast. They were times when even a man as large as life as McBride was checked in his stride.

'A good friend of mine played No. 8 and second row for Ulster in one game. A day after, he was shot, opening a new business.

'"Mistaken identity," they said.

'That knocks the stuffing out of you. It was heartbreaking.'

Even now, all these years later, the big man paused to draw breath.

McBride's attitude during the Troubles was, if they're going to get me, they will. So he carried on as normal a life as he possibly could.

'I changed my route to work a bit. I didn't have a set routine and I did that for four or five years. It does worry you.'

The worst happened on 21 July 1972, 'Bloody Friday' as it was afterwards known. Nineteen bombs exploded across Belfast in just over an hour that day, killing nine people and seriously injuring 130.

McBride's memory of it remains vivid.

'I walked up Royal Avenue, saw this van parked and thought to myself, *That's a funny place for a van to be sitting.*

'Of course, there was no one in it. I walked back to my office which was very close to where the van had been left, but no sooner had I arrived than the sirens started. There were police and soldiers running everywhere, clearing the streets. It quickly dawned on me, I shouldn't be where I was.

'I was the only one left in our office so I quickly ran down the fire escape at the back of the building...

'I was running, literally for my life. The bank had a big administrative office nearby, in Waring Street, and I decided to make for that.

'To start with, I ran in the wrong direction – towards the actual car bomb. I realised my mistake with the aid of shouted warnings from the Army and changed direction.

'But I didn't reach our office. When I was about 10 yards short of the door, this huge bomb went off. The explosion was massive. The ground shook like an earthquake, the air was filled with the aftermath of the shock and flying objects, and the windows of the building seemed to go out and then back in again.

'I was thrown against a brick wall and then on to the ground. For a moment, I lay there as the earth trembled. Until you experience such things you really cannot understand the sensation. It is scary, truly frightening.'

McBride talked of the terrible sights he saw when he stumbled out of his office that afternoon, hoping to get back to his home. Explosions were going off everywhere, he felt threatened whichever way he turned. He gambled by turning one way, not the other. Whether it was into the path of another bomb, no one knew.

Eventually, he ran on to some wasteland where a few cars

were parked. He heard a voice saying, 'Willie John, Willie John. Over here. Quick.'

It was a friend of his from Ballyclare and they jumped in the car, roaring out of the city and down the motorway to escape the mayhem.

It was a time he never forgot.

CHAPTER 12

Inishowen

There is a reason why some people go to their grave insisting County Donegal is the loveliest in all Ireland. They could just be right.

Early on this serene, sunny Saturday morning, it just feels great to be alive. I steer the car in the direction of the Foyle Bridge to the north of Derry city. As I soar over the top, the old river below sparkling in the morning sunlight, I feel liberated.

I'm heading for the Inishowen peninsula, the largest in Ireland. It is a wild, beautiful part of Ireland that goes as far north as is possible, until it hits the Atlantic Ocean. History litters both the land and ocean floor in this part of the world.

In Kinnagoe Bay, County Donegal, they found the wreck of *La Trinidad Valencera*, one of the ships of the Spanish Armada. She sank in 1588 in the rough seas, a fate that befell several other Spanish galleons after the defeat of the Armada by the English navy.

Dramatically, although the ship went down, 400 soldiers and sailors survived, making it to shore. Alas, they were not so fortunate on land. It is estimated that 300 of the survivors were then massacred by the Earl of Tyrone, Hugh O'Neill's militia.

In all, it is thought that more than twenty ships from the Armada fleet were lost off the stormy coasts of northern and western Ireland.

But today is calm, all but still. And I am taking a little diversion on this trip. I will return to Carndonagh, the market town and largest settlement on the peninsula, later in the morning. A thoroughly interesting rugby story awaits.

But first I make my way along the twisting roads and hedgerow-lined lanes that snake beside the inlets and open sea. Apart from an occasional local delivery van or passing car, most of the roads seem largely empty. It is nature and me, a sanctuary for the human soul.

The skies are a beauty to behold. They seem to stretch to infinity, coloured in by a collection of soft blues, whites and threatening dark greys.

My first destination of the day is Malin Head, the northernmost point in Ireland. It is also one of the wildest, bleakest parts in all Ireland. In 1885, a meteorological station was built here, close by the coastguard station. It's fair to say they would have seen some dramatic times. Ships were flung on to the rocks, lives lost in the frequent winter storms.

I am captivated by the fact that in late 1911/early 1912, those working on the telegraph station on the Head heard the words coming through the ether amid a winter storm: 'RMS *Titanic*, RMS *Titanic*. Do you hear us?'

The ship was on sea trials north of Malin Head. Tragically, barely four months later she would founder in another part of this vast ocean.

I ponder all this as I watch the fickle weather change. Where once there was a pale, wan sun, there are now dark clouds and the first spots of rain. The wind, too, is aroused. A storm is coming.

Back in Carndonagh, the rain is no more than a minor irritation to the members, players and supporters of Inishowen

Rugby Club. Rain and County Donegal are old companions, like grass and moss. Carndonagh is a gentle half-hour drive north of Derry. Mind you, don't be getting away with ideas of vast numbers flooding the streets. It has a population of around 2500; comfortable enough numbers for this exclusive, heavenly part of the world.

What I love about small, humble clubs such as this is their strong sense of community. Also, they are modest in everything except their ambitions. Which is exactly how it should be.

Inishowen Rugby Club was founded back in 1972. Local men like Jim McCarroll, Robert Scott and Noel Hunter, who had followed the game keenly all their lives, decided the town needed a rugby club. They put an ad in the local paper, asking for recruits.

At the time, one guy from Carndonagh played rugby for Letterkenny, another as far away as Connacht. But if these men were instrumental in helping get the club off the ground, so was another, most unlikely, hero.

Carndonagh is GAA country, always was. Yet one local man was willing to listen when McCarroll and his merry men knocked on his door one day and asked if they might play a few games of rugby on the Gaelic pitch he owned where the GAA boys played.

Tom Farren, who owned the land, was even chairman of the local GAA at the time. The cheek of it! You'd think if anyone would slam the door in the faces of the rugby guys, it would be him.

Especially at that time. But not so.

Farren agreed they could use the pitch. Which caused some furore elsewhere in Carndonagh. Farren woke one morning and found the word 'Traitor' painted across his front door. Feelings were running high in the town.

But the rugby followers shrugged off any sense of being unwanted. They stuck around for a good while. They played there for a few years and at other sites around the town before ending up at Moss Road.

The first time they played in a league was in 1974. John Merritt was involved by this stage and became the backbone of the fledgling club. He played for them, coached, drove the bus, got friends and family to wash the kit. 'He also pulled guys out of bed to come and play on a Saturday morning,' laughed 2024 club president Anne Scott.

Men and women like Merritt and Scott are the bedrock of many of these clubs. They do so much unseen work, keeping the wheels in motion behind the scenes. They urge, cajole, plead, beg, insist, organise or whatever when their club needs something to be done.

Scott went to college in Dublin, played rugby and had enjoyed the game. It was probably inevitable that rugby would run in her blood. Her father, Tommy Lindsay, was really into the sport. He was president of the Ulster branch in 1982/83.

'I grew up with the smell of Deep Heat in my nostrils,' she grins.

Anne 'discovered' Inishowen Rugby Club in 1984 when she went to Carndonagh to work as a student vet.

'I went to the pub one night with another vet. He introduced me to the man who would become my boyfriend, Stuart, and heard all about the club. That was it. I joined up. Stuart and I got married in 1987.'

She had come from one rugby family and now she had found another.

Fundraising was always important. They would raffle a car, donated by a sponsoring company. They ran rugby club discos in the local nightclub.

All the time, money was being carefully saved, put away to sustain their dream of one day buying their own ground.

In time, it came to pass. In 2013, they bought two fields on Moss Road, just on the fringes of the town. The land became the spiritual home of the club.

The area totalled 9.6 acres and cost €174,000. The deposit was €50,000, all of which had been saved. Buying the land was vital. They couldn't get grants until they owned a ground.

'When we bought the two fields it was a big job to make the site ready for rugby. We had an ex-player, a farmer with the expertise to plough it and level it before we reseeded,' said Scott.

'We spent nights down here lifting stones off that ground. There were twenty or thirty of us. That reflected the spirit in the town. The payment was juice and buns!'

For the opening match they had hundreds of people there. The buzz about the town was fantastic. The Ulster team came with guys like Tommy Bowe helping with the Under-8s. They had a great day.

The sense of pride at where the club had got to was palpable. But those driving clubs like Inishowen never rest on their laurels. Almost immediately, a new exciting venture took shape. They wanted to put up a new, changing facilities building.

In May 2023, it happened. Scott says, 'We got a Sports Capital Grant of €75,000 the first time we applied. We then applied again and got €110,000. Plus €70,000 from cross-border funds. Now, we have four changing rooms, two referees' rooms, storerooms and a kitchen. We are so lucky.'

It was arguably their proudest moment.

For this wasn't just some rough-and-ready concrete slab with a few very basic changing rooms squeezed in.

What they designed and created amounts to facilities that would be the envy of many professional clubs in France or England.

The changing rooms are huge. But the shower areas are something else. They have large, elegant, grey tiles as a backdrop on the walls and floor, courtesy of the design and choices of Anne Scott and her fellow lady workers, Angela Kelly, Ann Diver and Tara McConalogue.

'We decided that we were only going to do this once so we might as well make it as good as we could. There were a few suggestions that we could do it a bit cheaper by putting in basic furnishings. But we thought, *Why? Let's do the job properly with some style.*'

They have certainly achieved that. I should think visiting players queue up to play a match at Carndonagh these days. The dressing room facilities are more like a four-star hotel en suite. Meanwhile, the big storeroom offers the hot water for things like coffee and tea for which, back in the day, they had to carry flasks, plus the milk, to the ground.

A local SuperValu cooks the sausages and makes the soup for an after-match feed. Ann Diver makes the sandwiches.

It is, says Scott, a real community club. 'On 6 May 2023, for our official opening, we hosted an Ulster v Munster Junior Interpro match. We had a marquee up. Our secretary has hotel management experience, so we had a pre-match lunch for a hundred people. Nancy's Barn in Ballyliffin supplied the seafood chowder, SuperValu did the vegetable soup and club members brought bread, cakes and buns. The lunch cost the club practically nothing.'

They went through thirteen kegs of beer that day. But then, as Scott says with a mischievous smile spreading across her face, most teams remember going there but some don't remember going home.

'We met after games for years at Simpson's Bar. Then the Persian Bar in the town.

'The owner of that is our vice president Tony Diver. That is where we feed them. Since the new building opened, we now have a washing machine so we can wash the kit. Our lives are so much easier for that.'

But still they don't rest.

They are waiting to hear about more funding to further upgrade the 1sts pitch as they won their league last season and have moved up.

Building an extension on their own clubhouse, with dining facilities and meeting rooms in the future, is also on the agenda. It will have a function room, too, and be multi-purpose. But they don't want to take on more debt at present. 'We still have to pay off that money to the local council,' Scott insists.

'Now, we are looking at the next, more straightforward phase. We will stick up temporary lights. Brian McNally is a key figure. He is a teacher in the local Mayo community school, a GAA man who introduced rugby to Carndonagh Community School in 1992/93, namely P. J. McGarry. Several of his students such as Bryan Keogh, Alison McLaughlin and Liam Crampsey are coaching and now, their kids play.'

It is this sense of community and families in which everyone mucks in and helps in some way, that represents the strength of clubs like this. Truly, this is where you find the living soul of rugby clubs in Ireland. The visitor is inclined to the view that that soul, at clubs like this anyway, is in rude health.

'Rugby offers something special. I have always believed it is more important to get youngsters playing than winning,' says Scott. 'Youngsters are fiercely competitive. We make sure everyone gets a game to keep them coming back. So maybe they will do it forever. We want youngsters to learn rugby for life, and not just for this club.

'We have a St Stephen's Day match each year: John Merritt's team v the president's team. There would be about a dozen subs on each side!! Everyone pays €10 to play. There are glasses of hot port and mulled wine. The weather doesn't matter. It was freezing last St Stephen's Day.

'We are a grassroots club. Our ambition is to keep generating half-decent players who enjoy the game and want to come home and play. People are reared here but they go away to university or to work because there isn't enough local work.

'But every St Stephen's Day, they all come back. That's where you'll find the true spirit of this club.'

Today, the club is growing. Their Under-6s play Sunday mornings. They are four-to-six-year-olds. Rugby tots, they call them.

They also have minis, Under-8s, 10s, 12s, then youths Under-14s, Under-16s, Under-18s. Then there are girls Under-14s, Under-16s, Under-18s.

In mid-2024, Scott reported, 'We are expanding our girls' section. Now, we have Inishowen girls on the Ireland Under-18s squad and in the Ulster squad, plus another in the regional development squad – Erin McConalogue and Rachael Doherty respectively.'

Victories, whoever achieves them, are enthusiastically cheered. 'Our Under-16s beat Derry in the last minute in 2023,' said Scott, proudly.

There is one Senior XV. But in all, they have about 140 kids. Last year, there were around 160 members. Non-playing members amount to about fifty.

But of course there are difficulties, challenges that loom. What is the most serious problem they face? The GAA. 'We need more rugby in this area,' concedes Scott. 'We do compete with both GAA and soccer and those who come to us generally stay. For some of our players, this is their third sport.

'Many of our players play GAA as well, principally during the summer. It keeps them fit and we don't mind. But just think what a team we could have if we had the pick of GAA. Those boys have fantastic ball control. Then add on the boys' spatial awareness. Mind you, when we were introduced into the schools that was a big plus for us. There are secondary schools in Buncrana and Moville which we have not really tapped into as yet.'

But she is critical of the role played by some of the large rugby schools. 'They have too much power in Irish rugby. You should have school matches only during the week in school hours. But when they play on Saturdays, the local clubs lose some of them from their teams. That's not fair. There is so much prestige in schools rugby now, the boys are treated like gods. But those bodies are still growing.

'They are pushed on too far and too fast. They are bulked up too much. They end up with too much muscle for their physique. Where did the fun go? Our boys (at the club) are encouraged to have fun.'

Comparative geographical isolation was another challenge. They are in the Ulster branch but play mainly local clubs nowadays. The closest to them is City of Derry RFC. But in their league now they play clubs like Letterkenny, Donegal Town, Limavady and Rainey OB.

It is, says Scott, a distinct improvement. 'Our boys used to travel a minimum of one and a half hours each way. But other clubs coming here was the real problem.

'In the past we had too many cancellations. We had to try and combat that. Some clubs are very good about travelling. Last year, we travelled to Malone, over in Belfast, for a cup

(Some of) the hard-working women at Inishowen rugby club. Anne Scott, Angela Kelly, Ann Diver and Emma Rees-Donaghy.

match. That took two hours. Just five minutes into the game, the referee did his knee and we thought it would be a wasted journey. But a referee from a senior game played that day over there agreed to start another match under lights.

'Thank goodness we won that one!'

It isn't a surprise that Inishowen and Anne Scott have both been acknowledged in rugby circles. The club had a 'Spirit of Rugby' award and in 2022, she received an award for 'Services to Rugby' from the Ulster branch of the IRFU. So they know about them in the corridors of power!

Like a lot of selfless people associated with this game, she acknowledges the debt she owes rugby. 'It is a huge part of my life. I have been president since 2015 and as I frequently tell people here, I am willing to step down any time.

'What has rugby given me? A husband, and a second family (she has two sons and two daughters of her own) and friends. I love watching it. I love the sense of community we have here.

'When I lost Stuart, my husband, the club was there. I am not sure I could have got through that without them. That "family" is a treasured part of my life.'

It was a huge shock for her. 'He literally dropped dead on Christmas Eve 2017 – heart problems. The club was fantastic and I could not have managed without their support in the days and weeks that followed.'

There can be no greater testimony to this sport and the people who inhabit it, than Anne Scott's words.

But little things, small gestures by decent people who want to help, always lift spirits.

When the club had a fundraiser, they contacted some former members who had gone overseas. They caught up with one of them, Kevin Doherty, who was living in Australia. The suggestion was gently made that he might like to contribute a couple of hundred euros. He sent €3000.

It is gestures of that nature that epitomise the heart and soul of this club.

CHAPTER 13

Omagh

He runs his fingers through a shock of greying hair and tries to adopt an almost disinterested expression. 'Of course, I am not really a driven person,' he says. Mmmmmm…

Well, beyond dispute, *someone* at this club is.

Allan ('Chunky' to his so-called friends) Duncan is fifty-two years old and has been chairman of his local club for ten years. His association with the club spans forty-five years. But as for not being driven, I think I'll borrow that famous Shakespearean expression. 'He doth protest too much, methinks.'

One thing is certain. Someone, obviously with the help of others, is responsible for one of the best, most heart-warming stories to emerge from any rugby club in Ireland these last twenty-five years.

Today, Omagh Rugby Club is a beacon for other junior clubs all over Ireland and the UK to emulate. If they can. The sense of achievement at the club's grounds, in Mellon Park Drive, a short distance outside the county town of Tyrone, is tangible.

This is a rugby club defying talk elsewhere of diminishing playing numbers, fewer sponsorship deals and fears of the future. What Duncan and others like him have done here is to offer others a template on how to chart a path to success, even amidst the overwhelming attraction of other sports.

Quite simply, the financial sums accrued to back this club would be the envy of junior clubs almost everywhere.

Yet go back to the years between 2000 and 2002, and you unearth a very different story.

Initially, the club had accumulated £120,000 in club funds over the years leading up to 2000. It had a good Saturday night drink/bar business which then suddenly stopped as local clientele drinking habits changed with new bars opening in the town.

Then, in the years 2001–03, the club ran at a loss. Any surplus funds were quickly eroded, basically wiping out the cash reserve.

The club was largely unable to cover its annual running costs due not only to the large decline in bar turnover, but also a declining membership, little to no fundraising events and a poor uptake at any level of sponsorship.

Omagh Rugby Club was in a precarious position, apparently a dying club. They had been a senior club for three years from 1997 to 2000. But then they got relegated back to the junior leagues.

Most looked at Omagh RFC of that time and saw only its inevitable demise. The rugby club had precious little going for it in a town where depression was widespread after the terrorist atrocity of August 1998.

But one man didn't look at it like that.

Allan Duncan knew Omagh RFC like the back of his hand. His family had lived in the town for years, running a family hotel. Duncan junior had been taken down to the club from his earliest days. He'd clambered out of his pushchair as soon as he could and chased a rugby ball wherever it went. Like we all did back in the day.

But now, as the new millennium dawned, the then thirty-year-old Duncan spied an opportunity.

'What was required to turn the whole situation around was a buy-in from all our members. Oh, and a lot of hard work by a lot of people...'

The sheer scale of the ground is your first image when you turn into the lane which runs off the A5 road from Omagh to Strabane. Four and a half pitches are adorned with a plethora of advertising boards on the Thomas Mellon Playing Fields. One of the club's chief sponsors, Pat Kirk Ltd, is a local car dealership company that backs the club extensively.

But it is the number of advertising boards around this ground that speak of prosperity. Collectively, they earn £60,000 a season for the club.

The story of how the Thomas Mellon Playing Fields came to be is intriguing. The original Thomas Mellon came from near Omagh, but after emigration became renowned as an Irish-American businessman and lawyer who founded the Mellon Bank and was patriarch of the Mellon family of Pittsburgh.

Mellon died in 1908 at the ripe old age of ninety-five, but his heirs carried on the business.

In 1952, local people wanted to start a rugby club in Omagh and someone suggested writing to the Mellon Bank in New York because Mellon had come from this part of Ireland.

They wrote asking for help in the purchase of land and establishment of facilities. With hope in their hearts, they carried the vital letter to their local post office, duly paid for the stamps and watched it disappear into a bag.

From there, it would make its way across the Atlantic Ocean. Only to be discarded with a gruff laugh when it was opened and read, doubtless.

But sometimes miracles do happen. Someone at the bank read it, passed it to a higher authority and the bank's board convened. They sent a letter back to Ireland enclosing a cheque for about £10,500 to buy all 21 acres of land wanted to establish the club.

Two things happened in the immediate aftermath. Local postmasters in Ireland began to get an awful lot of letters addressed to the Mellon Bank in New York from a host of sports clubs throughout the country. None succeeded.

But the man who had addressed the original request began to get some stick himself. 'You should have asked for more,' they said. Honestly, some people are never satisfied!

But then, Omagh Rugby Club has always done things differently. It seems to be in their DNA. They were one of the first clubs to go on tour and played the Racing Club de France in Paris in 1956. Just getting there was an adventure.

Somehow, the plane ran off the end of the runway as it tried to leave Ireland. Not in the least deterred, the passengers, including supporters and players, clambered out and helped push it back on to the runway for another go. As you do.

Of course, the finances are hugely important at rugby clubs like this. But Duncan counsels caution. 'It isn't solely about money.

'The toughest thing to find at a club like this is continuity. You want to keep the people who have been long-time club servants. You want them to commit to five or even ten years' service. Then you have stability and can take it from there.

'So right now, the guys doing the work are in their late forties or late fifties. Which means the challenge for us will be to find another group fifteen to twenty years younger to come and take this forward. We don't want to be here when we are seventy.'

Today, Omagh has 600 members. At one stage, they were receiving £2000–3000 a month from members' standing orders. They also had 2000 people for fundraising at one point. Which emphasises Duncan's creed. You must seek the involvement of people throughout the town. It isn't enough just to keep relying on a few members to do everything at the club itself.

There are always jobs to do. Twenty years ago, they just wore random kit. Thus, organising their teams with proper kit was an early priority. Look the part, feel the part and there's a decent chance you will play the part, kind of philosophy.

The changing of the guard back around the turn of the century was a seismic moment. Duncan wanted others alongside him willing to share the burden, not just in hours spent working in the club's interest but in terms of innovation, ingenuity and ideas. Even those parts of the club that were bringing in revenue were closely examined to see how they could be improved.

They would have a pre-match lunch, perhaps on the last day of the season at an AIL game. It used to be a plate of curry in the members' bar. That would be for a sit-down meal for about thirty-five. But now things are different.

These days, they often have lunches, but with anything up to 200 people present. They would invite ten or more sponsors.

As many as ninety local firms sponsor the club. The key, says Duncan, is the lunches. 'But we don't just want their money. We want them to come and bring their family and friends and be part of the place. Most of our sponsors pay between £500 and £1000 a year.'

This is a process of what we might term load sharing. They're not reliant on a single sugar daddy to fund the lot. The perils of sugar daddies eventually getting bored and moving on are high. Then the club flounders.

Omagh RFC's driving force Alan Duncan (third from left, front row), whose hard work assisted by several colleagues, has transformed the club's fortunes.

'That is the danger of a club having one benefactor. If you focus just on the 1st XV, those players who don't make it move on somewhere else. But who comes in behind them?

'If you look at some of the Munster clubs, like Midleton and Sundays Well, they don't seem to have more than one or two sides. But here, there is a huge untapped reservoir of talent.'

They also have some strict philosophies that are non-negotiables. 'At this club, everything goes into facilities. We don't pay for players, but we do pay coaches. We want people who will play for the jersey. All the players live within a radius of fifteen miles.'

Omagh have been back as a senior club for the last five years. But better times on the playing field have not inflated egos, or spawned wild and unrealistic ambitions.

'We don't expect to be a First Division club. We're in AIL 2C. In all, there are five divisions. We play clubs like Armagh, Ballynahinch, Instonians, Belfast Harlequins, Bangor and Dungannon plus Clogher Valley.

'We want to play senior rugby but constantly going up is not the main ambition. What we want to be is the centre of rugby in the west. Then, when we go, we want to leave the club in a better place than we found it.'

Duncan believes that the better the environment and facilities, the better chance of attracting players. There is, he maintains, no loyalty in rugby in Belfast. They jump ship.

'Youngsters who were around eighteen from our club used to go to Belfast when they went to college. You lose them in that situation. But that is happening less and less now. 'Meanwhile, a lot of the Belfast clubs have declined. Belfast Methody is a good example. It is harder for the clubs in Belfast to get local buy-in. So the club is relying on big sponsors with big money.'

But there is something else to consider. A lot of kids tire of rugby by the time they become adults, he says. The intensity of schools rugby has become draining in some instances. This is a view of which I am hearing more and more in these pages.

'Besides, players here are unlikely to go and play for a club like Dungannon. We employ our own full-time rugby development officer. He is out there recruiting young age group boys and girls. Now, we have a good solid youth set-up.'

But there are difficulties, frustrations. For example, Christian Brothers School at Omagh has 1000 pupils. They won the GAA All-Ireland Schools Cup in 2023 and 2024. They are very successful. But Omagh Rugby Club has to sit on the sidelines and watch all that sporting talent drift elsewhere. Surely, they reason, there are enough numbers to spread the talent.

Duncan says, 'If you took just thirty players out of every year, they would still have 800. Not even in the first and second divisions of the school. But we can't get into the school. GAA takes precedence. That will always be the case. It's about popular relationships. The GAA jealously guard their players, present and future.

'It is like treading on eggshells trying to get access to any of these kids who might come and play rugby. But there are mutual benefits. The (comparatively few) guys who play GAA and rugby have better ball skills. These skills are transferable. We have noticed girls especially are much more comfortable with the ball. We have a women's senior team with twenty-five to thirty players. Also, Under-14s and Under-16s. In fact, we have strong numbers at every level – Under-14s, Under-16s, Under-18s.'

Has perhaps one of the spin-offs from Ireland's recent successes in the Six Nations Championship and in getting to number-one-rated nation in the world been to lure more youngsters, girls and boys, to clubs like Omagh?

'Yes, definitely. When we put on a special event at the club, we asked the IRFU if we could "borrow" their two trophies from the 2023 Grand Slam season.

'They agreed, so we invited whole families to come to the event. Countless snaps were taken of kids and families with the Six Nations trophy and the Triple Crown plate.'

Duncan was grateful but feels the IRFU could do more such things to get players and people joining clubs throughout Ireland.

Together with then club president Kevin Murnaghan, we head inside the large clubhouse. The extent of the first-class, plush facilities stuns me. It's more like entering a chic gastro pub recently renovated in the heart of Belfast or Dublin than a rugby club dating back to 1952.

They have heavily invested in two major aspects of this club. The clubhouse and the pitches. The so-called 'Great Hall' has been transformed with a new bar area and two viewing areas to watch sport on either a 5-metre screen or a 2-metre. There is an integrated sound system so there is always a cracking atmosphere in which to watch games.

It's not only rugby you can see there. Depending on schedules, English Premier League soccer matches are frequently shown.

As for the pitches, Duncan said, 'We identified very early on that investment in pitches was vital to a good healthy club. We're proud of our pitches, and we think they are some of the best in the whole country. We try to encourage playing fifteen-man rugby and good pitches are highly conducive to that. We have four pitches and two of them are floodlit.'

Disingenuous wags at the club allege that years ago, a directly converse philosophy was at work with pitches being watered to accommodate what they called 'the legendary fat forwards' such as Mal Hill, Glen 'Pogo' Patterson and Duncan himself from yesteryear.

There you are, that's the thanks you get for helping to revive and rescue a great old club. Nothing but abuse!

Total reconstruction of the bar and TV viewing area cost a cool £100,000. But more recently, they have significantly upgraded the members' bar in their clubhouse. How much did this one cost? 'We needed to raise about the same, £100,000,' says Duncan, calmly.

Here is the approximate cost of some of the work which has been done at the club:

- A sponsor paid to have the lane tarmacked. That cost nearly £20,000 or almost €23,000.
- They drained the original pitch: £21,500 (€25,000).

155

- They then did it again, properly. Another £21,500 (€25,000).
- The 1st XV pitch drainage was improved. Almost £13,000 (€15,000).
- Work was done on the fencing all around the ground. Around £26,000 (€30,000).
- Floodlighting was installed: £43,000 (€50,000).
- Upgrading of women's changing facilities: £43,000 (€50,000).
- New toilets were installed in the women's area: nearly £13,000 (€15,000).
- Work on a gym shed: Around £13,000 (€15,000).
- A completely new boiler system was installed: approx. £43,000 (€50,000).
- They got about £107,205 to £111,493 (€125,000 to €130,000) in grants from the council and sports organisations. Then there was €10,000 from Lottery funds.

For most, these are fantasy sums. Until you hear the story of an event they arranged at the club in spring 2023. They called it 'PIG RACING DAY & FAMILY FUN DAY'.

The details are remarkable. They wanted to raise £100,000 to put quality floodlights on their 2nd XV pitch (the 1st XV ground already had them).

So Duncan and all his other hard-working committee men devised an idea to have pig racing, a major raffle and a fun day out for everyone. They asked underage girls and boys, plus seniors, to come and play some matches. There were also about 150 minis and juniors there.

Imagine how many bags of crisps and drinks they sold behind the bar all day...

In all, they estimated around 2000 people were there and at one stage, someone counted 700 cars parked on the club's playing fields. It seemed like the whole town and local community had come along in support. The strong family element was quickly noticed.

But this wasn't some event put on at the last minute. 'It took months to organise,' said Duncan. 'Everybody bought into it.'

You can only do things like this with drive and energy from all those at the top.

The big attraction was a new car, donated by Pat Kirk Ltd., who puts in around €4500 a year to the club. The interest in this was phenomenal. Another prize offered two tickets to see Ireland's quarter-final at the 2023 Rugby World Cup in Paris.

The raffle tickets, priced at £10 each, quickly became the hottest in town. As Duncan said, 'a lot' bought tickets. Not just in Omagh, either.

Other clubs not too far away seized the invitation to sell tickets too, because they were offered a cut of the eventual profits. Duncan said, 'The most pleasing thing was the collaboration with the other two local rugby clubs.'

Strabane made about £50,000 by selling raffle tickets in their area. Ennis probably sold about 25–27,000 tickets and made about £17,000. Which was not to be sniffed at. The collaboration saw them raise collectively considerable sums to invest in local rugby.

Duncan added, 'This was a mammoth fundraising day which had been ten years in the making, whilst the event itself was turned round in less than five months as we had already run the same event seven years earlier. We followed the same template.'

By the time the day's multiple festivities had been completed and the people had at last made their weary way home, not to mention the delighted winner of the new car, Omagh were left to calculate their total 'take' on the day.

Their target was £100,000.

They missed that. But only by the smallest of margins.

Other sources of income have long since been identified by the club. They are due to receive around £80,000 from the government's levelling up fund at Westminster.

For a long time, you didn't go to Omagh, in County Tyrone, expecting to hear many good news stories. What happened in this town on 15 August 1998 was a cruel and depraved act. A car bomb parked in the main street exploded killing twenty-nine people and injuring more than 200. It represented the highest death toll in a single atrocity throughout the Troubles.

Among the slain were Catholics, Protestants, a woman pregnant with twins, twelve children and teenagers. It had been a normal, sunny August Saturday afternoon in the bustling town. It ended in carnage. Lives were destroyed. For what, local people asked?

Like so many others from Omagh, 2023 club president Keith Murnaghan remembers it vividly.

'We had played a pre-season friendly match at Dungannon and were driving back. We were suddenly aware something was going on, but we were back too soon even for the police cordons to go up.

'We actually drove right into the town. It must have been minutes afterwards. The scene was horrific: we were literally about 100 yards from it. We saw people coming round the corner with blood all over their faces. Thankfully, we didn't keep going. We went back into someone's house with one of our players whom we were trying to take home and started trying to make connections with our own families. The immediate fear was about them. I had a young family, and they would have normally been in the town on a Saturday.

'We tried to phone, but the lines were dead. So you couldn't reach them and in those moments, couldn't know their fate. You had to try and get back to your house. But by that stage the roads were cordoned off and it was quite difficult to get home.

'It was only when I managed to get there that I found my wife and child were safe. Until then, I didn't know whether they were caught up in it. It was the longest drive of my life.

'I had an office in town, and I can remember for days afterwards, the silence. It was so quiet. Life stopped in Omagh for about four or five days.

'The worst part of it was the funerals some days afterwards and the realisation that so many people's lives had been so badly affected. It was awful.

'For those of us who were remote from it, yes, the wounds healed. But for those who lost family members it is very difficult to get past it.'

What did the rugby club do to help in the immediate aftermath?

'We had a fundraiser. The Ulster team played Leicester Tigers here. Dean Richards came over and that all generated funds. Then we had a Sevens event and planted trees for people. We did a few things but...

'People felt very angry. That was the biggest emotion. I think there was a realisation that this bomb had come in from somewhere else. It hadn't come from within Omagh although there were probably people from close by who helped with it.

'You are always powerless against terrorists. It was a bad time for this town.

'But I think Omagh has grown, and it hasn't prevented us from developing as a community. It certainly didn't polarise things. In fact, it probably did the opposite and brought people together.'

CHAPTER 14

Dave Gallaher

Arguably the greatest rugby player ever born in Ireland never won a single cap for the country of his birth. The story might be predominantly one relating to rugby. That tale is well known.

But it is hard to get past the human tragedy element that underpinned it.

Try this for the toughest of tough upbringings.

Ramelton is a small, sleepy town 37 miles, or about an hour by car, north of Donegal town. It lies on the mouth of the River Lennon in an isolated part of the country.

There, on 30 October 1873, in an ordinary terraced house in an unremarkable Irish town, an unremarkable thing happened. A third son, David, was born of James Henry Gallagher, a 69-year-old local shopkeeper who ran a draper's shop, and his 29-year-old wife, Maria Hardy Gallagher.

This was a marriage of convenience. James married Maria, a local woman, in 1866, a year after the death of his first wife. Large families needed a figurehead, a mother.

James had two children from his first marriage, and David was the seventh from his marriage to Maria. The couple had three more children after David, but of their ten offspring, three died in infancy.

But life was cruel in Ireland in those days. Little money, meagre profit levels and too many young mouths to feed led James Gallagher to be seduced by promises of a better life. In faraway New Zealand.

They closed up the family home, part of it converted into a shop, and booked passages for the couple and six of their children. One, a tiny baby, was too ill to make the journey and died after his parents had left.

Can we even begin to imagine the thoughts that went through the minds of Gallagher and especially his young wife as they sailed away? He anticipated a better place to settle and more propitious work circumstances.

Alas, they were to be bitterly disappointed. If they thought they were leaving their troubles behind, little did they know they were taking them with them. But these years, this era, would go down in history as one of immense sadness and tragedy. All across the world.

After other family members and friends had tearfully waved them farewell in Ramelton, they reached Belfast and sailed in May 1878 on the *Lady Jocelyn*. The rough, basic emigrant boat would take twelve long, harrowing weeks to cross the world and arrive in Auckland. David was just four years of age.

The family was then taken on, again by ship, to Tauranga in the Bay of Plenty. Plenty for some, in Maori mythology, but not for arriving immigrants from the other side of the world, it turned out. The final section of the journey took them to Katikati, a small town that sits on an inlet of Tauranga harbour, 40 kilometres from Tauranga.

For someone coming from Ireland, it must have represented the back of beyond. Nevertheless, upon arrival in New Zealand, Gallagher senior altered the family surname to

162

'Gallaher' in an effort to reduce confusion over its spelling and pronunciation.

But if the long journey and arrival had lowered spirits, worse was to follow. The job James had hoped for with the company Donegal Knitwear failed to materialise. Meanwhile, the family was shattered when they viewed the land allocated to them. The settlement was rough and hilly with no access to water. An enormous amount of work would be needed just to make the land suitable for farming.

There was no living to be made from such poor quality land, which forced Maria to become the breadwinner. She accepted a teaching job at £2 a week.

But the job was lost when Maria became ill in 1886. On 9 September 1887, she died of cancer. David was just thirteen.

Before that, he had had surgery to treat stunted muscles in his left leg which had led to curvature of the spine.

But after his mother's death, he was forced to leave school and get a job to earn money for the family. His brothers did likewise, not least because the authorities threatened to put the younger Gallaher children up for adoption if their elder brothers could not provide for them.

Ireland, on the other side of the world, must have seemed a Valhalla for every remaining member of this broken family.

But the brothers managed to keep most of the family together. And when David joined the Auckland Farmers' Freezing Company as a labourer, he found himself carrying around heavy animal carcasses, which helped him build upper body strength and kept him fit. Little did he know it would be a critical factor in his rise to worldwide fame on the rugby field.

Gallaher's interest in rugby began at the tiny local club, Katikati. But when he moved to Auckland, he joined the junior club Parnell and later the famous Ponsonby club. From there, the international rugby legend was born.

But, it should be said, only after he had served in the Boer War where he saw action in various parts of the Republic and won assorted medals for his courage. In January 1901, he signed up as a member of the Sixth New Zealand Contingent of Mounted Rifles. Intriguingly, when he enlisted he gave his date of birth as 31 October 1876, three years later than the real date. It is not known why.

But from there, Gallaher's reputation as a potentially outstanding rugby player who played in the forwards took off. He first played for New Zealand on their unbeaten tour of Australia in 1903. He was already thirty years of age yet would go on to play thirty-six games for New Zealand, twenty-seven as captain.

By then, his qualities as a leader, full of courage, commitment and dedication to his team and teammates, had long been recognised.

But the tour that would put him into the halls of rugby legends came in 1905/06 when he led the so-called 'Original All Blacks', the first representative New Zealand side to tour Britain. Known simply as 'The Originals', their standards of strength, commitment and play saw them win thirty-four of their thirty-five matches, scoring 976 points and conceding just fifty-nine. Only Wales, who won 3-0 at Cardiff, beat them although New Zealanders have argued about a disputed try ever since.

In 1905 on that tour, Gallaher missed the Ireland international match through injury. But it is said he left Dublin to travel back to Ramelton to see his old family house and talk with some relatives. It must have been a highly melancholic trip for him.

What on earth would have been going through his mind? How such a visit must have catapulted painful memories to the forefront of his thinking. Or did he reflect chiefly on the four years of childhood he'd had before they sailed away to another world?

Gallaher retired after the 1905/06 tour, becoming a coach and selector. But he would enjoy barely eight years of peace and a happy life before the First World War broke out in 1914. His brother Douglas was killed on the Somme, prompting him to sign up, too, in 1916. He had no need to, for at forty-two he was officially beyond the age of recruitment.

But just as he had carved out a reputation for courage and leadership amid the horrors of the Boer War, Gallaher now made one last hugely courageous decision. He would sign up and fight in the First World War. It typified the man and his values.

Alas, Gallaher was one of 449 New Zealanders who were to be killed (by shrapnel wounds to the head, in his case) in the Battle of Passchendaele, in Belgium. He was forty-three when he died on 4 October 1917 and all New Zealand mourned.

Today, he lies in a simple grave among his fellow soldiers, down a quiet, leaf-strewn lane in a Belgian countryside littered with such cemeteries. An old, weather-beaten rugby ball remains, donated by someone paying their respects. Messages from visiting Kiwis adorn the grave. All around is peace and silence, broken only by the strengthening wind coming across the fields.

But outside one of the world's most iconic rugby grounds, Eden Park, Auckland, stands a huge bronze statue of Gallaher. He is remembered and revered, not least by the Gallaher Shield, the New Zealand provinces' major Inter Club competition.

Ireland can but imagine what a role he might have played in inspiring their young rugby men in the early years of the twentieth century, had he remained in Ramelton, County Donegal. But then, perhaps the New Zealand environment made the man. It is mere speculation.

The bronze statue of Ireland-born New Zealand legend Dave Gallaher outside Eden Park, Auckland.

What is known for certain is the depth of feeling for this man who endured such traumatic times in his life. There could have been no greater illustration of that than in 2015, the small matter of 110 years after he captained 'The Originals' on that famous tour, when Gallaher's tour jersey from that 1905 trip, was put up for auction.

It sold for £180,000, ten times the previous record for any rugby jersey.

CHAPTER 15

Heading West (Donegal)

Keith Anderson still remembers the shock of the diagnosis. OK, he'd had a good go at this rugby lark down the years. Had far more nights he daren't tell you about than the conventional ones.

Then there were the injuries. He'd had lens implants in both eyes when he was forty-four, so he'd had to give up the game. There was no way Anderson wanted to throw his boots into the waters of Donegal Bay. Far too young for that. Alas, he didn't seem to have a choice.

But then he went back to playing, when he was fifty, for a charity game and continued to play in the 1st XV until an eye injury stopped him.

They diagnosed a torn retina and the doc seemed sure. So, naturally, the members of this little club, Donegal Town, which overlooks the Bay, gave him a white walking stick as a gift! Most helpful, that was. Anderson admits he was very emotional, in bits.

About possibly packing up, not the walking stick, I think he meant...

'An eye expert said, "No more rugby," after I tore the retina. I was a bit shocked by that.'

But being full of ingenuity, Anderson sought a second opinion. He went to a consultant who knew rugby and said, 'Keith, how many rucks do you hit in a game?'

'Twenty,' Anderson said.

'Hit ten,' said the consultant.

And he trotted off back to the club happy as a sand boy, ready to pull on the famous jersey once again. So, fast-forward to autumn 2023, and Anderson finally played his last game for the club against Strabane. Mind you, he added a rider to that. 'I may yet tog out for the odd 2nd XV game. I'm still strong and reasonably fit.

'I have lost my front teeth and, as I said, have had a few issues with my eyes. I've had cuts and a few more serious things. But I've never broken a bone in my body in all the years.'

And he played the majority of his years as a hooker, tight head prop for the last two to three.

Meanwhile, others have also been making an impression down the years. It is said Gareth Marais, their South African coach who lives and works in Donegal, broke his hand six times – allegedly, three times playing rugby, three times fighting. It's also said he played one match with a broken wrist. 'He's a tough cookie,' says Anderson.

You see, that's the spirit which epitomises junior rugby clubs like Donegal Town.

Everyone buys into the reality of a fun Saturday down at the club. Even the wives and girlfriends. Anderson concedes, 'Years ago, our wives didn't even think of hunting us down in pubs after games. From the very start, they would say, "Talk to you on Sunday."

'It seemed to work out much better that way. My wife also got sick of people talking and saying, "He will get hurt."

Donegal Town club stalwart Keith Anderson.

'The way I look at it is, if there is a twenty-year-old player in the scrum, I'll stand aside. But a thirty-year-old must fight for his place. I get sick of ages. We have had a centre, Lee Mosby, who is forty-six or forty-seven; he played amateur rugby league in Wales. He is as solid as a rock.'

Nor does the rugby league link end there. Two other players, Kez McKeown and Tom Barker, both played league, for Widnes and St Helens. Not a bad pedigree.

You'll seldom find a lovelier location for a rugby club than Donegal Town. Jump in your car in the town centre, escape all those American tourists cluttering up the pavements and dragging enormous bags filled with Donegal sweaters 'for the folks back home' and head out on the Killybegs Road, turning left before the Texaco garage for The Holmes.

It is a small lane, signposted 'The Beach'. It twists and turns for the better part of a mile, passing bungalows and, increasingly, larger homes with views. Gradually, what was once mainly farmland, has been converted into building plots. And some of the properties they have built with sumptuous views to match are now worth megabucks.

A small hill rises from the old, flat farmland and opposite is the modest driveway on to the club's ground. Literally, 20 metres away lie the waters of Donegal Bay. They are three miles out of the town.

On a clear day you can see Ben Bulben in Sligo, 30 or 40 miles away across the Bay. Today, it is bright but cloudy. Calm, too, so the waters of the Bay lap gently on to the sandy shoreline. On warm summer evenings after a training session, the lads have been known to strip down to their shorts and race each other into the water.

You don't have a training facility of that nature even at mighty Munster! But of course, when the tide comes in, it affects the wind. The whole ground is surrounded by trees apart from the bottom end where the sea lies. Meanwhile, in late 2023, they erected new floodlights.

There was a rugby union team in Donegal as far back as the late 1800s. But they played most of their games seven miles away, at Ballintra, which, incredibly, hosted four other teams. Crowds of up to 1000 people would go and watch. There was a strong Army presence in those times.

It is believed a guy called Townsend Gahan founded the first club in 1887. At that time, the actual rugby pitch was nearly in the centre of Donegal.

Donegal Town Rugby Club was founded in 1973/74, and

Roy Irwin was the first captain. Trevor Johnston was the skipper who took them into the Ulster League in 1976.

After that, they rented various grounds for years. About 1983, they bought the present site for £10,000. It was just farmland with the ruins of an old house on it.

'We have had some great nights down there. Social life in general was more vibrant in the 1980s and 1990s before the breathalyser became a factor. But you find ways,' says Anderson.

Donegal has some pubs among Ireland's best. The Reel Inn, close by the river, and McCafferty's Bar are among them. We sup quietly at the back of The Reel, a genuine old Irish pub until the clock touches 7.30 p.m. Suddenly, a horde of tourists arrive. We're back in the good ol' US of A.

Free music is promised and the place starts to resemble the concourse of an airport or major railway station. We drink up and head into the night.

But whenever I begin to worry that rugby has completely lost the plot, that all the game's rulers are interested in is more international matches, more first and business class airline travel and staying even longer in five-star hotels of the world, my faith is restored by the thought of little clubs like Donegal Town. Here, as with certain others, you'll find the true soul of the game, REAL rugby people with all the values you associate with that breed.

These people are givers to the great game; not takers.

What they do for their communities and the game in general is incalculable. Take Laurie McCaughan who runs their youth team. He has played for years, and was still fit enough at the start of 2024 to tog out, but gives all his time to training and managing the Under-14s, 16s and 18s. In other words, doing vital work for the future of the club. He is helped by a few others but quietly gets on with what others, like Anderson, regard as vital work.

Everything you see at this club is paid for. They just have to meet the day-to-day running costs of their clubhouse and ground. Like Keith Anderson, Charlie McGinty (English Charlie), and now retired Trevor Johnston are both long-time servants of the club. Charlie has been president for the last twenty years, something not even Donald Trump could achieve. He is a member of the RFU board.

Anderson, long-time player and committee member, says, 'Our team is made up of almost all locals – local builders, tradesmen, electricians, painters etc. One guy does concreting. Then there is a stonemason. Many are self-employed guys, especially from the construction industry.'

Mighty useful it is too when the clubhouse needs a fresh coat of paint, or a shed at the back of the pavilion needs a bit of attention. Or some fencing put up or the lighting repaired.

As for Gareth McMurray, a past captain and current player, he played Gaelic before meeting someone in a local pub around 2010 who invited him to come down and try rugby. Just like Mark McFeely at City of Derry RFC.

They played all kinds of fitness games in training, and individuals never felt left out of anything. McMurray said he never had that feeling with Gaelic football. Here, people immediately feel part of the team, part of the club. They have never looked back.

Anderson, who played just one GAA game years ago and was twenty-one when he started at the club, said, 'GAA is very strong around here. Our region would span six GAA clubs in a 30 to 40 mile radius. The secondary schools play mostly Gaelic and soccer. But it's not a religious problem.

'We can go into the schools and ask the teachers if they have people who would like to play rugby. None of the teachers are interested. GAA is the national sport of Ireland, and we accept that. We can live with it as long as there are sufficient numbers to go around. The number two sport would be soccer, then hurling, then rugby.

'It is the structure they have in place that makes GAA so strong. It starts at school level where they recruit so many. A lot of players are privately schooled. It's not very often you get a guy joining with a country background.'

They have a juniors' section this year with Under-14s, 16s and 18s. They have also run a second team, started in 2023. They played four to six games before Christmas that year. New blood was needed and they seemed to find it. Now, they have young fellows starting and a team of four coaches. But there is an intrinsic problem.

Their difficulties are compounded by a maddening tendency from some well-known clubs to cancel their fixture at the last minute against a more junior club like Donegal Town.

'We travel for two to three hours sometimes to play these matches, but others don't always come to us. It is frustrating for these young guys who are all keen, when our opponents cancel, often on the morning of the game.

'Our guys have taken a day off work and lose a lot of money by doing so. But the other teams don't seem to care if they don't tell us they're not coming until Saturday morning. Of course, by then it's too late to do anything about it. It's like playing poker.

'At one stage, we had our games cancelled for three weeks running. If they don't travel, they forfeit the points. There is also a €200 fine for not travelling, but the wealthier clubs are not bothered by that. It has gone on like that for years.'

Again, as with others, they eagerly support the progress of the national side.

They tell you that Ireland's success has made a massive difference to them. 'Everybody is talking about rugby,' said Anderson. 'It took off when leading players like Rory

Best became household names. For the benefit of all Irish rugby, it is imperative that the national side continues to flourish.

'You want to feed off that success at national level. When Ireland won the Grand Slam in 2023 and then the Six Nations Championship in 2024, the amount of people watching in the pubs around here was unbelievable. We wear our club shirts on occasions like that and others. Little things like that can help.'

Finding and then holding on to players is an age-old concern. It affects clubs throughout Ireland because there is no inexhaustible supply coming through.

'We are familiar with this problem,' concedes Anderson. 'As for other clubs, Derry is struggling, while Letterkenny only have two teams. We have lost three or four good players due to our club not being up to strength. One guy from Ardragh won the AIL with Terenure in 2023.

'If they want to progress, they have to move away.'

In 2012, they lost a whole pack of forwards, maybe seven to ten guys aged around twenty-five. There were no jobs around then, and no money. There was a deep recession. They found themselves very vulnerable to trends in society.

'Most clubs have been struggling for numbers in the last few years. I think some guys used to think, *what's the point of coming down to the rugby club?* But now they have built up a good camaraderie and we have a four-year plan.

'Our ambition is to get back into League 3. We finished fourth in season 2022/23. And we had a good unbeaten run in 2023/24.'

But for all the problems, the club's heartbeat is vibrant. They organise events on a regular basis: dinners, competition evenings and barbecues (when the weather permits). They run a golf classic that makes £7000–8000. Then there are darts tournaments to raise more. There is always a need to find money for all sorts of things.

The most urgent was for floodlights on the field side of the ground. Originally, they could only see the ball on half the pitch, grinned Anderson.

Floodlights are expensive. But they could get a sports club grant from the government for €30,000. Then there are the tours.

In 2022/23, led by captain Gareth McMurray, they went to the USA to celebrate their fiftieth anniversary.

They played three games and spent seven days there. They visited Philadelphia, got a coach to New York, stayed at Times Square, then played the Blackthorn club on an AstroTurf pitch. Their American opponents were a big side, and Donegal lost 42-31.

'We had only two subs; they had thirty players. We had been drinking since Friday. A marching band welcomed us on to the pitch. Even that was a bit loud for some of our boys with hangovers,' joked Anderson.

Donegal has about forty-five playing members and thirty to fifty social members. Around forty supporters went over to America with twenty players. The friendliness of those at the club goes without saying.

Anderson says, 'It's not important whether you are fifty-nine or eighteen. You'll get a warm welcome at our club. Everybody has a bond; we are all friends. We also have the best stew in Ireland. Two of our former players, Eamon Friel and Victor Kearney, make it.'

Kearney is another of those loyal, long-term servants of a club. He has been involved from the early days. He works behind the bar, makes lunch or the post-match meal on Saturdays. He was voted 'Club Person of the Year' two years ago by Ulster rugby. He does the bar, sells lottery tickets and a hundred other things. He is irreplaceable.

They used to have three teams, then it came down to one. Now it's back to two most weeks. A lot of guys have connected to them through social media.

At the moment, they are playing the 2nd XVs and 3rd XVs from the bigger clubs. If they go back up to the higher league, they will be playing all the best teams in the West region.

Anderson suspects they need to get the schools more involved. 'There is a massive effort from the clubs going to schools. The GAA sent people into the schools long ago. If the IRFU came and did something similar it would make a huge difference. But they don't do that.

'Rugby is strong at mini levels, and we usually get about fifty on a Saturday morning. So overall, I think we give a huge commitment to this game.'

During the Troubles, they still travelled all the time. But they found several clubs up in the north didn't like going down there. 'You saw the news all the time and you got used to it,' said Anderson. 'We are a very mixed club. Maybe 75 per cent Catholic. But it's all changed. It's far easier down here now. Religion is no longer a strong part of the community. Everybody gets involved. Everyone can turn their hand to something.'

So what basically is a club like theirs all about, I asked him.

'I'd say, keeping players and finding new ones. It would be the same at most clubs in Ireland. The players are the club. Ballyshannon folded in 2022 although they're looking to get up and running again. They had good facilities: an AstroTurf pitch, floodlights, clubhouse. We played night games there sometimes. But they didn't have the players.

'If the 2nd XV doesn't get a game, you lose them. They walk away. That is why we need the 2nds up and running.'

Long-term clubman Trevor Johnston was forty when he finally stopped playing. One day, there was a collapsed scrum and he was taken off on a spinal stretcher. There was no long-term damage, but he felt it was time to stop. The scans showed old damage but nothing new. He had played prop and hooker during his entire playing career, which lasted from 1973 to 1999.

He joined the club in 1973, as a founder member. He was also PRO (Public Relations Officer) for the club from 1975 to 1995 and continues to support and advise.

'When I joined, we had nothing. There was no real history of rugby in Donegal. But quite a few boys went to Sligo Grammar School and played rugby there. They wanted to set up a club in Donegal and the first match was against Sligo Grammar. It was a 7-0 defeat for Donegal.

'There were four main guys who were the driving force behind it: Roy Irwin, Charlie McGinty (wee Charlie), Alrick Thompson and Jack Ramsey. Jack had no rugby association but was very keen. Somehow, it worked. We made a lot of friends, travelled and socialised together and had some great times.'

But Johnston remembers the difficult times, too.

'The Troubles had kicked off in 1969 so every match was an adventure. We had difficulty with some players. It wasn't easy for them to go to Northern Ireland. I'm talking about members of the security forces. We had half a dozen of them, and they couldn't always make a game. They always had to get permission to play so there would be plenty of 'A.N. Others' on our team list for a match.

'In those days, with teams coming from Northern Ireland it was the opposite scenario with members of the security forces. You would see plain clothes Guards around the club as they were aware a few security members from Northern Ireland were playing.

'At one time, we were in the same league as the PSNI (Police Service of Northern Ireland) so we had to go to Northern

Ireland to play them. But those guys couldn't go to Donegal, Cavan and Monaghan; they couldn't play there, it was too dangerous.

'Quite often, we chose a neutral ground between the two of us for a match. There was a lot of ingenuity going on. It's still going on; the threat hasn't gone away. But we're not in the same league as the PSNI now. We spent maybe twenty years in the same league as them.

'All through the Troubles, you never quite knew how safe you were or what danger you might be in. I worked in Northern Ireland, all around Ulster, my whole career and had to travel each day... across the border. We had a house in Donegal.

'Sometimes at night, you would see a strong light looming up ahead in front of you on the road. You imagine. You didn't know whether it would be the police, the Army or the terrorists who were stopping you. There was always a fear in the back of your mind.'

But just occasionally the fear turned to humour.

They went to RAF Bishops Court in County Down once for a match. In those days it was a radar control and reporting station. When they got there, the sentry on the gate said he didn't know anything about a rugby match and refused to let them in. The referee wasn't allowed in, either. Since a number of different military units were based at the airport in those days, security was always tight.

A lively discussion ensued between all parties over a period of time. But by the time the sentry finally got permission to let them in, it was getting dark and too late to start a match. So they had driven three hours to play a game that couldn't be played.

What do rugby people do in such circumstances? Easy. 'The lads were in good form and we retired to the bar. It was a great night. We were always treated very well.'

What of the club's future, I asked Johnston.

'We went through a bit of a shaky period a while back. But now, we own our own ground and we have no debt. We're going to put up some new floodlights and that is costing £100,000. Gareth McMurray does so much for the club in so many roles and the club is on a good solid footing.'

But as to progress of the game in general, he is not so sanguine.

'It is not obviously going in the right direction. The whole thing has to be thought through again. I don't think professionalism has helped grassroots rugby. The grassroots have not been thought of or considered.'

That, too, is a widely held belief at this level of the game.

CHAPTER 16

Sligo

Just outside Sligo, a little way past the village of Rathcormack on a coast where the North Atlantic crashes ashore with explosive power, stands a tombstone upon a simple grave.

As far as I am aware, William Butler Yeats never laced up a pair of rugby boots at Lansdowne Road, never made some brilliant corner flag tackle back in the day.

Yet Yeats is buried only about 7 kilometres away from another of Ireland's proud senior clubs, Sligo. Thus, it seemed absurd not to stop and pay respects at the grave of a man who became one of this nation's greatest poets.

His final resting place is in the graveyard of St Columba's, Church of Ireland at Drumcliffe. Mind you, he had to undertake some final journey to get there.

In his later years, Yeats expressed a desire to be buried in Sligo. Alas, when he died in June 1939 aged seventy-four, at Roquebrune-Cap-Martin, just along the Mediterranean coast from Monaco, in the south of France, there was insufficient time to make the arrangements to transport his body home before the Second World War began.

Thus, his last request had to be delayed until September 1948. Then, a coffin was placed on the Irish naval vessel

LE Macha and she sailed for Ireland, eventually docking in Galway.

Thousands of people silently lined the route to Sligo Town Hall and, later, to Drumcliffe where Yeats's plot was ready, close by the church door. There, you will find lines from one of his most tender poems expressing vulnerability in the face of unrequited love. Written in 1899, it says simply: 'I have spread my dreams under your feet. Tread softly because you tread on my dreams.'

The simplicity of his words arrests the reader's attention.

Behind the graveyard is the mountain of Ben Bulben. On this grey morning, it is covered in a light drizzle. The only sound is the cawing of the crows from trees encircling the graveyard.

A tenuous link with rugby? Probably. But it's not every day you drive past the grave of so esteemed a man. Like going to Paris and never trekking out to Père Lachaise cemetery to see Oscar Wilde's resting place.

Up here, on Ireland's wild north-west coast, you might think that, amid the omnipresent GAA challenge, rugby is spread pretty thinly on the ground. But you'd be wrong. This is no rugby backwater. History and tradition thrive.

For example, the good men and women of this club will continue to speak proudly of someone who became the only Sligo man ever to represent Ireland at rugby.

Angus McMorrow, a full-back, played against Wales at Cardiff in 1951. The match programme that day would have told you that McMorrow was a representative of the famous Garryowen club. 'But he was one of ours, a true Sligo man,' they'll still tell you, in these parts.

Alas, Ireland drew 3-3 that day and missed the Grand Slam. It proved to be McMorrow's only cap. Still, if he's the only Sligo man to attain the honour, you hold on to him for dear life.

He came from a small village near Collooney but didn't go to school in Sligo, instead attending a rugby-playing school and playing his club rugby for Garryowen. But blood is thicker than water. And the rugby community at Sligo won't be forgetting their man and his great honour. Even from the distance of seventy-four years later.

Nor is that this area's only claim to rugby fame. Nearby Ballisodare is where Ronan O'Gara's father was born. His grandfather had a garage there. His aunt still lives at Strandhill, just down the road from the beach where the powerful Atlantic currents have ensnared too many victims, young, inexperienced surfers especially. The rugby grounds are at the foot of Knocknarea which is supposed to be the burial place of the warrior queen, Maeve.

The approach to Strandhill and the club's HQ is beautiful on this mild day in May. Down twisting, narrow lanes, the gardens are beautifully manicured, shrubs in bloom in the sunshine. The white hawthorn bushes are ubiquitous. It is a lovely time of the year.

The great Bill Mulcahy, Irish rugby legend, remembers playing at Sligo long, long ago. 'It is an impossibly beautiful setting, opposite a very famous mountain,' he told me. 'Go there, see it.'

So I did.

They've been playing rugby around these parts for well over a century. For sure, they've had some high old times down the years. One of the club's most loyal servants is just the man to tell me about them.

Tom Gilligan is now into his eighties, no spring chicken, of course. But he walks every day and has a home gym to keep up his fitness. But the sparkle in his eye tells of a character, and I'm not to be disappointed.

I ask him about the good times, but also the tough times

here. He strokes his chin thoughtfully for a moment. 'Well, you know what they say,' is his response. 'A clap on the back is only 12 inches from a kick in the arse.'

Indeed, it is.

The club came here in 1968; they had no fixed abode before then. They were founded officially in 1879 and played wherever they could.

In 1910, the mighty Trinity College Dublin came to Sligo. They probably met them on a local farmer's field. That was the way it was in those early times. Tackle an opponent hard enough into the lush grass of an Irish field and you introduce your opponent to his first face full of cowpat.

Gilligan came back to Sligo in 1973 when he was thirty-one. He played for them from 1974 to 1982. Then followed a variety of roles, climaxing with the presidency of the club from 2006 to 2008. All the early presidents would have been British Army soldiers, he tells me, as we study the faces of those players and officials of long ago on the clubhouse walls.

I wonder what they could tell you, the men of those times, of their day and fate. The eyes stare back at you from the photographs. But the life has gone.

Gilligan's involvement spans half a century. Probably, most of a lifetime. But there are no regrets.

'It has been time well spent. We have had great days and great nights here. So you look back on the commitment with a sense of satisfaction. Leaving here Saturday at 9 a.m. for a match in Dublin, back at 11 o'clock at night. It is from September to April.'

Then there's the weather. My God, the weather.

'The wind? We like it here; we are used to it,' he smiles, somewhat mischievously. 'You can find a bit of a blow here, you know. Add some rain and sleet and it's cold enough, too. We get a lot of rain.

'We often play in January snow. From Under-6s upwards. It is a whole community that is involved here. Goodwill towards the club is very strong.'

The club, looking west, is on a high promontory of land. You pass by the old clubhouse, go down a narrow lane and there is the pitch. Or rather, the pitches. One is an AstroTurf that allows year-round training. There are two other conventional pitches.

The grounds look down to where the land runs away to the sea and there is the Atlantic. This location is surely something in the middle of a winter storm.

In 2008, Sligo RFC's committee agreed to sell the club's land when the Celtic Tiger was roaring, and to purchase a bigger area nearer Sligo town. Planning permission was granted but the deal collapsed when the buyer pulled out. The Celtic Tiger had crashed.

'So we stayed here and George Mullen was instrumental in putting in the artificial ground, where we train. That has been a great investment. The main pitch on our ground cost €100,000.'

As ever, there are plenty of other sports competing with them. Golf, soccer, GAA, hurling, surfing in Strandhill. There isn't a shortage of choice for young people.

'You do find fewer and fewer guys trying to play two sports because now it's too competitive. At one time they might have played three or four sports part-time. But they don't have time for that now. There are so many matches.'

Like a lot of clubs, they have been victims of the vicissitudes of society that have often plagued rugby clubs in this land. There were good times followed by fallow years. They would go ten or twelve years struggling all the while. Then they would get a bit of money again.

Gilligan says, 'It wasn't really until the mid-1960s that they started to get strong. Local youngsters might have gone away to rugby-playing schools and then they came back to Sligo from different parts of the country. They had rugby backgrounds and it grew from there.'

Comparative geographical isolation helped, too. Ballina is their nearest club, 56 kilometres away. But in AIL 2B the nearest club would be Dungannon and that's 145 kilometres away.

'We won a few Junior Club competitions from the mid-1960s but were given senior status from 1974/75. It was a Provincial League and Cups in those days, no AIL of course.

'We didn't do very well initially as a senior club. We joined the AIL in 1994 but got relegated in 1998.'

What of the health of the club now? 'It is healthier than it has ever been. We are playing in AIL. In 2023, we won 'Club of the Year' in Connacht. We have an underage group from six years of age. Our Under-18s won League and Cup a few years back and the Under-16s are good. So we are doing well.'

As for their women's rugby section, it is going great guns. Four Sligo women have been capped for Ireland at senior international level and they are very proud of their achievements. They are Thérèse Cosgrove, first capped in 1996; Anne O'Toole, capped in 1999; Aoife McDermott, in 2018 and Nicole Fowley, capped in 2019 and a current Ireland squad member.

Several Sligo players have represented Connacht at senior level and Ireland at Under-20 level. They reflect the contribution of the club to the promotion of rugby provincially and nationally:

- David McGowan was capped for Ireland at Under-21 level in 2005. He became Sligo's first professional rugby player.
- Former Sligo underage players Seán Henry and Cathal Sheridan played Heineken Cup Rugby with Connacht and Munster respectively. Another, Niall

Kenneally captained the Irish Clubs team in a 2018 international against Scotland.
- Three other Sligo players, Conan O'Donnell, Kuba Wojtkowicz and Donnacha Byrne were capped by Ireland at Under-20 level in recent years.
- Michael O'Hehir served as president of the Connacht branch of the IRFU in the 2023/24 season.

In the early 1970s, one of their members, George Draper, got underage rugby going on Saturday mornings. There were plenty of youngsters from non-rugby families. That remains a strong part of the club. As is tag rugby. Sometimes, says Gilligan, you can have forty teams playing there.

'The AIL as a concept is brilliant even though we have to travel. But it is a great day out from here and that fosters interest. We won the Connacht Cup twice in the last few years.

'We sometimes surprise people. Lansdowne were here once for a Bateman Cup game, as were Cork Constitution and Terenure College and it must have been like playing in the Welsh valleys for them. The kids from the private schools in Dublin and Cork had never encountered these wild men of Sligo.'

In 2008, they got a plan together. Their aim was to qualify to play in the AIL by 2013.

They were producing players, but the good guys were going off and playing for other clubs in the AIL. They were ambitious and wanted to play at a higher level. At one time, nine guys from Sligo were playing AIL for other clubs. In 2012, they qualified to play in the AIL, which reduced the loss of players to other clubs.

Of course, it wouldn't be Ireland and a sporting context without talk of the GAA. Yet Gilligan is far from morose at the constant challenge the rival game represents to rugby.

'There is a strong presence of GAA in Sligo and Limerick. GAA is the big thing in the country areas, always was. But there was always a sneaking regard for rugby. It was a physical game played all over Ireland. Of course, the GAA suspended you if you played another sport in those days. But from October to March there is very little GAA played and it would help rugby to give those lads experience of our game.

'To be honest, we do battle against a tide of GAA here.'

Oh, and one other tide on a wild Sligo day. That from the pounding ocean.

The club's recruitment processes have had to move with the times. 'We have two schools here, Summerhill College, which is a Catholic school, and Sligo Grammar School, which is Protestant.

'Over the years, the Sligo club has gone into the grammar school to recruit. But now we also go into Summerhill. We have made huge strides there. Now we get the guys who are really good athletes. So we are making progress as a club.'

Another factor is valuable to them. There are a lot of golden oldies close by and the rugby club is their life in many cases. Their support is greatly appreciated, especially when it comes to things like upgrading facilities.

On that topic, there were new dressing rooms going in when I visited as part of their upgrading of facilities. Four new rooms were being created. The government gives them some money for sports development. Otherwise, as with most clubs, it is down to their own efforts and ingenuity to raise funds.

Gilligan says that the Troubles in Northern Ireland never impacted Sligo RFC. Sport and politics were never subjects for discussion in the club, he adds. Of course, Sligo found themselves close to the Troubles. But they never had a fixture cancelled during that time, although they played plenty of games up north, places like Dungannon, Armagh and City of Derry.

Like so many other clubs from all over Ireland, Sligo found the hospitality was always outstanding from those clubs of the north.

'You might have been stopped at the border. There were checkpoints everywhere. Yet we always got through. But you wouldn't be talking to anyone after a match about this subject. It was the rugby that mattered. We all tried to get on with our normal lives.'

They always had Catholics and Protestants in their club and lifelong friendships were forged on the playing fields and in the clubhouse. They remain proud of that.

There is something else they feel proud of. Gilligan smiles.

'Rugby is a small game in Ireland, certainly compared to England. You would think it would be a numbers game. But perhaps things don't always work out the way you might think...'

CHAPTER 17

An Englishman's Words

In March 2017, the then Irish Taoiseach Enda Kenny nominated John F. Kennedy's speech to the Irish Parliament during his historic visit to Ireland in 1963 as his favourite speech of all time.

That's some accolade. It put him ahead even of South Africa's great freedom warrior, Nelson Mandela. Personally, when he spoke (and I secured an exclusive interview with him once at his Johannesburg home), the hairs stood up on the back of my neck.

However, far be it from this humble scribe to challenge the opinion of a former Taoiseach. After all, it's mainly in New Zealand that I call prime ministers to account and get it right. But if you were widening the field to include the world of sports, I suggest there may well be a challenger to Kennedy's words. And that man was a humble farmer from Bristol, in the West of England.

John Pullin wasn't speaking from the esteemed Irish Parliament building. He wasn't standing on a soapbox on St Stephen's Green. And he certainly wasn't talking about the freedom of an entire nation, in the inspirational style of Mandela.

What is more, Pullin also wasn't known as a public speaker – and didn't particularly relish it, either.

All the same, his words, spoken in February 1973, struck such a chord in the hearts of Irish rugby followers that there was an instant drawing back of chairs in the room where the respective teams of Ireland and England were dining, following their match that day.

Every man and woman in attendance rose to their feet and launched such a thunderous volume of applause that the occasion has gone down in the annals of rugby matches between the two nations.

Emotions were running high in 1972. Notwithstanding the sadness and anger of events at Derry just weeks before, by the evening of 12 February that year, in London, Irish rugby eyes were casting excited looks during the Twickenham post-match dinner.

Ireland had beaten England 16-12 that day, to follow their 14-9 win over France at the old Colombes stadium outside Paris.

No one had overlooked the fact that only two home fixtures, against Scotland in two weeks' time, and then Wales, on 11 March, stood between Ireland and a coveted first Grand Slam since 1948.

It was probably Ireland's best chance of a Grand Slam in all those years. True, not all Ireland was ordering cases of champagne to toast the impending, inevitable triumph. Wales had in their team a few who could play: the likes of Barry John, Gareth Edwards, Gerald Davies, J. P. R. Williams, Mervyn Davies and Delme Thomas.

Ireland would have to take them on assuming they could beat the Scots first.

But the story never had the chance to unfold on the playing field. Ireland's players and followers were stunned when news came through that Scotland had refused to make the journey in the light of events in Ireland at that time.

Less than a month earlier, on 30 January 1972, Bloody Sunday had erupted when British soldiers opened fire and shot twenty-six unarmed civilians during a protest march in the Bogside, Derry. Thirteen died that day, another some months later.

Even so, Ireland were shocked that their fellow Celtic nation, Scotland, turned their backs on the game and refused to fulfil the fixture. It hardly smacked of friendship and supporting those in their hour of need.

Then, some weeks later, Wales similarly pulled out of their fixture. The Championship was not completed; Ireland's hopes of a Grand Slam were over.

Willie John McBride has never masked his true feelings for those who made the decisions: 'I was very, very disappointed,' he said, years later.

The violence which erupted in the wake of the killings spread. On 2 February, the British Embassy in Dublin was attacked and burned down. The RAF Club was attacked, likewise many British-owned shops and businesses around the country.

By the time the new year dawned in 1973, events had hardly calmed. In fact, some called it the height of the Troubles.

So much so that in the light of the Derry massacre anniversary, obvious doubts existed as to whether England would travel to Dublin for their match. It was scheduled for 12 February but before that all manner of private conversations were held; Englishman to Englishman, RFU president to England captain, IRFU president to the RFU president and Ireland players to their English counterparts.

One of the latter involved Willie John McBride to the late England wing, David Duckham. McBride already remembered the years when so many rugby people had made such an effort to keep links alive either side of the border.

He said, 'They were troubled years. But rugby had made tremendous efforts to fulfil fixtures throughout Ireland and I told David that. Rugby people were making those efforts every Saturday to ensure matches were played.'

The pair had become close friends during the 1971 Lions' record-breaking tour of New Zealand. Now, McBride urged the flying England wing to make the trip. But Duckham wasn't convinced.

The RFU announced publicly that if the players wanted to go, they would let them. That may have masked a private determination by the RFU board to fulfil the fixture. Certainly, England captain John Pullin was left in no doubt from conversations he had that if he didn't go, someone else would.

In 2007, Pullin was invited to Dublin to receive an award from the Ireland Funds organisation for his part in those dramatic events. Amazingly – and remember, this was thirty-four years later – when he reached the lectern to speak, Pullin received another thunderous welcome with everyone standing up and roaring their approval.

Irish rugby people don't forget. There may be issues that continue to divide the Irish from the English. But there's a hell of a lot more that brings them together.

Pullin said on that occasion, 'I don't think we realised the seriousness of the situation at that time. But it was obvious to me that if rugby relations were to resume, they had to be done very quickly. The longer it went on, the harder it would have become.'

Meanwhile, at the height of the drama, Duckham rang McBride. The Irishman smiles at the memory.

'How a wing and a second row become mates, I don't know. But maybe that's rugby for you!

'David said, "My wife is not happy if I come, so I might have to cry off."

'"If you cry off, the game has gone," I told him. "You will never be able to live with that."'

Then McBride had an idea. He told the Englishman, 'Bring Jean over and I will guarantee the players' wives will look after her.'

'I might add that, at that time, wives were not considered by the IRFU. They didn't exist as far as they were concerned.'

With relationships strained and emotions running high, what would the consequences have been if England had joined Wales and Scotland in boycotting their fixture?

McBride says today, 'If England had not come, who knows what the consequences would have been? The economic loss of the fixture would have been substantial for a start. If England had not come, rugby in Ireland would have suffered even more. We would have been isolated and the Five Nations Championship would have been in trouble.'

Duckham rang back within thirty minutes with his decision. 'It's on, we're coming,' he said, simply.

McBride reflected on the decisions taken the previous year by the Scottish Rugby Union and Welsh Rugby Union to cancel their fixtures in Dublin. Could he not have held similar discussions with the players from those nations with whom he had toured in New Zealand in 1971?

'There was a lot of faffing about at that time,' he said. 'My understanding was that it wasn't the players saying they wouldn't come. It was the unions. I don't think it was political. I think they were just scared.

'The sad thing was, the players were not consulted at all.

'But I might have been on someone's wish list to be shot at. I am a Northern Protestant, I am a big target and I move slowly. And I was on the field...'

And what of Jean Duckham? 'She had a brilliant weekend,' smiled McBride.

No one was shot during the game, no pot shots were taken. No one in the crowd was spitting venom at the England players. Indeed, when Pullin led out his team at a heaving, highly emotional Lansdowne Road, the 50,000 crowd universally got to their feet and applauded. For five minutes, as the Irish team waited to enter the field.

Pullin, who died in 2021 at the age of eighty, said later, 'I never realised how pleased the Irish people were to see us.'

If ever a message was conveyed loud and clear it was surely this one. Rugby is a family that spans nations, seas, the entire globe. These are its core values: comradeship, standing up for what people believe in, demonstrating courage and commitment, support, friendship.

They were amply demonstrated that day. None more so than when the England captain gave his speech in a leading Dublin hotel that night, after his team's 18-9 defeat.

John F. Kennedy's speech all those years earlier contained many more words than those of the England rugby man. But Pullin had crafted a speech that contained sixteen words which would fairly fly at the hearts of Irish men and women throughout the nation.

'We might not be the greatest team in the world,' he told his gathered audience, humbly. 'But at least we turn up.'

It brought the house down.

CHAPTER 18

Westport

She's the gal from New York City who bust the trend of the Irish diaspora.

Liz Brady didn't pack off her family to the New World in search of a better life. She came the other way, over the Atlantic to Ireland, to settle in the land of her mom's birth.

Her mother was from Roscommon but Liz was born in New York. What is more, despite quitting America, the girl from New York with an Irish mother ended up being called 'president'. How's that for turning history on its head?

Brady has given loyal service to a rugby club in the West of Ireland. Yet when she arrived in Ireland from New York, she hardly knew one end of a rugby ball from the other. The key was her husband, who hailed from Westport.

'I would have spent a lot of my childhood over here,' she explained. 'But I was born in New York and after I'd got married and had kids, we were living in New Jersey, just over the bridge in Englewood. We were there for six or seven years.'

But by 1997 with their youngsters growing, the Bradys decided to relocate. All the way back to Ireland. 'The kids were at certain ages and we felt we had to make a decision.'

Westport's former president Liz Brady whose family travelled in the reverse direction to the diaspora.

They didn't find it difficult to choose Westport and settle beneath the gaze of Croagh Patrick, the holy mountain behind the rugby club and the site of great pilgrimage in County Mayo.

'We love it here,' said Brady. 'Westport is a tourist town and a little bit more diverse than other parts of the country. It's a lovely place to raise kids, a great place to live. Also, when your kids are in school, you meet people. I started working in services very quickly and it was a good time. Things were starting to get better in Ireland.'

Would she ever go back to the States? 'No. I think the States is not the place it was back in the 1980s and 1990s.'

The story of how Liz Brady and her family became such servants of this rugby club in the extreme west of Ireland over the last twenty-six years finds an echo throughout this land. The words we are looking for here include friendship, welcome, decency, optimism, fun.

Like so many others, both at this club and at others nearby such as Connemara RFC based in Clifden (they play in Connacht Junior League in Division 1A), she got involved through her children.

'My son played many years ago and I enjoyed going along even if I didn't know much about it. But when my daughter started playing, she was twelve and they needed women to supervise. I only live up the road and they said, "Someone is away, can you help?" They needed a female present.'

She admits that one of rugby's values especially attracted her.

'What particularly appealed were the people; they were welcoming. I liked the attitude, the fairness, the respect. Girls had started at that time, but it was new enough in the area and in Connacht.

'I felt the way the club embraced it was great. You didn't have to fight for equality, they were equal from the get-go. Even for myself, I was just there helping, carrying water bottles etc., but they were trying to encourage more women on the committee to take an active role.

'I was treated well, my daughter likewise and other people's kids too. I probably thought it was going to be a little bit elitist, but I don't think that happens here in the countryside. At rural clubs, it takes everybody to get involved.

'I loved the culture and the environment. The people were very supportive and it just grew on me. I loved sport before but not rugby. I didn't have any previous involvement with the game other than as a parent, helping out in the kitchen. So that's how I came into it.'

Perhaps a club like Westport has benefited from hearing different voices and perspectives in its committee room.

Different philosophies can be valuable in unravelling old attitudes.

I ask her if they find there is antagonism from the GAA.

'You're always battling against GAA and other sports. I love all sports, but I just found this to be a lovely club. There's a good community feel and everybody supports other sports, encouraging kids to be in other clubs and never to have to choose. Finish what you start; if you're playing Gaelic or soccer, finish out your league, and come to us when you're ready. That was very unusual from what I've been hearing.'

But one element concerns her greatly. 'We are seeing more injuries because of other sports and schools. They're just overloaded. So we aim just to support them and try not to add to the pressure they're under. If they're happy here and have a good experience, this is where they will end up when they're ready and that's how we have to approach it.'

This season, 2024/25 is Westport's centenary year, a magnificent achievement in a marvellous setting. Directly across the road from the club grounds is a steep hill offering a spectacular view across to the mountain and down to the sea, not far away.

Here is another club that has to battle the myriad challenges raised by the ocean. But it is a beautiful setting.

What is more, don't go thinking the star men have always passed them by. Like Sligo, they boast just one player from the club in their 100-year history who has played for Ireland. Charles Thomas John Lydon, known as Charlie, was born on 31 August 1931 in Lecanvey, Westport, and died on 16 February 2013 in Achill, Mayo aged eighty-one. A contemporary of Tony O'Reilly, Jack Kyle and Cecil Pedlow, he was a flanker and was capped in 1956 against Scotland at Lansdowne Road, although by then he was playing for Galwegians. Ireland won that match 14-10.

But Westport don't forget he started with them! They're still mighty proud of Lydon.

They began way back in 1925 with a single pitch in the Demesne Westport. They called it 'The Bog Field Gate' on the Golf Course Road. We can surmise from the name how humble it was.

But from small acorns grow mighty oaks.

Sixty years later, the club moved to a site at Carrowholly, three miles outside the town. There, they laid out and developed two pitches and a training area. Just two years after, a purpose-built clubhouse was erected and seventeen years later, they completed a new pitch improvement scheme which allows play in all weathers.

More recently, 250 tonnes of fine Wexford sand plus new grass along with the existing grass has been laid. It allows for a quicker turnaround after use.

'A natural pitch was the preference, but we had to look at options because we are in a very wet spot. The lads did a lot of research and came up with this natural, all-weather pitch which is sand-based.'

They did it over a summer and opened it for matches in the autumn. It was a big investment, about €110,000.

Where do they get money like that? 'Well,' said Brady, 'we had savings. The previous committee had been very good with money, and we restructured a lot of things that year.'

Finding a way. It is an inherent characteristic of rugby clubs such as this. But there are some that do it a whole lot better than others. Put Westport's name down on that list.

Brady completed two years as club president in June 2024, following her two years' service as vice president. As she says laconically, 'Then you finish in that role and move on to something else.

'Our club is like a great many others. It started with men's rugby but then embraced everybody, opening its doors to girls and boys. Now, we try to have as diverse a club as we can.'

She believes it is a big thing having this club in terms of the community. 'We have a huge catchment area. But other than Westport town itself, it's a rural catchment.'

Liz's two daughters are still involved. Laura is playing with the club and she's a senior women's player. 'She came to it a bit older and didn't start playing contact rugby till she was twenty-nine because there wasn't anything for her when she was younger.'

Her second daughter, Lily, is the out-and-out rugby player who has flown the Westport nest, if you can put it like that. She plays senior rugby for UL Bohemians and Connacht.

'She would have gone down to Limerick on a rugby scholarship from her experiences here and with Connacht. She played her rugby there and she's graduated from university now and is coaching down in Limerick with the college. We have a lot of girls come through our club playing for Connacht.

'We are very proud of the Westport contingent we have at other clubs.'

Brady's day job is as a day service quality lead within disability services. She works for Western Care Association which is a Mayo-based voluntary association. She has been there twenty-seven years.

She admits she's happiest donning a good pair of wellies, putting up goalpost pads or corner flags... getting things ready behind the scenes. She was doing all that even when she had the fancy title of 'president'. The reason? She loves the club and believes it's easy to put yourself out there.

Just mucking in is the creed at clubs such as this.

Do they get enough support from the IRFU? The question is usually regarded as akin to a walk on eggshells. But you'd expect honesty from a New York gal and you get it.

'We'd all like to say we could do more. The support we need is more time, probably; finances yes, but time. We're all volunteers. You have Connacht Rugby and you have the IRFU with a lot of paid staff who actually do give us a lot of help, but it's just time. Like everything, there are many more administrative aspects running clubs than there were years ago. I'm not saying it's because of the IRFU or Connacht Rugby. It's just the way we live, the way the world works now. But the onus is on the volunteers at clubs. Without them, there wouldn't be a club.'

The statistics suggest they must be doing something right. They got 240 people for a club dinner a while back and at the last count, had 470 playing members plus a few hundred non-playing members. It's a thriving place. But then, as Brady says, the groundwork has been laid for many, many years.

You sense the New York streak in Liz Brady is the driving force behind her determination. One thing's for sure. She has never looked back and wished she'd stayed in the States. Had she done so, she'd have never had her life so filled with the friendship and comradeship that runs deep through rugby clubs like Westport and Connemara in Clifden.

CHAPTER 19

Oughterard

You cannot have more basic facilities than they first knew at Oughterard. Even to call it a rugby club was stretching credibility.

No clubhouse, no changing rooms, no showers. They were, literally, the paupers of Galway rugby.

But it got worse than that.

The field they'd managed to acquire had a pronounced slope. Which meant, inevitably, water used to gather at the bottom. Of course, there was always plenty of it. Here, close by the so-called 'Wild Atlantic Way' north of Galway, you do get a decent drop of rain on a regular basis. Like, most days.

The youngsters knew instantly when training sessions were over. 'Right, guys, you can hit the showers now,' one of the coaches would call.

It was the signal for a headlong, aquaplaning rush down the slope towards the mini lakes that had formed from the lying water. Every youngster would slide, shouting and hollering, into the freezing cold water to try and get off the worst of the mud.

Complaints? You bet there were. Club stalwart Aidan O'Flynn said, 'The biggest complaint the parents had was that their washing machines were breaking down with the weight of the mud.

'Because we had no showers, we always said to the parents, "Make sure you bring something to cover your car seats, like a black bag," because they were literally covered from head to toe in mud and muck. All you could see were the little white eyes.'

Mind you, they have had a few deserters. Like the poshly dressed mother who turned up one time to collect her little monster after training. Before she had time even to cry out, little Liam had leapt into the front seat of the big, plush family BMW. Complete with its cream leather seats.

The Oughterard coaches could hardly bear to look.

Some passers-by were equally dumbfounded after one match when they saw the muddied oafs who represented the Oughterard senior team walk out of the ground, cross the road and plunge, boots and all, into the rushing Owenriff River that runs underneath a pretty little stone bridge on the outskirts of the town. Quite what the salmon that inhabit the river must have thought is not recorded.

All for the love of a game. But the enthusiastic rugby people at little Oughterard had a dream. What's more, they were determined to pursue it zealously...

Not that many people, beyond the locals, even know where Oughterard is. It's a small, increasingly chic little town, a thirty-five-minute, 26-kilometre drive out of Galway heading north on the N59, through Moycullen. It is close to the western shore of Lough Corrib, in County Galway. There are two superb butchers' shops, an elegant tourist gift shop, comfortable hotel and little coffee and bread-making shop. There's a lovely, cosy pub too, Powers Thatch, right in the town centre. On a Sunday evening at 6 p.m. in winter, the live Irish music fills the bars and a log fire crackles as a backdrop to your pint of Guinness. The quintessential Irish scene.

Aidan O'Flynn has been involved almost from the beginning of the club in 2004. Since then, he's acted as both chairman and president for two years. Now he's a retired president.

'There is no denying', he said, 'it was really raw beginnings. We even used to put cones over the stones so people wouldn't hurt themselves. To see it grow to this level is hugely encouraging.'

O'Flynn says Oughterard is a tourist town so it would always have had an influx of people. Some of the originators of the club would have gone to boarding schools in Leinster, giving them a knowledge of rugby.

'A lot of people who set up the club were blow-ins and we brought rugby with us. There was a sort of hunger for it.'

When they started, the field was hopelessly uneven. It belonged to a local hotel owner who, for a very small fee, allowed them to take it on and develop it. It was sloping badly so a general call went out – 'Bring your machines and help us.'

At one time, the machines were queuing up at the gate. They levelled it. There were local men who did it at a very low cost. Today, they regard the main pitch as probably one of the cheapest that's ever been developed.

'One thing you get in Connemara is a lot of people with machines and they were very happy to help. They basically levelled it, broke rocks. There was sand in some places, rock in others. They backfilled it and we just got it level. It took over six months,' said O'Flynn.

Their sense of pride at having found a possible site and then developed it into a rugby ground, was tangible.

On the last Saturday of October, on a cool, sunny autumn morning just outside the town, I spot a rough wooden board with the club's name above a gate and drive in. Immediately, you see activity all around the ground. On the main pitch, young boys and girls are throwing rugby balls about, running on to passes and chasing the ball wherever it is kicked through the fallen autumn leaves.

This is Saturday morning exercise for all ages, tiny tots and parents included. Further evidence, should it be needed, of how these junior clubs, whatever their size, contribute to the local community by offering such facilities. What is more, so many of these small clubs cater equally for girls as much as boys.

Season 2023/24 chairman Norman Tierney explains the importance of girls to the club. 'I'm more involved in the girls' rugby now. I've been here about nine years and they've been very successful over the last couple of years for such a small club. We supplied six girls to the Leinster Under-18s, one to the Under-20s and we had eight or nine girls in the Connacht Under-18s last year and five in 2023/24.'

In January 2024, the club had a big day. Their women's team, Tuam/Oughterard, played Barnhall in Mullingar in the All-Ireland Junior Cup final. It was the first time a Connacht team had reached the final in that competition. Only two players in the Tuam/Oughterard team were over the age of twenty, a phenomenal achievement.

The amalgamated Tuam/Oughterard team led 6-5 with just eight minutes left. But they got a bad injury and the subsequent break in play destroyed their momentum. They lost 15-6.

'Pints now to drown our sorrows,' reported my man at the game!

With three Portakabin-type buildings at the back of the ground, no one at the club could lay claim to providing plush facilities. But, typically of this club and those behind it, they constantly strive for improvement.

Tierney says, 'It's still small but it's growing and we've

started new facilities. We have now bought our own land, still in Oughterard but down near the lake so it's within walking distance of the town. We're quite a way into that development. The pitch was ready in March 2023.'

They had all the plans submitted for a clubhouse and were waiting on final planning on the second phase which will be the clubhouse, car park and other aspects. But in June 2024, news came that it was going back to planning with regard to the clubhouse. But Tierney insisted, 'Everything looks promising going forward.'

Tierney said, 'We get a lot of grants. There's a major wind farm just down the road here and they have a social commitment to provide money for clubs. They've been a big help and there are various supporting bodies whom we can lean on a bit for funding.'

What difference would a clubhouse make to them?

O'Flynn says that just having the basic facilities would be huge. 'To have the shower areas, a gym where we could have indoor training at times as well and just to have that kind of centre. The idea of the clubhouse would be a multifunctional space. It wouldn't be a white elephant sitting there empty all week.

'I've been involved in other organisations who work with retired people during the day. So the clubhouse will be used in the daytime for the community. When we put together the plan, we made that clear. We wanted it to be for the whole community, not just the rugby club. It's a bit like the French model where the community comes together around sport. We like that model so if we can facilitate that, we will.'

They have also done mightily well in the personality and character of some key operators behind the scenes. O'Flynn and Tierney are two such men. But another introduces himself to me.

Oughterard coaches (from left) Aidan O'Flynn, Jack Clarke and Norman Tierney.

'Hi, I'm Jack. I've been involved in coaching here. I was coaching the senior men's team. I've played here for a small bit too, I'd say about fifteen years...'

He is interrupted by O'Flynn.

'I'll tell you the real story now. Jack played for Ireland on the wing. He played for Munster for many years, but he came here and has been an enormous benefit to our club in terms of coaching and support. He's just being very humble there.'

It's true. D. J. Clarke of the Cork-based Dolphin club played six times for Ireland in 1991 and 1992, including at the 1991 Rugby World Cup. He also played for Munster. A wing, his debut came against Wales in the 1991 Five Nations Championship, which ended in a 21-all draw at Cardiff. His final cap, as a replacement, was against New Zealand in

Wellington, on Ireland's 1992 tour. A happy memory? Well, not quite. New Zealand won, 59-6, outscoring the Irish by eleven tries to one.

'They were in another league,' was Clarke's pithy comment. 'I would have called the Irish team of the nineties gloriously disorganised.'

Since those days, Clarke has devoted much time to this small club. He quickly made it a family affair.

'When Aidan started, he played and his son came along. It was the same for me and my daughter, Hannah.

'A lot of the coaches here had played before, and they brought their kids along. One of the big things that we do here is play for fun.

'Sometimes the kids are the ones who make up their minds. They're the ones who want to play rugby and I think that's where Oughterard, compared to some of the other rugby clubs, provides a real fun atmosphere. You can see some of the videos that Norman would have had with the girls, and you see the boys with the muck all over them in the evenings. They just love running around. It's fun and hopefully you'd hear that Oughterard do play for fun.'

They amalgamated with Tuam, partly because of the friendship between Norman and one of the Tuam club guys.

Amalgamation just made sense, said Tierney. 'I played with Tuam. They'd have always had a very strong youth and men's team – a bit like us – and were trying to get the girls up and running. So we played together.

'The girls developed big friendships over the years, both within our club and with the girls from Tuam. Jack's girl Hannah and my own girl, Karly, they started in the Under-10s here, but you couldn't separate them from the Tuam girls. Now, they've been eight years together. It's a very strange mix because we're 50 miles away! It's phenomenal the matches and

211

playing. They would be top of the league in most age groups so it's brilliant.'

The girls won the Women's Division 1 title in 2022/23. It was the first time they had ever been in a Connacht senior women's league. They were all youngsters, aged eighteen or nineteen, but they won it, beating Westport in the final. They also beat Sligo and Galwegians. By winning that, they qualified for the All-Ireland Junior Cup the following year.

The concept of links with other clubs has now expanded.

'Connemara is a very long-established club, one of the older clubs in the province. They're about 30 miles away over at Clifden and we've now started to join with them at youth levels where we've got a few teams. They may not all train together, but they play together, and the kids love it,' says Tierney.

'There was resistance from some people; you know, about giving up club identity. But in Connacht, we see those geographical links between these smaller clubs that are set up, and that's going to become stronger.'

O'Flynn enthuses at the community aspect to all this. 'All the parents gathered round here and met each other for a chat. Sometimes they were complete strangers. This was a town where a lot of parents wouldn't know each other, especially young parents coming here from other places.

'It was a great spot for them all to gather. A lot of clubs' parents just drop the kids and go, but here they hang around. We really encourage families, and the participation of parents.

'We often get a group of ten or twelve parents coming down and playing tag rugby. Especially if their youngsters are at training. Instead of standing around and doing nothing else, some parents like to get involved. Fitness and health are big factors nowadays.'

What would many of those youngsters be doing if they didn't have a rugby interest to pursue?

Sometimes probably nothing, thought Jack Clarke. The good thing about rugby, as he said, is that it can cater for all shapes and sizes whereas with some other sports, you have to be fit to start.

But what was the crucial factor that enabled them to succeed?

'I think it was our ethos. We were very child-centred, that was the whole thing. The ethos was that we were there for the kids, and I think even the schools got that. And it's lovely to see so many wanting to get involved.

'We really made sure that our training sessions were very well organised so when we came to 'littles' as we called the minis, it was very important that it was about fun, not results. We always made it clear, it wasn't about winning, but participating.

'The parents got to see that it wasn't what they see on TV, which is the professional kind of monsters; that their kids could do well here and be physical but also be well trained and safe by learning how to tackle, to fall etc. Over time they came round, which is proven by the number of women that have become involved now,' thinks O'Flynn.

'The number of mothers, who probably hadn't played before, is hugely encouraging. When the club started, all the coaches were parents who had played rugby. But now a lot of the parents are with Connacht doing coaching course skills. They get their coaching badges and then they can come here and coach their kids.'

This bringing together of the communities – and Oughterard is by no means the only club in Ireland that does this – reminds you of the long-held values of this sport and its support for communities.

Oxymoronically, what we are increasingly seeing at the top level of the game, the so-called window of the sport, with its serious injuries, threat of long-term brain damage, rapacious financial demands that have helped bankrupt several leading clubs, violence, abuse of match officials, boring and incessant kicking of the ball and, in this professional age, a total lack of loyalty to original clubs, bears no relation to the values being demonstrated at the lower levels of rugby.

Perhaps the greatest triumph of the Oughterard club, I can now tell you. From beginning as a youngster new to the game, Karly Tierney became the first international of the club. Then, Jack Clarke's daughter, Hannah, joined her in the Ireland girls' international team at their age level. They met in the Under-10s originally when Oughterard only had five or six girls playing. But from that small cluster, Oughterard produced two Irish internationals.

Remarkable.

Karly remembers clearly the time she went along to the club one evening to watch her brother, Nathan, training. 'I was standing on the touchline and after a while, Dad said to me, "Do you want to try that?"'

No one had a clue, of course, about what the future held. But from Karly agreeing to have a go in the Under-10s, years later she found herself wearing an Irish international jersey.

'Dad was good,' agreed Karly. 'When I had decided I wanted to join in, he helped develop me as a player. But he didn't pressurise me to play.

'I liked the contact side of it. It's more fun than a game without contact. But there is also speed, strength and skills. Rugby has all those things. You can be the fastest or the slowest, but you can still play this game and have fun. At that time, there weren't many girls... just five or six, maybe. Now the women's section has thirty or more from 10s upwards.'

She insists size is not the only essential factor. 'If we see a bigger team, we are pretty confident we can outrun them for speed. It is more about technique than strength half the time.

'I play No. 8 and I like to get the ball and run. There is a lot of freedom in that position.'

She played with Ireland in Edinburgh in the Under-18 Six Nations Festival in 2022 and again in Italy in 2023. She then made the Ireland Under-20s at the Under-20 Six Nations Festival playing against Scotland and Italy and looked forward to being involved in the inaugural Six Nations Under-20 Championship.'

She won the Connacht Rugby Women's Club Player of the Year award in 2023 even though she was only eighteen.

There was more good news for any rugby-mad young women around that time. It was announced that a British & Irish Lions women's squad will make a first tour to New Zealand in 2027, music to the ears of Karly. She wasn't saying she would necessarily get anywhere near a place in such a squad. But the concept thrilled her, and why not?

Hannah Clarke is a year younger than her closest friend. But they are both thankful to rugby for forging what has become a wonderful friendship.

Her mum, Heather Clarke, told me: 'Hannah's friendship with Karly came just from rugby. They met at training one night and it gelled. There was a great atmosphere.

'The girls had so much fun together.'

And where one goes, the other seems to follow. Exactly twelve months after Karly won the Connacht player of the year award, Hannah won the same award at the Connacht Awards night in May 2024. How's that for synchronisation?

Hannah has been playing since she was six or seven. But it didn't take over her life until she played for Ireland. Then it became a lot to juggle, especially when you are so young.

Heather said, 'As parents, we are super proud. But we are not pushy parents. Her dad helps with coaching, but the girls do what they want. That won't change.

Oughterard girls Hannah Clarke (left) and Karly Tierney.

'It is a big part of her life and she has made so many friends.'

Hannah, a wing or full-back, played for Ireland Under-18s Sevens team in two tournaments. In the summers of 2022 and 2023, she played for Ireland Under-18s. In summer 2024, it was for Ireland Under-20s.

Ask Hannah Clarke what rugby has given her primarily and she doesn't hesitate.

'All the friends that come with it. Then you make more friends from around the country if you are training with Connacht. These become bonds that you just wouldn't have with people if you didn't play the sport. Some of my best friends have come through this game. You go through a lot

216

in this sport; wins and defeats. But when you have friends, both tie you together.

'What I like most about rugby is meeting new people, making new friends.'

When she started playing, she admits it took a while to get used to the physical side. But that has come.

'We spend a lot of time building up our skills. It's very important to have a complete skills base before you play in a match. You always fall back on your skills.

'Both forwards and backs do passing skills regularly. The forwards work just as hard as the backs at this. They are expected to be up to the passing standards of everyone. It's about trying to get a constant skill base.'

'When you run, you look for space. Personally, I have always run away from people, not into them. Of course, it depends on the type of rugby you play and on what position you're playing. But I see my job as drawing other people in and trying to put others into space.'

She admits the opportunities within the game are attractive.

'That inspires me. It is great to see the women's game moving forward. A few years ago, that would never have been put on the table. But we are getting a lot more opportunities and it's good to see a pathway where you can go on in the game. You can see a real direction now. It would be great to be involved.'

CHAPTER 20

The Wild Men

He made a lasting memory at birth, and when he died sixty-two years later, 800 mourners accompanied the coffin to his grave.

It's fair to say that Maurice Ignatius Keane made a substantial impression in life. Not least on his mother. For when he was born, he weighed 14lbs.

This was no ordinary man. At his death, the Irish Taoiseach Brian Cowen announced him as 'one of the great gentlemen of Irish sport'.

The *Irish Times* called him 'an amazing, graceful giant of a character'.

Born in July 1948, Keane became the first Kerryman to play rugby for Ireland. As a youngster, he did what most young Kerrymen did. Played Gaelic football. He was good at it, too. Playing for University College Cork (UCC) he won several medals and represented Kerry at Under-21 and Junior levels as a full-back.

He was then tempted to try rugby, but the raw relations between the two sports at that time meant he needed a false name. So Moss Fenton stepped out for the UCC junior rugby team as a second row forward, and his path to Ireland's national side unfolded.

What did he make of his first experience of rugby, someone asked him? 'Ah, well,' he replied after a moment's thought. 'It was like watching a pornographic movie. Very frustrating for those watching and only enjoyable for those participating.'

That gave birth to a multitude of Keane tales, both true and apocryphal. The late Tony O'Reilly told one at an Ireland Funds gala dinner one year.

With his masterly command of mimicry, O'Reilly told the tale of Keane sitting alone one night at a pub, nursing a very lonely pint when a very attractive woman came in, saw him and came over to him.

She says, 'Gosh. Are you Moss Keane?'

He says, 'I am Moss Keane.'

She says, 'Moss Keane the footballer?'

'I am Moss Keane the footballer,' he replies.

'But you are enormous,' she says. 'What height are you?'

'I am 6ft 5 and a half inches,' he replies.

She says, 'But are you built in proportion?'

He says, 'If I was, I would be 9 feet tall.'

In 1978, Keane was part of the famous Munster team which beat the touring New Zealanders. The late All Blacks lock Andy Haden recalled forming up for a line-out which was Munster's throw.

The code came clearly from the player throwing in... '22, 34, 22,' he said.

To which Keane replied in a loud voice, 'Oh fook, not me again.'

Big-boned, strong, prominent facial features with large ears and protruding teeth, with eyes that seemed to dilate when he looked straight at you beneath a healthy shock of hair, Keane could be a fearsome sight on the sports field. But his friends always said he was in truth as soft as a kitten.

Which was perhaps the cause of Trevor Ringland's

misunderstanding when he was engaged in conversation with him at the time he made his Ireland debut as a wing.

'Big Mossie', with those large, wide eyes, came up to him and started talking earnestly in his heavy Kerry accent. Ringland, the Ulsterman, didn't have a clue what he was saying.

'He then said something else, but I still didn't know what he was on about. But I thought he said something funny, so I laughed.

'One of the other boys turned to me and said, "Why are you laughing? He has just told you his dog has died."

'You can imagine how I felt. But of course, it was a total wind-up. Mossie was a good character to be around all the time, a nice man.'

Plenty would testify to that view.

Starting rugby late meant Keane didn't make his Ireland international debut until he was twenty-six. But when he did, few ever forgot it.

He was playing club rugby for Lansdowne and joined the throng in their clubhouse after a game that afternoon. At 6 p.m., the Ireland selectors would announce their team to play France in Paris on 19 January 1974.

The names were duly read out. M. I. Keane (Lansdowne)... the place erupted and the night began. It was to be his first cap.

Fast forward to 2 a.m. the next morning and the clubhouse looked more like a war zone. Bodies strewn out in various poses and conditions, others seeking the bar to hold them up.

A small, old man spied Mossie and said, 'Now, Mossie, there's a last pint for you; you're in there.'

'Ah, no,' replied Keane. 'I'm on my way home; I'm back to Kerry.'

Those sufficiently compos mentis were horrified. But Keane assured them all would be well. Some twenty minutes or so later, a Gardaí radio crackled into life in the city centre, telling of a car being driven the wrong way up a one-way street at 5 mph.

The car was stopped, the window wound down. The officer immediately recognised the driver.

'Ah now, Mossie, we've heard your news tonight and I expect you've had just a pint or two to celebrate.'

Keane looked at him aghast. 'A pint or two, officer,' he repeated. 'Are you feckin' mad? I've had twenty-two feckin' pints and I'm on my way home.'

To which the officer replied, 'Ah, Mr. Keane, I wish you hadn't told us that.'

But they persuaded him to let the police hold the keys until morning. Sense prevailed.

Today? You wouldn't contemplate it. Utter madness. But back in the day, standards were more lax compared to now.

A week later Ireland got to Paris for the match. Keane made his debut alongside Willie John McBride in the second row but Ireland lost, 9-6.

McBride decided to keep an eye on his new colleague that night. They went to the banquet, all dressed up in dinner jackets, and they offered big Mossie a wide-rimmed, delicate crystal glass with a liquid inside it full of lively bubbles.

'And what might this be?' he enquired.

He seemed to accept the explanation that this was France, this was champagne, and a few glasses wouldn't be out of order. Then came the fine wines at dinner. Keane muttered to a colleague, 'Can I not get a feckin' pint here?'

By midnight, the dinner was over and McBride found himself in Montmartre with Keane in tow.

The new cap told his pal he felt awful hungry, so they found a shop cooking and selling sausages in rolls. Alas, there was a queue.

Keane waited a while, then made his move. Going into the shop, he approached the counter and saw a couple of sausages. Grabbing them in a mighty mitt, he made his way out of the shop against a background of shouting by the owner.

No one had told Keane his two sausages were attached to about twenty more...

Brian McCall remembered a time when, although still at university, he was chosen to play in an Irish trial at Lansdowne Road.

After the trial, the selectors named twenty-six players for extra training the next day and he was one of them.

'Our coach, Noel Murphy, had called a team meeting for the next morning. But it was delayed because Moss Keane and Willie Duggan had not turned up. They delayed it for an hour, but they still weren't there.'

Someone was despatched to their room but an inspection revealed neither bed had been slept in. The plot deepened...

Meanwhile, the players hung around, waiting for developments.

'Noisy, (Murphy) (the coach), was effing and blinding but decided we had to get on with it. As we were running out on to the pitch at Lansdowne Road to start the training session, round the corner came Keane and Duggan. They'd been drinking all night. Murphy gave them a bollocking.

'We were running lengths up and down the pitch and when I turned round, Keane, together with Duggan, was being sick behind the goalposts at Lansdowne Road. I thought to myself, *These are my legends.*'

But 'Big Mossie' never lost that legendary status, in McCall's eyes. 'Great man, great heart,' he said.

McBride concurred with that, calling him 'one of the great characters of that time'.

223

And his record was immense. In a ten-year spell from 1974 to 1984, Keane won fifty-one caps for Ireland and rumbled over for one solitary try. He was only the third Irish forward to reach the fifty caps landmark. Imagine if he had started his rugby Test career at twenty rather than twenty-six.

Even so, McBride added, 'He would have been a very good player if he had got himself fit. But he never disciplined himself to be fit. You had to do that yourself.

'He came into the game very quickly; he was a huge man, very strong with great hands. He was good in the scrummage, too. He was willing to learn and was a big addition to the Irish team. He was aggressive and never stood back from anything. He went to New Zealand in 1977 with the Lions and didn't do himself any harm there, either.

'I remember he never had much control of his feet. He would step on everyone else's feet.

'But alcohol became a problem for him. He went off it for a period of years but then started drinking again.'

How good could he have been? 'Well, he had a lot of skills and he was quite fast too when he ran. But you had to be fit then. He never really was, so it's hard to know how good he might have been.'

McBride was invited to Keane's wedding and the Ulsterman never forgot that day, either. Keane was a bit like that. Just about everything he ever did or signed up for became unforgettable.

'There were a few priests there but no matter, Mossie got up and sang one of the filthiest songs I had ever heard.'

All doubtless delivered with that incorrigible, shy-looking trademark grin.

Long, long before he died, on 5 October 2010 from bowel cancer, a legend had written forever its own name in the archives of rugby football in Ireland.

THE WILD MEN

Irish rugby has known some great characters down the years. But few stand comparison with Maurice Ignatius Keane.

The world, never mind just the game itself, was a better place for his presence.

* * *

Ireland's capacity to churn out top quality second row forwards has long since become legendary. An almost continuous line of tough warrior men ready to do battle in the famous green jersey has emerged from all corners of the land.

Many have gone on to captain or represent the British & Irish Lions on their overseas forays. Keane, who toured New Zealand with the 1977 Lions, was just one of them.

Each man brought a particular quality to the role. In no particular order and with apologies to the unfairly omitted, these are some of those who have given Irish and Lions teams a hard inner core from the engine room of the scrums.

Jimmy Nelson, Tom Reid, Ronnie Thompson, Bill Mulcahy, Mick Molloy, Willie John McBride, Neal Francis, Donal Lenihan, Willie Anderson, Malcolm O'Kelly, Mick Galwey, Jeremy Davidson, Paul O'Connell, Donncha O'Callaghan, Ian Henderson, James Ryan and the outstanding Tadhg Beirne. Their combined efforts have offered a sound underpinning of so many Irish packs.

But if the exploits of men like Moss Keane might be regarded today as controversial, consider the rugby activities, lifestyle and extraordinary achievements of an Irish second row forward missing from the above list.

Robert Blair 'Paddy' Mayne was as far from a conventional rugby man of the 1930s as it was possible to be. Mayne came from Newtownards and was the sixth of seven children. From an early age, his intelligence, aptitude for dismissing fear or danger, especially on the rugby field, and sheer devilry marked him out as special.

At his school, Regent House Grammar School, established in 1924, those in charge at a later time wrote: 'At Regent House we believe in setting the bar high and helping every student reach their full potential.'

Paddy Mayne was to do that in bucketloads.

He joined Ards RFC, later Nigel Carr's club, and played for Queen's University, Belfast, after school. There, his skill and courage at rugby catapulted him into the Ireland national team, starting with a first cap against Wales in 1937. He won five more caps and was chosen for the 1938 British & Irish Lions tour of South Africa.

This was a phenomenal rise in anyone's language.

On the tour, he played in seventeen of the twenty provincial matches and in all three Tests. The Lions lost the series 2-1, winning the final Test. After the first Test, a South African newspaper called Mayne's performance 'outstanding'.

But events off the field in South Africa became a precursor to Mayne's extraordinary war years. He cheerfully conceded that wrecking his teammates' hotel rooms was a particular pleasure. He also managed to free a convict he had befriended and, at one point, after a game against Natal, he came back to the team hotel carrying the head of a slaughtered antelope. It was duly dumped on a teammate's bed.

It was said he and a teammate also enjoyed slipping away from their colleagues and heading for the docks in Durban, Cape Town and East London. There, they would pick fights with the local sailors.

Fine sport, one imagines, was had by all. Except the poor sailors who would not have known Mayne had been Irish Universities heavyweight boxing champion in 1936.

But if his rugby activities were different, his wartime

pursuits and achievements were astonishing. Utterly fearless in the face of the enemy, he was posted to North Africa and became a founding member of the Special Air Service (SAS). He led one raid on a German airfield that saw twenty-four aircraft wrecked, most of them by Mayne single-handedly.

He served with 11 Commando and fought Vichy French forces in North Africa.

In July 1942, he took part in the most successful SAS raid of the desert war when, with eighteen armed jeeps, he and his colleagues raided an airfield and destroyed up to forty German aircraft, escaping with the loss of only three jeeps and two men killed.

In January 1944, Mayne was promoted to lieutenant colonel and commanding officer of the re-formed 1st SAS Regiment. He subsequently led the SAS with great distinction through the final campaigns of the war in France, the Netherlands, Belgium, Germany and Norway,

One report of a rugby match played by Mayne before the war talked of his 'ruthless efficiency'. He adapted that quality to warfare, becoming one of the British Army's most decorated soldiers. Remarkably, Montgomery recommended him for the Victoria Cross after one outstanding act of courage.

But the wild side of Mayne's character had surfaced when he hit a senior officer, Major Charles Napier, who was second in command of the battalion, apparently over a dispute about the man shooting Mayne's dog. Mayne was dismissed from 11 Commando the next day.

The Establishment back in the UK could not stomach such a man receiving the ultimate award in battle. Montgomery's advice was rejected, and Mayne was turned down for the award.

He died in December 1955 in Newtownards at the age of only forty, after a road accident, and was buried in Movilla Abbey graveyard in the town.

CHAPTER 21

Rugbaí Chorca Dhuibhne (Dingle)

A raging, boiling ocean thunders close by; a tearing wind blows down off the hill at the back of the ground. Rain showers come at you horizontally.

Rugby in Kerry is not for the faint-hearted.

But there are compensations. The field itself has a nice covering of grass. They make sure it's not too long. With a mower? No. The groundsman's flock of sheep.

I stand outside a crumbling brick building, the rusting metal door and its hinges under fierce attack from the salty, sea air. They call it their changing facilities. In truth, it's a converted cow house.

Even the concrete on a wall is cracked and rotting, from the water that seeps inside. The shrubs and bushes nearby, bent in one direction like old men, reveal the source of the howling winds.

There is more. A field with two sets of basic rugby posts, gently sloping down towards the ocean some few hundred metres off, looks barren, bereft of facilities. But not of hope.

Around the time I stood on this vivid, soaked sod, around 12 kilometres outside Dingle in a deserted corner of West Kerry and the peninsula that runs into the Atlantic, members of Kerry County Council's planning committee were deciding the fate of this tiny club.

You just hoped that the committee members had half the hope, optimism, vision and enthusiasm that infuses these men in the far south-west of Ireland. Outsiders visiting the land they call a rugby ground probably see only decay. Perhaps a tinge of dismay, too.

But the rugby followers of Rugbaí Chorca Dhuibhne, to give it its full, proud title, see it differently. And thankfully, Kerry County Council bought into their vision. Planning permission was approved in late 2023. The hard work began almost at once.

There is a strong reason why this club is not called 'Dingle RFC'. The Irish language is central to their existence. 'We wanted to get over the parish rivalries,' explained club official Paddy Fenton. 'The name is trying to be inclusive, to reflect the whole peninsula, not just Dingle. So that everyone is pulling in one direction.

'We speak Irish 100 per cent. It is written in the club's constitution. It helps create a means of communication; it's not a problem.'

Hope is eternal in the hearts of these men. They see new, match-quality floodlights, a levelled up, sand-based reseeded pitch and, in time, work beginning on a clubhouse. At a cost, of course. General estimates range from €250–300,000 for the job, although they think 80 per cent of it could come from grants. Buying the ground cost them €150,000.

In October 2024, Paddy Fenton was proclaiming 'probably the best week in the history of the club'. The seniors won the McElligott Cup for the second time, beating Tralee 29-28 in the final. Then came news that €178,500 had been granted by central government, plus a €62,000 grant and another €1400 grant, both from the local council. Plus, the Under-14s, Under-16s and Under-18½s all won.

An optimistic future, then, for the most westerly club in all Europe, never mind Ireland.

They hope that such facilities will enable them to play on Friday or maybe Saturday nights. Then, opponents could travel and stay for the weekend, providing a knock-on effect to local businesses. If that were to happen, they would hope for something reciprocal from those businesses in terms of sponsorship for the club. It would be a two-way street.

Then there are the comfortably-off owners of the many holiday homes that cling to the fields and hills of this beautiful region. Many of those owners are not seen for perhaps ten months of the year. But, says Fenton, we would be happy if they were to support the club more. 'We are trying to attract them down to the club. We think it has untapped resources in that respect.'

But you have to be a born optimist to share such a dream. At the last count, the club had six non-playing members.

'It's hard to get people to sign up. Our facilities are very basic,' they admit.

If you picked up a copy of *The Kerryman*, a newspaper covering North Kerry, West Kerry and Tralee, in early November 2023, you found twenty-five pages devoted to sport. There was a multiplicity of stories covering just about every sport ever invented. Except rugby.

Yet in that first week of November, there was a local sensation. A rugby story from the region made it on to the paper's back page, an almost surreal experience. But there was a simple explanation. Among the back-up staff of the South African rugby squad that had just won the 2023 Rugby World

Rugbai Chorca Dhuibhne coach Paddy Fenton (foreground) with friends.

Cup in Paris was a Kerryman, Paddy Sullivan, whose role was as a senior performance analyst.

The story of Sullivan's success filled one column. But that was about it for rugby in the paper.

To be a rugby lover in this part of the world is to plough a lonely furrow.

But all you need to have your spirits revived, a warm glow return to your soul, is to pull up a stool in one of Dingle's renowned pubs or coffee shops with a rugby devotee. Almost instantly, optimism returns. You begin to share the dream.

They founded the club in 2001, Paddy Fenton tells me with a twinkle in his eyes, as we sit in the James Long bar. But why would you set up a rugby club in an area known as one of the strongholds of GAA in all of Ireland?

'Now therein lies a tale,' says Fenton, one of the senior figures at the club and a highly regarded coach. 'I think they only did it to get tickets to Munster matches.'

232

They credit the late Danno O'Keefe for his role in establishing the club. A local publican, it's thought he might have been influenced by some of the South Africans who had found their way to Dingle to work at a fish factory. When they began to look for players, a few Gaelic footballers also showed interest.

Of course, it all started in wonderfully haphazard style. They turned up for their first match against Tralee needing to borrow a few players to get the game played.

Early on, they found a site extending to 17 acres near Ballydavid, way out on the Peninsula. 'A wild and lonely place' as Private Fraser was fond of saying, in those *Dad's Army* TV classics. Even Fenton, a man with a wonderfully dry sense of humour, admits, 'It is very isolated.'

Well, America is the next stop going west.

Their geographical location decrees their fortunes. They have struggled in recent years because it is so far to travel for most matches. Even their home games can cause problems because referees from places like Tralee and Killarney are not particularly keen on the long drive west, especially when they have to negotiate the mountain pass to get home.

Yet out of all this, the club is gathering goodwill and a swell of support. Their seniors play in the Munster Junior League and their team includes outsiders no one knew existed. Like wing three-quarter Deividas Uosis, a former All-Ireland medallist who was born in Dingle but of Lithuanian descent. He found himself in Australia at one time and played Australian Rules for two years. He had also played underage Gaelic football but has switched to rugby with conspicuous success.

'He is an incredible athlete,' Fenton tells me.

Fenton seems confident. 'We are getting there with the forwards and we've built a really good team. The seniors are doing OK.'

What is more, when the GAA programme finishes every November, around 50 per cent of the team return to their roles from the other code. They feel the loss when GAA resumes in the new year, he admits.

But they have built good relations with their hugely popular rival. As you would need to in what Fenton calls the heartland of Gaelic football. 'It's very important we co-exist. They like the way we keep their players fit during the winters. Also, Gaelic football coaching is very similar to rugby in some ways. Like breaking the tackle, passing before contact. As for rugby, we benefit from their spatial awareness, ball-handling skills and general fitness.'

There is something else, too. The Gaelic football pitch is twice the size of a rugby field, yet they have the same number of players. It is, says Fenton, a full-on game.

You measure the success and future potential of clubs such as this by the interest at youth and minis level. If a club can attract a steady stream of youngsters, there is a good chance the whole structure of the idea will flourish. So if you acknowledge the fact that the club has twenty-nine players in their Under-18½s, then there must surely be optimism for the future, not least because in season 2023/24, those youngsters were at one stage top of their league.

As for the Under-16s, who are coached by Fenton, they twice reached the Munster juniors final at their age group, despite confronting the junior teams of some famous clubs. Each time they drew but were declared losers because their opponents had scored the first try of the game. Thin margins...

Imagine the pride, then, when their local school, Pobalscoil Chorca Dhuibhne won its first ever provincial rugby title in May 2024, beating Kinsale Community School 47-7 in the Giles Shield Under-16 B final at Cork's Musgrave Park.

Kieran Keane (remember that name, say the experts) scored three tries.

The school was only founded in 2007 and they have also won three All-Ireland titles in Gaelic football. Led by captain Jack Grealy, the Dingle school put on a masterclass in the final to lift the trophy.

The *Kerry's Eye* newspaper, in a May edition, proudly announced: 'It's not every day a Kerry school wins its first provincial title at rugby.'

There could have been another triumph for the Dingle school. The same teams had met in the semi-final of the club plate. Alas, when no referee was appointed, a Kinsale official generously offered his services.

He did his best, God bless him. But it would be stretching credulity to say his performance was roundly applauded by all present.

A Dingle man shrugged and said, 'His performance should have earned at least an audition for a Monty Python stage production.'

Kinsale won 16-12.

Paddy Fenton calls it 'a golden age' for underage rugby in this part of the world. 'Even the local secondary school has bought into rugby. But it's a premium Gaelic football school. Back in the day, those that didn't play Gaelic football got no sport. Rugby has changed that.'

But the distances are always forbidding. They've played Kanturk, a Cork team, not to mention the likes of Killorglin and Killarney. Two years ago, they played a couple of away games that totalled 1124 kilometres, all without the expense of hiring a team coach.

'We try to avoid buses,' says Fenton. 'We like to get the parents interested and involved if we can with car shares. It helps build the spirit in the club.'

The biggest problem they have, according to Fenton, is that their potential numbers are really small. He has four boys and jokes that they have been the backbone of a few teams. 'But families are getting smaller, and some people have been apprehensive about playing rugby.'

Good quality coaching, which he insists is a hallmark of Munster rugby, is critical. 'It is up to the coaches to eliminate any risk,' he thinks.

You grow clubs like theirs, he believes, by doing little things well. They pride themselves that everyone who turns up gets a game. No leaving youngsters out of it all, isolated and feeling rejected on the touchline. 'Rugby has an ethos that you don't put Johnny on for the last two minutes. You must give them a good chance. We want to attract, not lose players.'

A brilliant ethos.

Such talk is heartening and goes to the core of junior rugby. People like Gary Curran who was a founder member but now looks after the minis, plus Australian Rob Williams, who has settled in Dingle after marrying a local girl and now coaches the Under-14s and Under-18s, have both played key roles. Fenton says, 'They have shown amazing commitment and done a lot of good work.'

They feel their senior team was neglected for a time. But they demand respect, not least for the fact that they produce a lot of kids for Munster underage teams. Two at Under-16 level, one each at Under-17 and Under-18. That is a good representation from a small club.

The memorable victory achieved by their Under-16s against their esteemed Cork Constitution counterparts, emphasised the point.

Fenton is a qualified vet. He went to University College, Dublin to study and played his rugby there. 'Mainly for the pub team, not the firsts,' he smiled.

But back in the day, he also found time to play Gaelic football.

Fenton's status, as a former pupil at a top rugby-playing Irish school (Newbridge College), then university and now the father of four boys, qualifies him to comment on an issue that troubles many in Irish rugby. The increasing intensity of the game at schools level.

'I was a decent schools player, although it all went downhill for me thereafter. But today, it's all about the intensity. These youngsters at some of the schools are living the lives of professional sportsmen. The aim is not to win the match for the kids, it's for the school.

'But sport has to be fun. So when they reach eighteen and leave school they are tired of that intensity. It's like playing professional rugby before you are developed physically and that is very challenging, a really big ask.

'Some of those schools have a €1 million budget. Is it bad for the game? I don't know. But it is working for Leinster and Ireland.'

The schools in places like Limerick and Cork, he believes, would not have such resources. But he's sure of one thing. 'This focus on the top, the peak of the game, has narrowed the base at the club level. The whole professional thing has stolen the support base of the senior clubs. It doesn't affect us very much, but it certainly does the bigger, senior clubs.'

They run the club on a strictly controlled budget of €25–30,000 a year. It has made them a lot more efficient insisting on those parameters. But Fenton warns it would be dangerous to become ambitious.

'We just want to compete and to contribute. We also aspire to speaking as much Irish as we can. That attracts parents to us. They appreciate that we have a commitment to the local culture.'

They put on fundraising events like a golf day and also an event to coincide with the world-famous Dingle Food Festival which is held on the first weekend of October.

They also benefit from an important sponsorship. Just eleven years after the rugby club began in 2001, a company named 'Dingle Distillery' opened its doors for business, just overlooking an inlet on the outskirts of the town. Traditionally, Irish whiskey had trailed far behind in the wake of its Scottish counterparts.

But the last decade has been a propitious time for the Irish industry. Small, individual companies like Dingle have been set up and their products have become much in demand. So much so in this case that Dingle now markets its own distinctive whiskey, gin and vodka and sells its whiskey to twenty countries worldwide. They might not yet be frightening the life out of the likes of Scottish giants such as Macallan and Johnnie Walker, still less the leading vodka names like Smirnoff.

But in Dingle, Kerry and indeed increasingly across all of Ireland, Dingle whiskey and gin especially have become hugely popular. What is more, two of the Master Distillers at the company have been avid rugby supporters. Now there's a helpful coincidence.

Michael Welsh was also a senior coach at the club. As Fenton says, 'Between fishing and the distillery, we have had half our pack of forwards! Their founder was very generous to us and that has continued after Michael left.

'They are a great success and a fantastic company. They have given a lot of support to players through jobs.'

The present Master Distiller at Dingle, Scotsman Graham Coull, attributes the close links between business, town and rugby club to the original founders of the company.

They had a huge passion about supporting Dingle Town overall, he says.

Dingle was established and began making whiskey in 2012, but turned its attention to gin production whilst waiting for the first whiskey casks to mature. He joined in October 2019.

'It was a chance to join a distillery that was coming of age. It was not yet seven years old. It is not often you get the chance to join a new distillery.

'Dingle was the first new distillery for 100 years. Now, over forty small companies have started up across Ireland. There is more craft in the Irish whiskey scene.'

Coull understands the game well enough to know where the club may struggle.

'Holding on to people. It is difficult for youngsters to stay and work in rural Ireland. Accommodation is expensive in Dingle. It will find its own equilibrium. If business can get the staff, they will have to sort things out. It is very difficult in rural areas everywhere.

'Most youngsters here will go to work in the USA at some stage. Youngsters in Ireland are much more able and keen to travel. They have always had to.

'We can work on our general support for the club and make it attractive for youngsters to join.

'But you have to be a tough player to play in these parts. The rain and wind generally come at you horizontally. You do like your rugby if you play in Dingle.'

Or, God willing, if you just support the club. Standing on one of those wild, windswept touchlines is a bit more than just supporting a team. It's an act of faith.

Club trustee John Holstead isn't even Dingle-born. He hails from Wakefield in West Yorkshire, although he just about qualifies for inclusion in the Dingle rugby story. He's lived in the town for over fifty years and first got involved with the rugby club right from the off.

'There was an event and I went along to have a look and promptly got roped in. I was president for many years but now I do reports and radio pieces for *The Kerryman* to help get the club's news out there.

'I was seventy-seven in December 2023 and thought I would never see rugby played here. This is the best place in the world to live. I have been here almost all my adult life and wouldn't dream of living anywhere else.'

We repair, not to one of Dingle's unique pubs, but to Bean in Dingle, the town's most popular coffee shop in Green Street. Everyone seems to migrate here from early in the day to later afternoon. The coffee is that good.

In those early days, Holstead tells me, the club was run on a shoestring. It wasn't too organised.

'In the mid-1970s, we had a club here although it was more a drinking club than a rugby club. I think we have moved on since then. But ironically, there was rugby here on the Dingle Peninsula before GAA in the late 1800s. It was hard for a while but there was a team here until the late 1920s. They won a county cup, the McElligott Cup. We won it again just three years ago. We were in the Munster Junior Cup.'

'The fun element has always been a central feature of this club's soul,' says Holstead.

'We had two pitches, one for Senior Cup games, the other for regular games. We were due to play Bandon in the first round of the Cup some years back and Tom Kiernan, the great Ireland and Lions full-back, came down from the IRFU to check on the pitch. There were no posts up when he came because the farmer wouldn't allow us to put up posts during the week. But Tom still passed the pitch for playing. He said, "I assume the main pitch will be perfect."

'A week after, when we played, the weather was terrible, yet it was the only game played in that first round. All the

240

other games were called off because the pitches were in a dire condition.'

Holstead comes from a rugby league background. But rugby and this small club right at the end of the Dingle Peninsula has captured his heart.

'It is a family affair for us. My son coaches all the minis. Friendship is the thing. Kids have more friends from the rugby club than from anywhere else. They play GAA too, but they don't seem to get the same sort of friendships from there. It's a really good atmosphere. Particularly with the minis.'

There is one thing men like Holstead and founding member John Curran, whose grandson, although not yet four, plays every Saturday morning, lament about modern times. Back in the day, they say, when Munster were lording it in the Heineken Cup, there was a very close connection between the province HQ and all its clubs. Everywhere you would see Munster jerseys and that attracted people, thought Curran. What's more, there was a good reason for Munster to draw close its many clubs all over the province.

Even this small club has had a few who have gone on to play senior rugby. 'We have a couple with the Munster Academy. Every year someone has come through. But if they have to travel to Limerick three times a week, it is a huge commitment for parents. That is two hours thirty minutes each way,' says Holstead.

He thinks it will be hard for Munster to come back to those levels because the competition is so tough. But he hopes they don't bring in loads of overseas guys. He would like to see fifteen Munster men in the provincial side.

'There is not as much talent as there was. There is still a lot of rugby played in Munster, but the schools are not as strong as in Leinster.

'It can't be healthy if Ireland are choosing 75 per cent of

their team from Leinster. The danger in Munster is that you are losing the crowds. Back in the day, you always knew someone in the Munster team.

'But there is not so much connection now between Munster and the clubs. Everyone used to feel part of the Munster set-up. There was this lovely connection. But there is now a drift away among the professionals.

'Professionalism hasn't done the amateur game much good. It has got the exposure you get from TV. However, youngsters who don't make the grade now consider themselves not good enough and give up the game. But clubs rely on all those youngsters who have come through their playing days to get into the administrative side of their club.'

Lose them and the club may lose its future. As they say, winning things is great, but the best thing of all is to have a full set of players and members.

Ask John Holstead and John Curran where they expect their club to be in a few years' time and that rich Munster humour shoots back.

'Probably halfway out into the Atlantic, given what's happening with climate change,' says Curran.

These are guys who love the game like their own families. And humour is never very far from their lips.

They remember the night they went to faraway Toulon for a Munster match in the early 2000s. The place where they were drinking ran out of beer halfway through the evening so the barman served Curran a mug, filled with champagne!

Holstead recalled one of the best nights.

'In 2006, we had a wonderful night after Munster won the Heineken Cup, beating Biarritz in the final in Cardiff. One of the Munster players that day was the South African centre, Trevor Halstead.

'We were staying at a hotel in Ross-on-Wye, the nearest we

could get to Cardiff. But we met some other Munster fans. Things developed as we had a few beers, and we introduced ourselves. They thought I'd said Halstead so, for a bit of fun, I said I was Trevor's uncle.

'That did it. They bought us drinks all night long.'

And he didn't even have to put on a fake South African accent.

CHAPTER 22

The Men of Munster

He can hardly believe it. But it is now forty-four long years ago.

So many memories, so much water under the bridge. The clock of life ticks on. Remorselessly. Ever louder.

But he will always remember one thing above all else from that day. The people.

It was the start of the 1980s and Irish rugby was still convulsed in a selectorial wrangle for the national No. 10 jersey that divided families, split the nation. Should Tony Ward, architect of Munster's historic 1978 victory over New Zealand at Thomond Park, wear Ireland's renowned outside half jersey?

Or should it be Ollie Campbell, the Old Belvedere man who won just his second cap in 1979, a player with a wafting right leg that landed penalty goals from almost anywhere in the opposition half? In essence, Ireland had two supreme outside halves for one position.

The minds of the selectors had seemed as jumbled as the supporters. But a glorious opportunity to make the definitive judgement came one winter's day at Dooradoyle, home of Ward's famous Garryowen club.

Campbell's Old Belvedere club were the visitors, ironically on a day when a League final was being played across the city at Thomond Park. Bohemians and Cork Constitution were the contestants.

Unusually, Garryowen were not involved. So, an old-fashioned Irish club match was arranged. Garryowen home to Old Belvedere. A. J. Ward against S. O. Campbell. And they came from far and wide. After all, Campbell was later to call Ward 'the first absolute star of Irish rugby'.

Ward cannot remember the exact attendance figure for that day. But he estimates it must have been something like 8000, maybe more, who were crammed into the place. Then there were the supporters who had climbed up trees overlooking the ground and now balanced precariously on a few branches. Down the open touchline, they stood several deep for a glimpse. This was Irish club rugby in its halcyon days.

'I couldn't tell you how big a crowd it actually was,' he said. 'But you couldn't get near the place. So many people were up trees, just hanging on to get a view.

'It was an exception because of the novelty of the Ward/ Campbell thing. Perhaps the biggest irony was, it was a really bad day weather-wise, so Ollie and I cancelled each other out.'

Near the end of 2023, I find a very different scene at the famous old Dooradoyle ground. The big, rambling clubhouse is still there, of course, and a modern improvement project of a new gymnasium and girls' changing rooms has made good progress. As usual, a friendly welcome is extended to all-comers. The 2023/24 club president, Dr Jim Fehily, makes no pretentions regarding the pride he feels at his role.

'I am very honoured to have been elected as president of this great club,' he says.

But there is one thing missing. The people.

That army of long ago, not to mention their descendants, some of whom joined the swell of supporters that famous day, are nowhere to be seen. The big clubhouse, warm and enticing, lacks just one thing. A noisy, cheerful throng. Only a few pockets of players, friends and supporters have drifted in.

Perhaps Old Wesley, today's opponents for this AIL Division 1B match, do not represent the crème de la crème of Irish club rugby these days. But then, who does?

Interest, that indefinable element without which no club or organisation, sporting or otherwise, can survive, has withered. The crowds long ago stopped coming to places like this. What you are left with is a hard-core rump of committed, industrious volunteers; decent, honourable people like Jim Fehily. Still in love with their club, of course, but surely saddened at the decline they cannot fail to see around them.

As Tony Ward says, 'The club game is nothing like it was. There is no coverage of the games nowadays. You don't even get results of AIL games here on a Sunday, never mind a match report. To get AIL results now, you have to go on to the Irish Rugby website.'

But back in the day, Ward remembers a different ambience. 'The spirit and atmosphere at Garryowen in those days was superb. They were a top club, and they still are. At the moment, they are suffering somewhat lean times and not winning leagues or cups.

'But along with Cork Constitution, they are the two top clubs in Munster in terms of cup wins.

'We were incredibly strong at that time when I joined them. Seventeen of our players were on the Munster provincial squad. It was a star-studded outfit by the standards of the time. They were certainly the club everyone wanted to beat down south. They were very much on top and loaded with internationals, such as Shay Deering, Seamus Dennison, Mick

Sherry, Larry Moloney, Pat Whelan and future Ireland coach Eddie O'Sullivan etc.'

The alumni here represent intimidating levels. Munster, the name alone, was and still is synonymous with pride, fire, physical commitment and dedication. Munster men are warriors, fighters. They wear their hearts on their sleeves. This is a tough tribe, unwilling to take a backward step, no matter who the foe.

No one epitomises that better in modern times than Ireland's 2024 Six Nations captain, Peter O'Mahony. Here is a man who goes to war with a grim expression upon his face that no opponent can misunderstand. Physical pain, to which he is inevitably destined by the very nature of his game, is nothing more than a minor irritant. It is the quid pro quo for his pride at wearing the famous jersey.

It has always been thus. The great Garryowen club of Munster built its name on the backs of such men who would fight to their final breath. Ward remembers particularly Shay Deering, the open-side flanker, and scrum half John Moloney, both of whom would go on to captain Ireland. Both had a huge influence on Ward.

'John was an incredible track athlete too. Off the base of the scrum at school level he was almost unstoppable. And after Deering left to go to Dublin and study, his younger twin brothers, Davo and Kev, took over. They also looked after me so it was no surprise the defensive part of my game was the least conspicuous element come representative time. I'd also had Shay wrapping me in cotton wool for Garryowen. I still have an enormous respect and awe for those guys!'

All of it, says Ward, was sustained by the crowds that came. 'They were very, very big. For Limerick was a passionate city as far as club rugby was concerned.'

Former Garryowen, Munster and Ireland legend Keith Wood with the author at Garryowen RFC.

It has changed in recent times, he says. What it means is that the emphasis now is very much on the provincial side, rather than the club game.

My day at Garryowen is enhanced by the arrival of another old friend.

The Wood family's roots go deep into the soil at this famous ground. Keith's father Gordon, born in Limerick and a Garryowen man most of his career, made twenty-nine appearances for Ireland between 1954 and 1961 and won two Test caps on the 1959 British & Irish Lions tour of New Zealand.

Keith would more than emulate his dad's legacy, winning fifty-eight caps for Ireland between 1994 and 2003 plus five caps for the Lions on their 1997 and 2001 tours. He also played

TRIUMPHS, TROPHIES AND TROUBLES

for Garryowen from 1991 to 1994 and represented Munster and the London club Harlequins.

Today, in 2024, he has three sons, aged twenty-two, twenty and eighteen. One of them, Gordon, who has trained with Munster, comes off the bench in the match I watch and makes a crucial try for his team in their victory.

But what of his beloved Garryowen and its future? Indeed, does Keith Wood believe it has one?

'I felt under David Nucifora, (the IRFU performance director until 2024), the club game in Ireland had been marginalised. I don't like that in medium terms. You now have a situation where there are three legs to this table. In Ireland, the professional game and the schools game are flying. The third leg, the club game, is not.

'There is a solution because an awful lot of people in this country want to play. The club level has got to be part of the process, not an afterthought. I think David Humphreys (now performance director) understands the importance of the club game. I think he will be good as performance director and will address this issue.

'When you look from the outside, there needs to be a coming together of those three legs to try and keep the structure and support for the club game. I believe that is necessary. It is not just about money. Several factors come into this.

'There are huge amounts of young men going to Dublin. There are better jobs there that lure them. But we need to manoeuvre the game more than it has been.

'After 1995, the IRFU made a huge number of clubs senior clubs. What was originally one or two divisions became four or five. I don't think that has worked. You want a cracking junior club system; there have to be tiered levels of the sport.

'Financially, I would really worry about all the clubs. Most are only surviving by the benevolence of individuals. Of

250

course, it's not just in Ireland. Most English clubs have losses of about £4 million a year which means the vast majority are insolvent. As a business, none of the clubs have cracked it.'

Ward accepts the problems that have arisen at club level. But he acknowledges the work done by Nucifora at the highest levels of the game in Ireland.

'Keith's point is valid regarding the club game. But Nucifora has brought the provincial and international teams to a new level in terms of organisation and success.

'But care from the IRFU for the club game has been hugely absent despite encouraging words from each and every successive president (coming as they do from a club background).

'The club game has been very much the victim of Irish rugby's professional success.'

Kieran Ryan is officially in charge of communications and marketing at the club. Unofficially, he'll turn his hand to anything to help out the club he loves. There are Kieran Ryans alive and flourishing right across this country. Trouble is, many of the clubs they revere are in nowhere near such robust health.

Even as a light drizzle threatens to turn into steady rain, Ryan is prowling the touchlines, searching out the best angle for his photographs. When the game is over, he is the reliable one sending reports and scores to the IRFU website to put up.

But even his love for the club does not blind Ryan to the reality.

'I'd say our situation right now is scary. Really, we are just hanging on by a thread. We are a community club, and we have always attracted all sorts of players. But what has happened is that the professional provincial sides have mopped up not just all the best players but almost all the sponsorship monies.

'Because we don't have large sponsorships, we cannot compete with Dublin. All the jobs are in Dublin. Straight after

Covid, we lost ten players; four to Blackrock, two to Terenure, two retired etc. For a club our size and with our player pool, it is very hard to replace those guys.'

Like Ward, he remembers the old times, when Garryowen was a focal point of the local community and a young man's education was regarded as incomplete until he had experienced the challenges of club rugby.

'We had eight internationals at one time back in the day. Then, after 1995, the IRFU pillaged clubs like ours. We were winning AILs etc. But we didn't win again until 2007.

'What the professional era has brought are the tentacles to stretch out to the Dingles of this world and getting players that normally would have played for big clubs. Natural progress had been to join a senior club.

'I came here in 1988 after living in London. They played a style of rugby I loved. Running rugby. Strong men up front punching holes in a defence and the backs released. I remember Keith Wood played back row in his early twenties. He typified everything about Garryowen.

'But today, like most clubs, we are struggling. It is incredibly difficult. The other thing is, we don't get crowds any more. In the Wood era, we sometimes had around 10,000. In the early 1990s, there was cash coming in left, right and centre. We could afford to get people like Andy Leslie, John Mitchell and Andy Earl (all from New Zealand) to come here and coach.

'Local derbies were big games. We would be putting up the "Sold Out" signs for those matches.'

In 2007, the club enjoyed a spectacular year. After seasons of disappointment, they won the AIL crown and also the Munster Senior and AIL cups. It was an unprecedented clean sweep of all domestic competitions in Irish club rugby. Overall, Garryowen have won the Munster Senior Cup thirty-eight times in their 140-year history.

But today, those happy times are mere memories. As Ryan says, their support base is dying off. All you get now are the diehard club types and that's pretty much it for their crowd. A combination of Munster and professionalism is threatening to kill off even clubs with such glorious histories as Garryowen whose home, Dooradoyle, translates as 'The Paddock of the Blind Man'. Presumably, someone was thinking of referees when they named it...

So, a great old club falls on hard times. But is this heartbreaking? Does it signal the end of society? Is it the end of civilisation as we know it? Of course not.

But it leaves many rugby greats immensely saddened. As Tony Ward says, 'Unfortunately, it is also my reading of the situation that the club is just hanging on. In every way.'

Wood believes that radical changes to the game are necessary, not just to improve its health at lower levels but right up to the very top. Typically for a man who always sought a positive slant on any topic, Wood has strong, forceful opinions about the modern game and where it is heading.

'It's a game and we want to keep it a game at this level. What you want is a valve, a sport to enjoy. But we need to get radical. You will never get a true solution if you only look at one piece of the equation.'

The Wood philosophy boils down to these salient points regarding the modern-day game.

- Too many substitutions
- Too many backroom staff
- Too many players on the field
- Get rid of both wing forwards plus a centre and you would have far more space
- Putting fresh players on for the final twenty minutes is a bastardisation of the spirit of the laws of rugby

These are his words, not mine. So, with characteristic vigour, not to say passion, Wood makes his point.

'Sure, these people say they operate within the laws. Yes, but the spirit of the laws is something else. The spirit of the law was a Victorian concept, but the game still has a Corinthian concept at its core.

'I do think that any time you bring back elements of that spirit it would be unbelievably beneficial to world rugby. Now, they have players playing all sorts of positions. Coaches won't like that but it's proven it can work to be able to change the game.

'As for bringing on fresh subs, it is inherently unfair. It's like being in a fight. After eight rounds, someone new comes out to fight you. That is against the spirit of the game.

'I understand the issue of player welfare. But the real issue is, if you are 22 stone as a player, it is going to be very tough to handle the last twenty minutes of a game if you cannot be replaced. Maybe you would need to be just 18 stone so you can last the game.

'If you keep players on for the whole eighty minutes, it is inevitable you are going to have more space available in the last quarter. Space, or the lack of it, is a fundamental flaw in the game today.

'Safety for the players, looking out for player welfare is key. If we do that, we can get a lot of younger people playing. It would make the game better. Right now, it is incredibly complex.

'Also, it is wrong to have more teams in a World Cup. I would rather see sixteen teams playing a higher standard than twenty-four with so many mismatches and one-sided games which we saw at the 2023 World Cup in France.'

Beyond dispute, the key to so much of Irish rugby has been, and will continue to be, at schools level. Tony Ward pinpoints some critical factors that created a gap, some might say chasm, between the schools system in Munster and that of Leinster.

'In Munster, it's a slightly different schools system which nobody can figure out. Therefore, it is very hard to read whether the passion for the game is still as strong. In Leinster, they have really maximised a fantastic schools rugby underage system. They always had it, but they had never optimised it. But over the last ten to fifteen years, they have done that and the talent coming out of the schools is remarkable.

'That talent goes directly into the Academy. In fact, it is so good that a player like Joe McCarthy goes straight through the Academy system, He is typical of so many of them now. They no longer need four years in the Academy. They are almost ready when they leave school. After one year in the Academy, they are getting contracts. It's all because of the system.

'The problem is, Munster don't have that same system. The other difficulty Munster still has with schools rugby is that it has always had a battle, even in the good times, between club and schools rugby with the underage players. In Leinster, they always gave priority to a school. You had to represent your school before a club.

'In Munster, to this day, they still have that problem and by and large the clubs tend to win out.'

Also, he warns, hurling's renewed advancement in the schools, in Cork as well, represents another problem down in the south-west. Partly, says Ward, that is a consequence of the enhanced physicality of rugby as a game.

'As regards hurling, it has always been a powerful sport in Limerick, particularly so in the county. But right now, in tandem with soccer, it is stronger than ever and impacting upon rugby. In the city, the latter is close to its weakest point ever. When I was there, hurling was still strong (All-Ireland winners in 1973), but both rugby and soccer were at their zenith. The Eoin Hand days for Limerick United were loaded with success.'

Ward does not seek to minimise an issue that could, in time, prove ruinous to rugby's entire future.

'It is clearly the case that excessive physicality has damaged rugby in some people's eyes. As director of rugby at St Gerard's School in Bray, I realised through talking to parents they are worried about their kids because of the increasing physicality. I get that, I absolutely get it.'

Ward says he also understands where rugby is coming from when it talks about the need to deal with collisions involving the head. Indeed, many fine, stirring words on the subject have emanated from senior officials' mouths. But as Ward says, 'The trouble is, when a guy of 6ft 5ins (1.96 metres) tackles a guy who is 5ft 6ins (1.68 metres) it is a complete mismatch. This is something you often see in rugby and how is the game going to solve that? I don't know. But rugby has got a huge problem.'

It has, and sadly, many of those charged with leadership in recent years have proved hopelessly inadequate for the task. *In extremis*, radical thinking beyond the box and firm action is needed. Urgently.

Too often, it would appear that rugby's chief concern is about getting bums on seats. Is it not the case that, in a sport where financial pressures are beginning to translate into crises, money matters will always take precedence?

Tony Ward underlines the vacuum in leadership by highlighting two controversial elements of the game. 'Look at the scrums and line-outs and the amount of penalties now being given. You can't have constant scrum resets because people paying to watch don't want to see that. So we are getting penalty after penalty after penalty.

'It is almost "your turn, my turn". Yet I talk to ex-pros, guys who have played the game, and they haven't a clue what the penalties are for; not the first idea.

'Another thing that drives me insane is, the only way tries are regularly scored now is through a kick to the corner, get the maul right and someone crashes over for a try.

'But when the ball is thrown in, the hooker goes to the back behind seven forwards who are all obstructing the opposition in their attempt to get to the ball. It is blatant obstruction. Yet out in the backs, referees give penalties for crossovers. Where is the logic in that?'

Is rugby still the focal point of the community in Munster, I asked him? 'It is a mix. It was always strong in the city, but it shared the limelight in the country. Soccer is struggling in Limerick. But hurling has really taken off and it's creeping more and more into the city. Yet there is still a huge passion for rugby.'

Even so, is the passion not dying at club level? He hopes and prays that doesn't happen.

'The memories we have, all of us, are so special. If we don't have our memories of those times, what have we got? I would hate to see that.'

Ward echoes Keith Wood's radical thought that team numbers should be reduced to create space on the field. 'I hate saying this, but because of the size of the pitches which they can't make any bigger, I think you will have to look at reducing numbers on the field.

'Many years ago, rugby league had to address this problem and what did they do? Take out the two wing forwards to create space. How can rugby (union) keep bums on seats with the claustrophobic state the game is in at present? Without reducing players, how are they going to create space? I don't think there is any doubt about that. Keith Wood is right.'

257

Tony Ward was born and brought up in Dublin. He remembers the time when he and his old pal, scrum half John Robbie, subbed together for Leinster against Munster at junior level at Thomond Park. Both went on to become British & Irish Lions on their 1980 tour of South Africa. Ward played seven years for Munster and then two for Leinster, near the end of his career. What was the difference between the two provinces at that time?

'They were playing very different games. At Munster, there was a much heavier emphasis on forward supremacy, on minimising mistakes and not taking risks. Whereas at Leinster, it was about moving the ball wide and bringing the backs into play. Theirs was a much more balanced approach to the game.

'It wasn't difficult playing for Leinster after Munster until we went to Thomond Park for a match. I found that the strangest experience of my career. But the fact is, I will always support Munster ahead of Leinster. That is the impact playing for Munster has, even on a lad born and brought up in Dublin.'

Ward is confident that, in the present times, Ireland's stream of young talent will continue to come through. With one proviso. 'My only concern is the one we touched on earlier, about parents and their worries that rugby is becoming too physical. When you get a mother, with her child coming through junior school, the prep school and you compare hockey to rugby, from a practical point of view you have a problem. There is definitely a concern and understandably so over the physicality.'

Garryowen RFC was founded in 1884, ironically the same year as the GAA in Ireland. Imagine if the GAA had embraced rugby. The game would have had so many incredible Gaelic footballers.

Kieran Ryan smiles at the thought, at what might have been. But his brow quickly furrows. 'Everything grows from the grassroots and if you cut that off, you will have trouble down the road.

'Now, Munster rule the roost in everything. The club loyalties we had don't exist any more. And the player pool has become so small. Maybe there are only sixty to eighty players in the Limerick area. The player pool here is so small those boys wouldn't get into the Dublin teams. We have front-row players aged twenty-one in today's team.'

Professionalism was inevitably destined to change rugby. But the threat of extinction for some world-famous clubs, like Garryowen, was hardly envisaged. It surely falls upon the shoulders of the IRFU, the ultimate administrators of the game in this country, to investigate what has gone wrong. Even better, to devise a solution to some of these problems.

If they cannot, they must surely relinquish control and allow a separate body, run solely by the clubs for the clubs, to take over.

Innovation and creative thinking will be needed to bring those crowds thronging back to Dooradoyle and the other grounds of Munster.

CHAPTER 23

Kinsale and Clonakilty

Some places are forever destined to be associated with famous people.

James Joyce, Oscar Wilde and Bono of Dublin; Kenneth Branagh and George Best of Belfast.

In the far south of Ireland, a town renowned as the gourmet centre of West Cork became synonymous with a famous British chef. At times, it seemed as if Keith Floyd put the 'K' in Kinsale.

Floyd, a notorious bon viveur as well as celebrity chef, certainly lived the life. You'd have to say he had a flair, not just for living but dying, too. Cleared of bowel cancer, he went out to celebrate with some pals and got through so much food and booze he promptly dropped dead from a heart attack at sixty-five.

But there was something else in Floyd's life for which he was passionate. And I don't mean the four women he loved, left and lost.

Floyd loved rugby, which was why, one morning back in 1994, I found myself knocking on the front gate of his cottage nestled beside the water on one of the lovely narrow inlets, just outside Kinsale town. It might have been no more than ten or eleven in the morning, coffee time to you and me. But

Floyd was already well on his way through a good bottle of Burgundy, his favourite tipple.

But wherever he was, he'd make sure he quickly located the nearest rugby club. Which was why he eventually became a vice president of the Kinsale club.

That morning, we helped him put away a couple of bottles of Burgundy grower Louis Latour's excellent Bourgogne when the cry came, 'To the town.' Keith was entertaining, buying lunch and he knew just the spot. We tucked into hot, oak-smoked salmon as a starter and a beautiful grilled fresh fish for the mains. The Sancerre was on tap. Or so it seemed.

Typically, no meeting with Floyd ever went to plan. The photographer and I were booked on the afternoon flight back to London from Cork. Time was short, especially after a brandy to wash it all down. But the TV chef wouldn't dream of letting me go until we'd gone into the local butchers across the street and had a cheery chat with the owner who was ordered by Floyd to cut a piece of his finest beef 'for my good friend here and his fine family'.

As the beef was cut, I grabbed a notebook and scribbled in shorthand Floyd's cooking instructions. Grabbing a tape recorder, notebook and chunk of beef, we dashed for the taxi, as Floyd lifted his trilby and waved in departure.

It was the last time I ever saw him. But the salt beef lunch that Sunday was superb, and I never forgot his words on the game he loved. 'In my view, rugby remains a sport unique in the camaraderie it inspires. It is a sensational way of getting on with people. It is like eating. Good food and good people create an ambience which is wholly pleasurable.'

He bemoaned the fact that he never scored a try in his playing days. But he did break his nose. He suffered the second attempting the first. 'It was a very rare occasion for me; it looked as though I was about to get that first try. The problem

262

was, I was so excited I ran into the goalpost, broke my nose and the ball squirted out of my grasp so I didn't get the try either. I never again came as close to a score as that.'

Floyd was always warmly welcomed at the Kinsale ground, a short distance from the town wrapped around a beautiful natural harbour. From close by the club, there are views of Kinsale harbour and Oysterhaven Bay. Some of the most spectacular views on the entire Ireland south coast are to be found around here.

In the years he lived there, Floyd took an active interest in the club. He played a few games, ran teams (one of them called Floyd's Vikings) and helped stage fundraising events for the young club. 'The Keith Floyd Association' was set up and all kinds of worthy efforts on the part of individuals have contributed to the whole.

But the hilarity, bonhomie and generosity Floyd brought, not just to Kinsale but myriad other gatherings, was destined to end in sadness. By the end, he basically had little money. Some found it sad after his passing that many of his things were sold off cheaply at auction.

He had a magnificent 400-piece train set, complete with engines, passenger cars, goods, stations, tunnels and lights with which he used to love playing. A local man in Kinsale bought that.

One of his suits was put up for sale for just €20. His two dogs, both Alsatians, went to different homes. The party was long over. 'It was all very sad to see,' one member told me.

Kinsale's history mirrors that of so many clubs in Ireland. They reckon matches were being played here well over 100 years ago. A club, Kinsale Green Rovers, was said to be a pub team playing as far back as 1888. But that club folded around 1902, in part because most of its players had gone off to fight in the Boer War.

When enough of the players came home, it started up again, around 1904. By 1927, a stake in the club bought by the government had kept it going, but in 1937, they folded again, this time for forty years.

The club in its most recent incarnation was not founded until 1982. They didn't have a clubhouse until 1993 but you have to say, the strides they have made in just over forty years are astonishing. Junior clubs such as this are the essence of club rugby all over Ireland.

There were seven or eight local men who came together to try and get the old club back on its feet. Jim Good was one of the founding members. 'Eli Lilly, the chemicals company, gave us use of a decent pitch. But the trouble was, it was three or four miles out of town.

'But eventually we found a very nice six-and-a-half-acre site at Snugmore.'

That was in 1985 and today, Snugmore has four full-size pitches including a training ground. Three of the pitches are fully floodlit.

Initially, they were short of changing facilities, which forced attention to focus on the need for a clubhouse. Keith Floyd used his contacts book extensively in bringing over some renowned international players for invitation games, as fundraisers. He also arranged several celebrity fundraising dinners.

So, by various ways and means by 1993, Kinsale managed to build their clubhouse. It cost €120,000 but Keith Floyd paid the architect's fees.

By then, too, someone had come up with the idea of staging an annual seven-a-side tournament. It would prove to be a master stroke. They found a chief sponsor of the event, Heineken, who would be so loyal and consistent in their support that in 2024, they sponsored it for the thirty-sixth year running. It is said to be the longest sports sponsorship anywhere in Europe.

'The Sevens has been the making of the club,' says long-term supporter and official, Jim Good. 'This is how we run our finances.' The club now has nearly 1000 members but on the Sunday of the Heineken Sevens, finals day, as many as 5000 people will pack into the ground to watch the action.

The combination of a weekend's rugby at an idyllic location with the attraction of one of Ireland's best gourmet centres on the doorstep is an alluring one. Support for this event has been worldwide with people flying in from all corners of Europe, the UK and the USA. They've even found a few mumbling, incoherent Aussies and Kiwis in some dark, deserted corners of the clubhouse after the event finally concluded...

In the early 2000s, the arrival of an overseas rugby star for the Heineken Kinsale Sevens set the entire town buzzing. Waisale Serevi was a pocket-size little Fijian genius, born with twinkling feet and a sudden injection of pace. He read a rugby field like a book and scored tries against some of the greatest players the game had ever seen. Sevens was his forte although he did play fifteen-a-side, winning thirty-nine caps for Fiji. He was called 'the greatest Sevens player ever'.

Serevi was the quintessential 'Have boots, will travel' character. In a bewitching career, he played club rugby all over the world, starting with the Nasinu club of Suva, then to Mitsubishi in Japan followed by spells with two French clubs, Mont-de-Marsan and Stade Bordelais and then the Staines club in England. He played for Fiji at the 1991 Rugby World Cup and won gold medals for the national Sevens team at the Rugby World Cup Sevens of 1997 and 2005.

Kinsale club officials met Serevi in a Dublin hotel after an Ireland v Fiji Test match in late 2002. He agreed to go to Kinsale the following May and play for a team called 'South

Sea Drifters' comprising mainly Fijians. Indeed, some of the players were related to him.

They hadn't always had the best of luck with the Sevens. In 2001, they had to cancel the event due to an outbreak of foot-and-mouth disease. Now, in 2003, they managed to get through the first day, the Saturday, albeit amidst wind and rain. But the forecast for Sunday was grim.

Alas, one thing you can normally rely upon in Ireland, especially if it is forecast, is bad weather. It came in the form of a storm that made the pitches unplayable and forced the event to be cancelled.

You might have thought that was it for the Fijian's visits to Ireland. But Serevi had such a good time in discovering the unique welcome Irish clubs and rugby people in this country reserve for guests, that he agreed to return the following year. He was as good as his word, helping his team to victory in the 2004 final.

In the summer, the club runs three-day camps with as many as 1000 youngsters involved. Each pays €60–70 for participation. 'Local business people have been very kind to us,' says Good. 'Financially, the club is very sound. But how some clubs survive, I struggle to see, for expenses at all these rugby clubs are extensive. We involve an awful lot of people from the local community. Plus there are about 150 people from the club who give their time to run the Sevens each May. John Walsh and his team do a superb job,' says Good.

Then there was the club's fortieth anniversary dinner, which 220 people attended. All these activities raise funds to ensure the club runs as smoothly and professionally as it can in a financial sense.

*　*　*

Just a thirty-five-minute drive along the south coast in a westerly direction from Kinsale brings you to a town with a population almost exactly that of Kinsale. In 2024, the latter had an official total of 4099.

Clonakilty, famous all over Ireland for its black and white meat puddings, had 4154 citizens although they believe if you include the hinterland around, it could be closer to 8000.

'Clon', as they are widely known, insist they are the biggest rugby club by numbers and membership in Munster. And they admit they have done it by putting a huge emphasis on girls' rugby. Club official Eoin Hurley told me, 'We always had a few girls in the club, but they tended to disappear at about thirteen or fourteen when the game became more physical.

'But seven or eight years ago, the girls started coming back and we decided to form a female side of the club. We hired coaches and went to the local schools. There are fourteen primary schools in our area. The coaches spent two or three hours each week in every school, developing awareness of the game and ensuring everyone had fun. We did the same with the secondary schools, targeting the twelve- to seventeen-year-olds and we had a very good response to that.'

The response was so good Hurley believes they are the only club in Munster able to field double teams. In some cases, even more. For example, their Under-14 squad has about fifty girls available.

They keep most of the girls happy by ensuring nearly all of them get some game time. In all, they have about 250 girls from the age of five up to seventeen and eighteen, playing the game. The boys' situation is even healthier: about 550. And in season 2023/24, another seventy-five joined up. Yet they have got only two playing pitches.

Ireland has many attractions, but these two southern coastal towns seem to have an endless appeal to visitors.

They are linked by other factors. Like Kinsale, this club didn't really get going to a serious extent until 1977. Even so, there were still tough times ahead. As recently as 2013, when they were relegated, Clonakilty hit trouble. The countrywide recession forced several players to move abroad. The overseas signings the club had recruited left with them. Star centre Darragh Lynch was among them.

Yet today, as with Kinsale, local support means everything to Clonakilty. From a population of only just over 4000, they boast more than 700 members.

These levels of local support are quite extraordinary. They speak of two things. Firstly, the desire of local people in both centres (and many more like them right across Ireland) to help sustain a healthy local club offering myriad values and sporting advantages for the local community.

Secondly, that club is seen as much more than exclusively a rugby club. Rather, a centre in the respective towns where local people, especially youngsters, boys and girls, can come together and meet others.

Clonakilty were re-formed in 1977 during a meeting of rugby followers at the town's Kitty Stone Tavern. They are the only West Cork club to have achieved All-Ireland League status. In 2006, they won the AIL Division 3 title, winning the final at Lansdowne Road. But they fell back into the Munster Junior League in 2013.

However, they boast two playing pitches, a clubhouse/ changing rooms complex plus a gymnasium/health centre and meeting rooms.

What is more, they now have a new 4G all-weather AstroTurf pitch which has hugely enhanced team preparations at every level. Hemmed in by the river and roads, they used to send groups of kids to train in a small farmer's field (mind the cowpats) or on Inchydoney beach. Depending on the tide, of course...

It took two years to bring the AstroTurf pitch project to fruition: one year of fundraising events, followed by a year of preparation and construction. More than 600 people were there for the official opening.

But the financial figures involved are eye-watering. The AstroTurf pitch cost €750,000, 'a phenomenal amount of money' in the words of Eoin Hurley. How did they do it?

They got a grant of €175,000 from government, they set up a lotto with a new electric car as the prize. That raised €190,000. Savings over several years contributed a further €100,000. Then there were smaller individual donations and legacies plus income from more fundraising events. Oh, and a bank loan of €120,000.

They have a general committee of twelve, six men and six women. That balance, says Hurley, helps enormously with the thinking when it comes to girls' rugby. He smiled. 'When you want a grant, if you can demonstrate your committee is balanced in that way, it helps no end. You get brownie points!!'

Hurley says there is 'a small army' of people doing all kinds of jobs. He estimates there are more than a hundred volunteers in the club.

This is how some of these clubs work. Most importantly, how they prosper.

So now, Clon's three men's adult teams, their Under-20s, two women's teams plus underage teams from Under-8s to Under-18s can use the AstroTurf facility. Not to mention local schools and others in the community. It underlines how this game and its philosophies benefit communities throughout the vicinity.

Not only that, it speaks of the vibrancy of interest in the great old game throughout Ireland. It also tells of how so many girls and women have come to this game in recent times. This

269

attraction of both genders is a triumph of rugby's resilience and appeal at all ages and levels.

Hurley says, 'We have improved vastly. Rugby is getting a lot of good hype. From the Munster point of view, there was always a lot of interest in the game. But overall, the exposure of Irish rugby has increased so much.'

Despite, as he says, the fact that in almost every town or village, there is a soccer team. In Clonakilty alone, there are three soccer clubs. Yet the town's rugby club seems to be going from strength to strength.

'We are thriving,' says Hurley. 'Our competitors are watching our success. It's great to have such a strong rugby club in the area. But in general, as long as the kids are playing sport, that's the main thing.'

CHAPTER 24

The Leinster Conundrum

Believe it or not, there was a time when Leinster did not lord it over everyone at provincial and European rugby level.

Founded in 1879, they played the first inter-provincial derby against Ulster that year. In 1899, the first Leinster/Munster game was played.

As for Leinster Schools, their inter-provincial games have been going since 1888.

The Inter-Provincial Championship ran from 1946/47 to 2002. But in that time, it wasn't Leinster who notched the most titles.

Ulster stand at the top of that table with twenty-six Championships, with Leinster and Munster on twenty-two each. Nor was entertainment necessarily the order of the day in those times. There was a cracking contest on 15 November 1947 at Lansdowne Road.

Leinster 0 Ulster 0.

It was a Leinster side that included 1948 Grand Slam captain Karl Mullen and an Ulster team containing the legendary Jack Kyle. Greats of the game in their day. Yet a pointless affair.

Leinster knew some barren years. From 1965 to 1972 and then from 1984 to 1994, they didn't win a single inter-provincial title. Even after professionalism arrived, Munster were beating Leinster in 2005/06 in the European Cup. In 2007/08, Leinster didn't even get through their pool in the competition.

Long-time failures then, these Leinster men? Well, in a sense they are of late. They have lost three European Cup finals on the bounce in 2022, 2023 and 2024.

In fact, they have not won the United Rugby Championship for the past three seasons, nor the Champions Cup since 2018. But then there is the counter view. Reaching three successive European finals and being narrowly beaten each time hardly represents systemic failure. Perhaps Jordie Barrett will help get them to the 2025 Champions Cup final... and then over the line.

Today, as befits notable residents of Dublin 4 (and as Barrett's signing emphasises), there is as strong and vibrant a cash flow at Leinster Rugby as the surging springtime waters of the nearby Liffey. Top southern hemisphere players recruited by Leinster include the likes of Jamison Gibson-Park, James Lowe, Rocky Elsom, Felipe Contepomi, Isa Nacewa and Brad Thorn. All Black Barrett has been the latest star recruit.

But Leinster learned something else at crucial moments in their history. Finding the right people to fill crucial roles was key.

Just before Christmas 2001, a new CEO walked into the Leinster offices. Not everyone agreed that Mick Dawson, a stalwart of the Lansdowne club, was the right choice for the job. Indeed, with the benefit of hindsight, you might say that even Dawson had some misgivings about his qualification for the role.

He had come from a background of amateur rugby and been a salesman in his working life. He hadn't got a huge amount of management experience.

'I was naïve to the responsibilities of the whole thing. I would be much more aware nowadays of my responsibilities to sponsors, season ticket holders, staff and supporters. It is a very wide-ranging, complicated job.'

It was widely acknowledged that Leinster had the players. So coaching became key. They had been through a lot of coaches, never a good sign. They started off with Matt Williams then he went to Scotland. Then came Gary Ella but he didn't last very long. He didn't really seem to get the respect of the players.

Then Declan Kidney came in, but he went back to Munster after nine months.

They were now heading into their fourth coach in four years. But then Michael Cheika arrived, and according to Dawson changed the entire culture and the way players thought about the game. 'He was the right man at the right time. We always had good players, but I am not sure they had that hard edge. Michael brought that hard edge into it.'

It was the turning point not just for Leinster rugby but Ireland as a whole.

In his naivety, Dawson had seen the team win the old Celtic League in his first few months in charge. 'I thought it would all be fun like that,' he winced.

He was to learn differently. After winning that Celtic League, they didn't win anything else until 2008/09. It was a long time to wait.

Besides charting an improved pathway to success for Leinster, Dawson looked at Ireland's increasingly painful period of adaptation to the demands of professional rugby. He wasn't very complimentary about the start they had made.

'It was like the train had left the station, but Irish rugby was still standing on the platform. People didn't understand how much it actually cost to keep a rugby team going. Ireland didn't want professionalism and we weren't ready for it. We were way off the pace, and it took us seven to eight years in the professional game to get up with it. For example, our players needed a long time to understand the physical preparation required.'

When they had done that, they had to sharpen their act in commercial terms off the field.

'The grounds we were playing on weren't good enough. You needed seats and proper facilities for people to attend matches. We were way off the pace in just about every respect.'

To transport your impressions from those stumbling times to the present-day scenario is not elementary. He might have had to wait 'long years' to taste the true elixir of success. But Leinster's (and Dawson's) cup all but overflowed as they won four Heineken Cups in 2009, 2011, 2014 and 2018. They also lifted the European Challenge Cup in 2013.

There are other aspects to it. Leinster's new home, the RDS Arena, has a capacity of around 18,500 with 16,500 seated. It is currently being enlarged still further. But for the biggest games, they move to the Aviva Stadium.

In the 2023/24 season, for the Investec Champions Cup quarter-final match against the European champions La Rochelle, Leinster sold 40,000 tickets in the first three days. Eventually, the match was a 50,000 capacity sell-out.

Then, for the semi-final against Northampton staged at Croke Park, 82,300 tickets, a capacity audience, were sold in just a few hours. If ever the Irish people's raging love affair with this game at the top level was being demonstrated, it was at this time.

Less than a week after that quarter-final triumph, Leinster announced they had beaten off rival bids from wealthy clubs in France and Japan to sign All Black centre Jordie Barrett, one of the most coveted players in world rugby.

Standing outside the RDS Arena, you could almost hear the groans of dismay and howls of disapproval from Leinster's contemporaries in Munster, Ulster and Connacht. Leinster, supreme on the field and financially healthy off it, have steamed away over their opponents' horizons.

Irish rugby's most powerful provincial team and much the wealthiest is in Dublin. The majority of the population is in Dublin, most of the best jobs are in the capital. The top businesses, obvious sponsorship targets, have their headquarters in Dublin. This is simply not a level playing field. On or off the pitch.

Mick Dawson acknowledges the differences that threaten to become a chasm.

'Leinster will continue to produce the majority of the players because of the demographics. It is the biggest province. Dublin has got money and the population. It's a different world here. Dublin is where the jobs are and the school system is so strong here. Players want to be here.

'Of course, I am completely biased. But Leinster like their position, they like the fact that they are producing good players.'

But this seemingly unending stream of quality young players has made Irish rugby lopsided. All the power, all the possibilities are in the capital. There is a production line somewhere in the Wicklow hills to match Max Boyce's famous 'fly half factory' in the Welsh valleys.

Except that the other three provinces don't see the funny side of it. And, if Leinster are being honest and open, do even they believe it is good for the long-term future of the game in Ireland that just one province dominates? How can there be worthwhile competitions if one side has almost all the best players?

Ireland's team for their final Six Nations fixture of 2024 against Scotland underlined the point. Leinster had ten representatives, Munster four, Connacht one, Ulster none. Of the eight replacements, six were from Leinster.

So sixteen of the twenty-three players in that day's squad were Leinster players.

All of which leaves me to wonder, how long will the IRFU continue to accept this absurdly uneven field of playing personnel? Because it's not just the top fifteen at Test level we're discussing. For example, how many Munster players would have got into the Leinster 1st XV in the 2023/24 season? Tadhg Beirne, for sure. Jack Crowley? Perhaps. Peter O'Mahony? Probably. Calvin Nash? Doubtful.

Dawson has an interesting take on it. 'In this country, we have challenges that nobody else has. Nobody else plays hurling and Gaelic football. Now you have got Limerick, which was a hotbed of Irish rugby, containing the best hurling team in the country and they have the biggest backer in the country in JP McManus.

'So good players could be gravitating to hurling. That adds up to a lot of challenges.'

In his own mind, Dawson is crystal clear on one issue. 'I don't think there will be any accommodation at all in the relationship between GAA and rugby. I believe they will have a fight to the death. The Gaelic season has been extended now and they are serving two masters. There is a club Gaelic player and a county Gaelic player. They don't want the two to overlap.

'Long term, I think Gaelic will fight their corner valiantly because Gaelic games are in the DNA of the Irish people. We have got a lot of good Gaelic players who have come across to play rugby because it is professional and you can earn a real living out of it. A very nice living, too.

'So you have to make sure that what you are providing is the best possible facilities, because if you are a good player at both codes, you will have a decision to make at some stage. It means that rugby needs good coaches and good facilities. Gaelic are doing the same and soccer is always with us.'

But how to address the pressing issues concerning Irish rugby that have been highlighted by many in this book? Especially in the case of Leinster's domination.

Would it not make greater sense for the IRFU to decree that a levelling up in player strength is needed right across Irish provincial rugby. Of course, some players in the past have voluntarily moved to try their luck at another province. But thus far it has been a trickle, not a trend.

This would be an enforced act by the union. Reduce the power and supremacy of dominant Leinster by decreeing that maybe three or four players move to other provinces.

Dawson claims that can happen already under the present system. But that claim is flawed by his words. 'I think the system works in the sense that if a young fellow at Leinster is not making the team, he *might move* (my italics) and go to another province.'

Sure, he might. But there is scant evidence of it, and even less chance of it becoming a trend. How many young players comfortably ensconced for years in the Leinster set-up from young ages would cheerfully turn their back on the location and the lucre, not to mention their mates?

Unless they had to by order of the union. After all, they pay the centrally contracted players' wages.

Dawson says, 'I admit, it is lopsided with all this success in Dublin and I would think the IRFU would probably be looking at it. There are definitely people in the union who will be thinking like that. But it won't sit well in certain Leinster circles. I think it would be strongly opposed by them.'

Nor is he certain that such a policy would work. 'The danger is, you lower the standard overall, so everybody just becomes average then. The standard could drop everywhere. Leinster has set the standard, it's up to everybody else to try and get up to that standard. So I don't think it's a good argument to say Leinster should give away some of its best players.'

Nevertheless, the realist in Mick Dawson does not deny one fact. Munster rugby has a problem. He says, 'In recent times, Munster sides have had hardly anyone from Limerick on the team and that is extraordinary. That is no good for Irish rugby.'

He doubts the notion that passion for rugby in Munster is diluting. 'I don't think so. The passion is in their DNA. But they just haven't been producing as many good players as they had in the past.'

He remembers when he began with Leinster, Munster were providing six or seven of the Ireland pack. Only lock Malcolm O'Kelly was flying the Leinster flag among the forwards. The reason for that is, in past times, quality players came through from the great clubs of Munster – Cork Constitution, Young Munster, Garryowen, Shannon, Dolphin, Sundays Well etc.

Now, with the declining level of those clubs, the best players have come through the schools system. Leinster, of course, is by far the strongest region in the country for that. And correspondingly, the majority of Munster's youth players are now coming out of West Cork.

'I think the Limerick success in hurling has taken away a bit from rugby over there, too. And they are fantastic physical specimens these guys in GAA.

'When you look at Ulster, they have always produced a huge number of good players. But again, Gaelic sports have got stronger up there as well. So how do we make this better? Will it improve Ulster and Connacht if they get a few more players from Dublin?

'I think the fact is, there just aren't enough players to go around.'

Besides, Dawson doesn't believe this is the biggest problem facing rugby in Ireland. In one word, it is concussion.

'Rugby doesn't own concussion. But it seems to have had more than its fair share of comment on it. Gaelic and hurling are knocking lumps out of each other. But we have got to look at that in rugby and make sure it is an attractive game.

'There are a lot of young mums now who would be happy if their son never picked up a rugby ball. People are getting laid out in tackles now. That is the biggest danger we have. But it's not just an Irish problem.

'Some people will never start an involvement in rugby if this issue is not addressed and solved to some degree. We have a very vibrant amateur game here as well. You can't have people not able to go to their work on a Monday morning because of concussion issues from rugby on Saturday.'

There is another issue, too, raised by several long-standing rugby devotees, some of them close by in parts of the Dublin metropolis. Would not the amateur game be healthier if it were run as a separate entity from the professional focused IRFU?

Dawson, perhaps predictably, is a defender of the status quo. Leinster, he says, works very closely with the IRFU and the clubs. He sees them all under the one umbrella. Splitting the two would not be a great idea, in his opinion.

'You need to have a handle on both sides of the fence. We had some very good people from the volunteer side and the executive side. The two are interlinked.'

Besides that, he rejects the notion that the professional arm is largely deaf to the needs of amateur club rugby. 'Leo Cullen wants as many of his younger professionals as possible playing in the club game. These young players are told to go away and play for the clubs. To be good at anything, you have got to go and play. Only twenty-three can start. Leo has forty-five players on his books plus twenty-two in the Academy. That's a lot of fellas kicking their heels.

'The players can decide what clubs they want to play for. We encourage them to make sure they get a place in the first team of a First Division AIL club. It's great experience because the standard is good.'

But there is a problem. Even Dawson acknowledges that.

The difficulty with the Academy kids, he admits, is that they're not sure they are going to be available because there could be an Under-20 match coming up for Ireland, or for Leinster. They might have to go on a rest week or Leinster might have an A match. Or internationals coming on.

'So, it's a difficult one to make it work well,' he concedes.

The people in the clubs know this; they're not fools. They have seen the reality. Once inside the Academy or the Leinster structure overall, the clubs know they're rarely going to see their players made available for a club match.

If you allow the heart to rule, you're on the side of the clubs. It would surely make sense to split amateur and professional rugby, not just in Ireland but anywhere. Apart from an oval-shaped ball, two goalposts and a crossbar, the two have virtually nothing in common.

Yet, as Dawson says, professionalism has been an extraordinary success in Ireland. 'From an Irish point of view, it has gone from zero to one hundred. Professionalism has worked in this country. People might argue the game has lost that camaraderie. But players now live and understand their responsibilities under professionalism.

'That is what they have chosen to do for a living. Under

that scenario, you have got to perform, you have got to live the life. It is almost monastic, but it is what it is.'

However, he doesn't seek to deny the obvious. 'There is no doubt the big loser from professionalism has been the amateur game, the club game.'

* * *

The Schools Man

For the rugby purist, there is an intrinsic pleasure in watching a good standard of schools rugby. In most cases, the focus is on running, passing, seeking space. Showing ball skills. Enjoyment, too.

Wow! How revolutionary is that, players actually freed to attack and enjoy the game?

In March 2023, I found myself in Dublin, lured to the RDS by the prospect of the Leinster Schools Senior Cup final. Good judges had urged me to attend. Blackrock College, from Dublin 4 v Gonzaga College, from Dublin 6.

Blackrock has dominated these competitions, at senior and junior level since their inception. The school has now won the Senior Cup seventy-one times, the Junior Cup fifty-three times. No one else has ever come near that.

But in this final, Gonzaga brought a bright, breezy confidence on to the field. Their attacking intent, a clear mandate to have a go, was soon rewarded. Blackrock responded and we saw a superb exhibition, not just of attacking determination but of doing the basic skills.

Gonzaga ultimately prevailed, 35-31, but long after the score was forgotten, I shall remember the delight of watching young players searching for space, ensuring they did the basics to maintain continuity and flow. They offered old-fashioned attributes such as making the ball do the work, taking opponents out of the game by means of timing and accuracy of the pass and the vision to unlock well-structured defences by a variety of means.

Compared to today's ultra-macho mentality and endless, aimless kicking in too many senior rugby matches, it was a breath of fresh air. But more than that, it was a triumph, a reaffirmation for those who continue to believe in the skills set required by this game and the potential to delight an audience when played with attack and positivity uppermost in the contestants' minds. Perhaps subtlety, too, that long abandoned quality too often crushed by overt physicality.

One of Dublin schools rugby's most experienced men is Bobby Byrne, at one time games master at Gonzaga and coach to the senior team for many years. However, he has not been involved with the team in recent times as he has been on a career break.

Declan Fassbender is the present coach of the senior team, supported by George Naoupu who is the overall director of rugby. Both played crucial roles in Gonzaga's Leinster Schools Cup triumph.

Even though he now takes a more distant role, Byrne remains a highly respected observer of the Leinster Schools scene.

Given that he first went to Gonzaga as far back as 1984, I sought his views on that school and others. But first, I asked him straight out about this Leinster conundrum. Isn't there just too much focus on Leinster Schools rugby to the point of obsession?

'There is an element of truth in that. Historically, Dublin was the main source of numbers for the professional game. St Michael's in recent times have also contributed significantly to that conveyor belt, but now there are also a lot more middle-ranking schools competing at a higher level than before. Many have invested heavily in their rugby programmes and overall, more players are being developed.'

Also, there have always been a couple of schools that have prioritised rugby, like Blackrock. It is a huge part of their history and tradition.

But Byrne clearly differs from senior personnel at some Irish schools who now appear in danger of taking rugby education as seriously as maths, science and history.

His view is simple. 'It is very important the amateur spirit is retained in schools. There is a danger the boys might be put under unnecessary scrutiny and pressure.'

But let's not be sanctimonious about this. Most schools rugby facilities have been enhanced almost out of recognition in recent years.

At Gonzaga, there has been significant investment in all-weather pitches and a weights room which caters for youngsters from twelve years all the way up to eighteen.

Even Byrne admits, 'We took small steps for quite a long time. Now we hope to be competitive on a regular basis.

'Strength and conditioning, nutritional advice and a significant amount of video analysis for teams and individuals are now part of most schools' programmes, particularly for Under-15s and Under-18s. It is the knock-on effect of professionalism.

'But it is still an amateur game in school.'

Well, at some schools maybe. But with all this 'professional' preparation that allegedly, as I was told during my journey, includes the use of drones by some schools to monitor the efforts of every player, it's hard to believe it.

When Byrne first arrived at Gonzaga, they were different times, in both a social and sporting sense. Back then, Gonzaga had small numbers. They were competitive but not really challenging at the top table of Leinster Schools rugby.

But there has been a significant change. The senior school increased in numbers over the years. It is a Jesuit school, a sister college to Clongowes, Belvedere College. The Jesuits like to promote rugby in their schools as part of their education programme.

But the dividing lines between obsession and adopting virtually a professional approach for boys has become ever narrower.

Byrne admits, 'There is no doubt there is significantly more pressure now than fifteen years ago. Some of that is generated by the amount of attention the cup matches generate. The media coverage hypes it up. A lot of cup matches now are televised. But youngsters are playing competitively from a very young age.

'I don't accept it is just about winning. Perhaps in some schools, winning is hugely significant. But it's important not to lose sight that these are young boys playing rugby as a pastime. Only a very small percentage will ever go on to become professionals.'

Gonzaga are one of the schools that can lay claim to the mantle of playing far more sports than just rugby. They don't make rugby compulsory and offer a host of other activities.

'A lot of Gonzaga students have played Gaelic football and hurling from a young age. That has helped them a lot in rugby because the skill base is very transferable. The benefits include hand/eye coordination, spatial awareness and competitiveness. Some Gaelic football is played in the school in the summer term.'

At Gonzaga, there are four rugby pitches. Their artificial pitch, which allows training in all weathers, is floodlit, there is an indoor sports hall and a fully equipped gym.

'We try to make rugby or any games enjoyable for the students and not put them under unnecessary pressure and we would emphasise promoting good sporting values and not tolerating poor behaviour at matches,' says Byrne.

But as regards Gaelic and hurling, he admits there is protectionism at work in some places. 'Some of the bigger schools would say if you are playing rugby for us, you can't play Gaelic football.

'But my own view is, the more sports they play the better for their overall development. If they want to play Gaelic or hurling, we accept it. We don't have hard rules about it. We can be flexible.'

What's more, he is forthright as to the effect the boys with Gaelic football and hurling backgrounds can have on a rugby team.

'We would not have won that Leinster Schools Senior Cup without four of our guys. Our captain had played underage Gaelic football for Meath. Lots played Gaelic football. One guy played hurling.

'We would have been significantly weaker without them. So, if they want to go and play those games, you try and manage it. You have to be a bit flexible. If they are training with a Gaelic team, I am very much in favour of letting them.'

Essentially, what are the qualities of those sports that participants bring to rugby? Byrne confesses, 'I have one regret in life and that is that I didn't play hurling when I was young. It is an incredibly skilful sport. But if you don't play underage, it is very difficult to acquire the skills you need at a later stage.

'Those guys that play it have great peripheral vision, handling skills and hand/eye coordination. You also need to be incredibly fit from a young age as they are playing a very fast-moving, highly skilled game.

'I could watch a schools rugby match and see a full-back and know he played Gaelic games.

'Their positional awareness, movement and kicking skills are often exceptional. Several top players including Hugo Keenan, Rob Kearney and Mick Galwey had a background in GAA. The conditioning requirements are very high and it is physically very demanding.'

But why does he think so many young players get to nineteen or twenty and walk away from rugby? After all, he admits he is concerned at the trend.

'I have been involved for a long time in rugby, and it's true. There is a high drop-off level in club rugby.

'Some may play Under-20 rugby but very few play into their mid-twenties. Today in life, young men have so many options and things to do. Rugby isn't necessarily their choice.

'As for the boys that don't make it when they are nineteen or twenty, those guys would have continued to play socially for fun… in years gone by. They have got used to such good structures in schools where everything is laid on for them. They can come in for training sessions before school or after school. It's right there in front of them.

'But when they leave, club rugby is different and does not necessarily provide the same structures. Also, some are pursuing different courses of study or starting new careers, so they are not as self-motivated to continue playing rugby after school.

'There is often parental pressure too, to focus on a job and career. So they give away rugby.'

If Byrne were president of a decent club in Ireland, would he be concerned about its future?

'Yes, I would,' he admits.

He claims club rugby at AIL level is still healthy and at a good standard. But really only the top two divisions.

'However, social rugby is perhaps diminishing, and most clubs are fielding fewer teams than in the past. That reflects the way society has changed. Also, young lads today don't hang around sports clubs now. It's not always the place they socialise. And rugby is increasingly a spectator sport so rather than play on a Friday night, they go and watch a Leinster game.'

What of the positives? He shares my view that one element that has emerged in the sport is to be encouraged and celebrated.

'It is fantastic the way the women's game has flourished. Clubs all over the country are making a big effort to have a women's section. They contribute immensely.'

He has a mixed message about those concerned that schools playing midweek *and* on Saturdays are being unfair to clubs. It is a view I heard all over Ireland at club level.

'I have heard that argument. There are arguments for and against it. I can understand the frustrations of those in the clubs who can't get the players they want because they're playing for their schools on Saturdays.

'Clubs like Terenure and Lansdowne have huge underage sections in their clubs. They try to work around it by training on Sunday mornings and going on tours. They do that quite successfully. It is very important these young boys are not overburdened and not over-stretched physically.'

But let's be honest. In many cases, they are. As several club officials have pointed out, many young players are being subjected to training schedules and physical exercise programmes more akin to professional rugby. But at ages as young as fourteen or fifteen. That might be wonderful for their progression up the ladder of Leinster Schools to senior rugby in the province. But it does not bode well for still developing young bodies being physically hammered to prepare them for still greater physical challenges that lie ahead.

Think on this, too. Who steps up with job opportunities when some young bodies break under the strain and a young man who devoted most of his youth to a mythical dream of playing rugby for his province and country, perhaps at the expense of a more traditional education, ends up in pieces? On the scrapheap at twenty.

Byrne admits, 'Now, in Leinster, there is a conveyor belt from schools and clubs. There is a talent identification programme where Leinster will identify boys from fifteen and bring them into camps to develop them. They get control of them from a very young age.

'So the overall rugby success is more likely than not to continue in Leinster. There are so many players coming through in that province alone.'

Much of the pressure inherent in rugby union in this country to develop streams of talented players for the future has come about partly because the GAA recognised they could be in danger of losing their eminence in sporting circles in the face of rugby's burgeoning reputation post professionalism.

Years ago, the GAA was not as well organised in Dublin as they are now. But Byrne says, 'They put in a huge effort to build some grassroots from the ages of five or six years. But twenty years ago, very few of our students were playing Gaelic games.

'The competition from Leinster Rugby encouraged them to be more active in recruiting from a very young age. Two-thirds of youngsters are now playing Gaelic football and hurling.'

So does he envisage what others have termed 'a fight to the death' between the two sports?

'I suppose everybody is trying to look after their own interests by trying to discourage their best players from playing other sports. We have had a couple of guys playing rugby and Gaelic from a young age. This can potentially cause friction with local GAA clubs, but it is usually possible to find a compromise.'

* * *

The (Ex) Player

Gordon D'Arcy was on the winning side in a Leinster Schools Senior Cup final, when Clongowes beat Terenure in the 1998 final, after losing to them the previous year. Of course, his pedigree flourished, both at school and then throughout his long career in senior, first-class rugby.

Between 1999 and 2015, D'Arcy made eighty-two appearances for Ireland and formed, with Brian O'Driscoll, one of Ireland's greatest ever centre combinations. He toured with the British & Irish Lions in 2005 and 2009.

Together with O'Driscoll, he brought an elevated level of cerebral matter to the playing field. D'Arcy was quick-thinking, neat, accurate and clever in his play in the midfield. His eyes could spy openings not in the orbit of others. And his defensive attributes surprised some.

Today, D'Arcy lives the epitome of a comfortable, middle-class life in Dublin. He is married with three young children, two girls and a boy, and works in insurance. He hasn't entirely turned his back on rugby because he coaches his club, Lansdowne's Under-8s. Lucky kids. But as he says, 'I gave twenty years to professional rugby, and I am quite happy with that.'

He comes to meet me on this bright Dublin day, clad in comfortable chinos and a crisp white shirt. He's been retired nine years but still looks as fit as a fiddle.

We sit at a local coffee shop and rekindle a friendship from way back in the day. These were times when top rugby men were not pre-programmed to speak robot talk. They were allowed views of their own, permitted to judge with whom they could and couldn't share them. Frankly, they were a pleasure to know. You could spend time with them, get to know them. Trust was implicit.

D'Arcy could usually look at a situation and analyse it correctly. Calmly and thoughtfully, too. On or off the playing field. Thus, I sought his considered views on some of the issues we have touched upon in this book, and especially this chapter.

He was an integral part of the Leinster senior set-up from 1998 to 2015, during which time he made 257 appearances for the province. But he also played club rugby for a while, for Lansdowne, and understands the differing voices being aired regarding the handling of the club game in the era of professionalism.

'Club rugby is really good but it is disconnected from the professional game which is a shame. The IRFU is a professional organisation, however it is mostly run by those from the amateur era at the moment and their focus has been on the revenue generating areas of the Irish system.

'I think we do a p*** poor job of supporting the clubs. How do we improve that? By coaching. In my opinion, it is one of the simplest ways we can improve the standard in the club game. We have 209 clubs in Ireland and we had one player representing those clubs in the Irish team during the 2024 Six Nations.'

Prop forward Tadhg Furlong came from the Horeswood club in County Wexford and he also played Gaelic football and hurling at school.

'Just a handful of players in the professional era have played rugby for Ireland from a club background. That's a dreadful return from 209 clubs. They make it despite the system, not because of it. People like Furlong, Horgan, Frawley – they are the kind of standouts.

'The clubs represent the highest playing population in Ireland. Yet they have the smallest representation in the elite game. Of course, the majority of these clubs will not have a player that becomes professional, let alone becomes an international. Most players come through the school system.

'We need to support club coaches at the underage level in the same way that the GAA have here. The standard of club rugby would go up and you would get players playing longer. More players would be taken up by the Academies.

'It's a crying shame when young players give up playing with the clubs. But the appeal of other, better organised team sports is hard to resist. But it's everything that is wrong with that type of pathway.'

If you could create a perfect Irish rugby ecosystem, he says, you would be thinking about players coming in at a young age, say eight, nine or ten, being given the skills for how to play rugby and just enjoying the game until about fifteen or sixteen. Then, they would really focus on competition and at eighteen you would definitely see players coming through.

A single phrase sums up the current system. Muddled priorities.

D'Arcy explains: 'A lot of coaches today haven't played the game, and in a perfect world we would have a guide that sets out the format for each season for them, right up to fifteen or sixteen years of age. Giving kids the skills to play the game from as young an age as possible. Improved skills would lead to a higher standard of rugby that would see improved participation and retention in the club system.

'For today's Under-10s, 11s and 12s, the focus every week is predominantly on winning. Not about how do we play, how do we get better. This type of approach rewards the biggest or fastest kids, where physical attributes dominate like this. So you see kids losing interest in playing because they can't compete. We haven't given them the skills that play to their strengths, which could be a great passing or kicking game.'

D'Arcy warns of the long-term consequences of what we might call this rush for results. At any age. 'If you don't build the fundamental skills at that age, you have a void. So for me, the skill level of players in Ireland is not comparable with a country like New Zealand or South Africa.

'A lot of young kids now like to focus just on the things they are good at. They don't want to focus on the things they're not good at. I saw that in professionalism right the way through.

'Players like to focus on fitness, gym work because getting stronger is quantifiable. Trying to improve your skills is much harder and requires hours of dedicated practice and it is almost impossible to show an improvement.

'People don't like being on a training ground throwing a hundred passes a day. But they will go to the gym and lift weights because they can see instant returns from that. With skills it's different, not so easy.'

He offers an intriguing comparison with New Zealand. 'They grow up playing touch rugby. From five or six years old, playing at school every day. The competition in mastering those ball skills means New Zealand end up with four really high-quality players in every position.'

But, he adds, there is a fine balance between preparing kids to play rugby and winning. 'If winning is the sole focus, you cut corners on the other side of the development.'

It is manifestly apparent that the Academies and production line of young players has been hugely beneficial for Irish rugby. But D'Arcy is concerned that at underage levels, there is a widespread replication of what the professional teams do without really understanding the intricacies.

'Go back to Ireland around 2012/13,' he says.

'We had pre-prescribed, multi-phase plays where we knew where we were going for the next six or seven rucks and that dominated the landscape for a while. But that fed down to the lower levels.

'We created a generation of whiteboard rugby players, like figures being moved around on a chess set. That makes players want to be told, "Go here, do that, don't think."

'The problem comes when you take someone out of that and drop them into an environment that is unstructured. Then they struggle. They do not have a bank of experience of having to deal with things on the fly in a match. Players prepared in that way may not thrive in professional rugby.'

He offers an analogy of himself, to make the point. 'I changed position at twenty-three years of age from wing to centre. My whole game had been built on broken field running. It meant I had to learn to pass at twenty-three. That is not easy. To be honest, I don't think I ever truly mastered it. It was something I was never overly confident about in my game. I knew technically as well as anyone how to pass the ball, how to get the ball away in one or two steps.

'But in a game that is completely different. In a closed environment you are focusing on the ball, but it's not real life. When you go into a game it is so dynamic and if you don't have your eye to the ball when it's coming and you look at the defender coming up, that's two steps.

'Because I didn't grow up with that as a player it became quite hard for me. I got more confident as the years went on. But it was always a thing I was aware of. Under pressure in a game, the first thing that would go would be your passing. It is a skill that is not as well practised as it should be, or even used to be.'

For someone who made eighty-two appearances for Ireland, this is an extraordinary confession. But it is not made simply for the purposes of self dramatisation; rather, to underline his insistence that all young rugby players should master the basic skills before anything else.

He concedes another thing, too. He is not in love with the structures laid down for young players in school rugby. 'At that level, the less structure you put on it, the better. There is too much structure at the moment and I find it hard to wrap my head around that.

'I would say to the schools, are you trying only to win matches or are you trying to give kids the skills to enjoy playing rugby?'

There is, he insists, a fundamental difference between the two. 'The trouble is, the system is overpoweringly towards winning.'

All of which interlinks with the topic of my next question. Can Ireland get better and go forward from here? It is, he says, a very broad question.

'The short answer is yes. But we would have to change a lot of structures in Ireland to do that. In the wider system, we are still heavily reliant on one province. That is not healthy. If Leinster's quality starts dropping, what happens then?

'There is no comparable school system in Munster, Ulster or Connacht. It begs the question even more, why have we not invested in the club game?

'Every corporation talks about diversity and how powerful that is. The more individual personalities you have in an organisation, the more people try different things and different ideas. The same holds true for sport.

'If you have players that just come through one particular

pathway, they end up thinking and acting very similarly.'

From about 2000 to 2010, there existed what he described as 'a really healthy tension' between Munster and Leinster players. That became a big driver for Ireland. But he doubts that tension is there any more. Then there is the fact that not a single Ulster player made Ireland's matchday twenty-three in the final game of their 2024 Six Nations campaign.

This might seem irrelevant to some readers. But in his quiet, analytical manner, D'Arcy explains just why these aspects matter.

'The other side of this is that we massively and consistently over-perform. Andy Farrell is there for a while, so all the structures are in place and they're not going to change. So I think we are as close to the ceiling as we have been. Getting better is relevant to our performances of late. By April 2024, we had lost four games in twenty-four.

'Then we went to South Africa and beat the world champions in Durban to tie that series 1-1. So I think we are doing pretty well.

'But as for winning a Rugby World Cup, that goes back to the structures. At some point we will get to a semi-final. But I don't see us ever having a squad deep enough to win a World Cup.

'We have only four professional teams and rugby is not a number one sport in Ireland. We lose players to Gaelic and soccer. That means we have only 120-ish professional players and twelve of them are not available as they will be overseas players. It is a small playing pool.

'The reality is, a portion of players will not be good enough. So it's quite a small playing field to pick from. Look at the South Africans. They talk of a group of around 400 players. As for France, they have two or three quality players in every position.

'Realistically, we have one player in fifteen positions and probably another seven or eight players below that of comparable quality. Plus, we have been really well coached (at the top level).

'But it could be done better in Ireland. Imagine if we had four provincial teams at Leinster's current standard. To me, that would be Ireland at its peak, bringing the other three provinces up to Leinster's level. Then you might be capable of winning a World Cup. But you need to have real competition with a minimum of two quality players competing for every position.

'I don't think we have that today.'

So, as things stand, Ireland may well be close to their zenith in international terms.

But if he doesn't necessarily see further great progression in Ireland's fortunes, then he does urgently want to see an overall improvement in skill sets. Nor is he referring solely to Ireland.

'In the game everywhere, I would prefer to see higher skill sets from players rather than just this overt physicality... in the modern game. I'd love to see more players like Matt Giteau, Quade Cooper and Jack Crowley.

'Centres now have become battering rams. I'd love to see a genuine second five-eighths there.

'A lot of northern hemisphere players have a big deficit in their skill sets. As for all the money that has vanished from the game under professionalism, imagine what the quality of players would be like now if all that money had been invested in quality coaches and grassroots coaches.

'I would love it if, by the time my son is twelve, all his peers know how to catch and pass and why they are throwing a pass. Then you can teach them about rucking, mauling and scrummaging. All that stuff is add-ons.

'The fundamental parts of the game are: can you pass, and do you know why you are passing? That, and enjoyment. Some of my most enjoyable rugby was school rugby.'

He smiles at the memory. From another day, another time. 'I spent three years playing senior rugby at school with my friends and absolutely adored it. We didn't have any patterns; we had a spirit of play and after that it was just go out and have fun. Just catch and pass stuff; that was the rugby I played. My favourite rugby.'

What of his favourite player? He saw a few, not least the great Brian O'Driscoll close up many times for Ireland. He thinks the question is hard because he played in three different decades. Nevertheless, one man stands alone.

'At that time, Keith Wood was on a different level, so far ahead of everyone. His professional approach, clear strategy and vision for what was required put him apart from others.'

One central issue concerns him in the modern game. 'The club game is losing support and that is reflective of what we are putting into it. Unless you can change that dynamic, it will continue to decline. I see a situation where a lot of those clubs could close. If we don't do something the worst will happen. But to get people back to club rugby, they need to increase the standard of the game.

'Right now, the clubs are just treading water.'

But on a positive note, he foresees the possibility of change. 'Maybe the lifeline will be as players who played in the last twenty years filter into the decision-making process in the IRFU. But one thing is clear. Club rugby absolutely has a place in the modern-day rugby calendar.'

As for that perennial old chestnut, the GAA, D'Arcy agrees with Mick Dawson's assertion that it will be a fight to the death between the two codes. 'Absolutely. I agree with that. But the consequence of that is that the players suffer, it becomes either/or as far as they're concerned. Players will have to choose one sport only.

'Whereas you can see now some players enjoying playing both sports, I don't see that in the future. I don't think the GAA are scared of rugby. It's just about not losing your best players and trying to recruit the best.

'There are only 70,000 kids born each year in Ireland so everybody is fighting for the same new bodies every year. They are just defending their patch. Ireland is not unique where there is conflict between sports for bodies.'

He says that Ireland is so small he would like to see joined-up thinking across different organisations. Schedules should be more friendly and flexible so that there could be more harmony in the sporting field.

A pipe dream? Probably. Not least because both sides defend their territory like animals their young. 'Let's not be naïve. Rugby would be talking out of the side of its mouth if it pointed the finger at GAA.

'We don't even have our own house in order. I have friends' kids who enjoy playing Gaelic and rugby. But it is rugby that is saying, "You can't play Gaelic as well."

'This is at ages fifteen and sixteen. Meanwhile, other kids that are playing school rugby are not allowed to play club rugby. That is ridiculous. It is one of the most ridiculous things I have ever come across. I would struggle to let my son play for a school that had that attitude. I would prefer him to play club rugby.'

D'Arcy's words on the self-centred schools banning their youngsters from also playing for clubs are an echo of the words of former Monkstown president David O'Brien, expressed earlier in this book. These are the views of rugby men with the health and prosperity of the game at all levels uppermost in their minds.

They offer a revealing contrast with those who seek only to preserve their own corner of the rugby community, still less advocate what is best for young people and the game in general.

CHAPTER 25

Tommy Bowe

Y ou wouldn't think that Gordon D'Arcy's background and upbringing, in the rarefied sporting air of Leinster, would have much in common with that of Tommy Bowe, the Ulsterman who became D'Arcy's colleague both in many Ireland teams and with the 2009 British & Irish Lions.

But you would be wrong.

Indeed, there is one very powerful link between the two men. It goes to the heart of why a great number of rugby players possess skills of handling, catching and on-field vision that bring an added dimension to the four provinces and the Ireland national team. It is their background in GAA.

As a youngster, before he went to Clongowes Wood College, 30 kilometres out of Dublin in County Kildare, D'Arcy played hurling.

Furthermore, when we talked, he made the point forcefully that he thought playing more than one sport was hugely beneficial to most young people. He believed he learned several valuable traits from his time with another code.

On the face of it, Tommy Bowe had a very different background to Gordon D'Arcy's. Bowe, although born in

Monaghan just south of the border, was to attend the Royal School, Armagh and go on to represent Ulster.

D'Arcy, born in Ferns, County Wexford, grew up in a part of Ireland hardly renowned for its rugby heritage. In fact, poor little rugby trails in fifth place on a list of the most popular sports in County Wexford.

Number one is hurling and Gordon D'Arcy played it for several years in his youth.

Meanwhile, up in the north, a young Tommy Bowe also played another game. Gaelic football. He started playing it from seven or eight years of age. It was the only sport in Monaghan and all his friends played. It wasn't until he was seventeen that he made the decision to choose rugby.

But by then, he had learned so much, and understood fully the value of that experience.

'It was hugely beneficial to me when I chose rugby ahead of GAA. You learn a lot of skills in Gaelic and I never once regretted my time playing it.

'Pigeon-holing yourself into one sport at a young age is not healthy because, certainly in rugby, there is a huge attrition rate of players that don't make it.

'Also, the cross-skills you can get between different sports is unbelievable.

'In Gaelic football, one of the things you really learn is about catching a high ball. Shane Horgan was brilliant at this. Rob Kearney and Girvan Dempsey, too. All were good GAA players. It was about running on to the ball and catching it above your head or catching it at full momentum. Whereas rugby is very much based just on jumping straight vertically into the air and catching it in your breadbasket.'

But it wasn't just one attribute Bowe took from his time with other sports.

'I think there are a huge number of skills applicable to each

302

one. Like the vision you see soccer players have or GAA guys have, looking at the bigger pitch rather than just straight up and down with rugby. I think there are a huge amount of transferable skills.'

Bowe pinpointed one other in particular which he always felt served him well when his time came to play rugby.

'There was a big area in attacking the ball at speed, running on to the ball. It was about timing in hitting a space, particularly when the gap was so small. I put a lot of that down to Gaelic football. If it was you against the man marking you it gives you that competitiveness, that sort of timing to see where the ball is going to bounce and try to pre-empt it. Competitiveness to get to the bouncing ball first and come away with it. The ball is there to be had in those circumstances.'

Does Bowe see GAA as an ongoing threat to rugby or are there improved relations between the two?

'The GAA sees rugby as more of a threat than rugby is threatened by GAA. GAA is still the national sport of the country. When I was growing up in Monaghan, there was little to no rugby being played.

'But now, I see Monaghan Rugby Club is packed with youngsters every weekend. The club is going really well, plus a lot of people watch Ireland in the Six Nations and watch provinces like Leinster and Ulster in the European Cup and the URC.

'That was never the case in my young days.'

Mind you, figuratively speaking, he doffs his stylish cap in acknowledgement of many of the GAA players.

'There are a lot of unbelievably talented GAA players out there. If we could get them to play rugby, the Irish team would be in a different stratosphere. But GAA will obviously want to keep its own and it's very important to keep that competitiveness.

'The more I see now, the rugby Academies are picking up players of thirteen and fourteen, and they are training three or four times a week. They're training in the summertime, training through the Gaelic football season and the soccer season. I think that's a bad thing. It's not beneficial. Sports do this, take youngsters at thirteen and younger, to get their own players in their sport. They are scared of losing them.'

Bowe had a glittering career, playing for Ulster, Ireland (sixty-nine caps) and the British & Irish Lions on tours in 2009 and 2013. But he always felt that he had to be that slightly better player when he was with Ulster to win a place in the national side. He sensed this was a unique challenge confronting all players beyond Dublin and Leinster.

When he moved to Wales to play for Ospreys from 2008 to 2012, he felt an even greater need to stand above his competitors for the starting role with the national team.

'I kept telling myself I had to be 10 per cent better than the players from the other provinces in my position if I wanted to get picked, particularly when I went to Wales. I knew that if there was a 50/50 call to be made, I wasn't going to get it. That is why I had to be a bit better.

'It's still the same now. If there were a 50/50 call between a Leinster player or a guy from the other provinces, I would imagine the Leinster player is going to be getting it.

'You have all those Leinster players playing together on a regular basis. Will Andy Farrell stick with players that know each other inside out from club level because it brings out the best in them, or can the Ulster, Munster and Connacht players be 10 per cent better than their counterparts in Dublin, to force their way into the squad?

'In the past, there were guys like Andrew Trimble, Rory Best, Paul O'Connell, Donncha O'Callaghan etc. because in those times there were strong Munster and Ulster squads. But to get yourself into that Irish team today, particularly as an Ulster player, there has to be quite a margin.'

What is the long-term cost of having so much talent from just one province?

Interestingly, in one sense, Bowe refutes that scenario. 'But it's not, if you look at the Irish Under-20s. They have won three Grand Slams or the Six Nations in the last few years. They are very close to the top and there are a lot of players from those other provinces within those teams. You only need two or three players to come through and represent their province and maybe their country.

'The problem is, are they getting the opportunities? We are churning out an awful lot of very talented players at underage level, but how many are coming through to be in the Six Nations and win Grand Slams?

'This is where I think the worry is. We are not seeing these young players playing enough rugby after the Under-20s. Playing once a month isn't any good for them.'

He thinks back to when he was playing. You needed to play two, three or four games in a row to get a feel for things and see if you could really compete at that level, he remembers. 'Nowadays, coaches are happy to take them in training, but I think there is a big difference between training and actual matches.'

His solution to the problem is almost exactly akin to the one I have proposed earlier in this book. He cites the example of former IRFU performance director David Nucifora who persuaded promising youngster Joey Carbery to move to Munster after two years with Leinster.

Bowe says, 'If we are going to see players get the best out of themselves and get more opportunities, they have to be willing and open to moving provinces.

'Obviously as an Ulster supporter, I want to see home-grown players coming through the system. But from a big picture, the Irish point of view, they have to be more open to moving. They might be fourth choice at Leinster and winning medals in Ireland and Europe.

'But they would be better off going and pushing themselves, challenging themselves, if you like, in another team. It must be quite easy to sit there as the third or fourth choice player for Leinster and lift a medal at the end of each year. But they haven't played much rugby.

'I don't think that's great for Irish rugby. Is it really the best for them in the long term? Likewise for the other provinces, it's important they give those younger players an opportunity to step up.

'I know it's a big thing, certainly at Ulster; they want to see home-grown players coming through the youth system and then representing the province and eventually their country.

'It's a tough one but it's a good position to be in because it shows we do have the player pool and the quality of players. It's just how do we get them there?'

Despite his views on the Under-20s and emergence of talent at that age group from all provinces, Bowe admits there is a problem higher up in the system. Does Leinster's dominance concern him?

'As a former Ulster player and Ulster supporter, yes, it's a massive worry. To have one team completely dominating the national team is not great for the three other provinces.

'But the standards of rugby in the last couple of years from Leinster, the quality of players coming through their Academies and schools and a few players from the youth system, it's putting it up to the other provinces to compete with that.

'At this moment in time, I see a couple of very talented Ulster players who could and should be pushing to get themselves into the Irish squad. But from an Ulster point of view, they are not playing well enough whether it be as a team or as individuals to make a case.

'Ulster have a strong schools set-up. It's not quite at the level of Blackrock or St Michael's, Dublin, where you look at someone like James Ryan who has pretty much been professional since the age of fourteen.

'In Belfast, we can't compete with those Dublin schools. Ours are not quite at that level and they don't have the same number of players coming through. Then of course there is the strength and depth in the Leinster Academy. The competition for places is just unbelievable. What Leinster are doing at Academy and school level is what we should all be aiming for.

'But because our rugby schools in the north are not private schools and because rugby is not the be all and end all for the principals of those schools, maybe their attitude, the standard of professionalism and the structures that are given to school kids in Dublin, would not be at the same level in Belfast and Ulster.'

This scenario is an old conundrum. Isn't it just being sentimental to hark back to the days when there were so many Munster players in the national squad and Ulster, too, contributed significantly?

Bowe isn't sure it is just about sentimentalism. 'Munster have an incredible history, but you have to look at that squad. Jack Crowley has come through that system and done unbelievably well. But realistically, it won't be the same in another two or three years because they are going to lose the likes of Peter O'Mahony, Conor Murray; a number of players who have been stalwarts of that Munster and Ireland set-up for a long time.

'So the question is, where do they go to, which players are really going to push themselves into that Irish set-up? They are very much like Ulster. There are few positions available.'

Looking at the health of Irish rugby, he cannot see Ireland's supremacy changing for the next decade. The quality of players coming through is an obvious reason. Then you look at the coaching available to the schools and the standard of rugby at that level. That, he insists, is incredible.

'Then there is the funding they are getting, particularly in Dublin. The likes of private schools and the money that is in the system down in Dublin is only going to improve.

'But can the other provinces keep up with that? I think that Leinster will get stronger and stronger and Ireland will benefit from that. My worry is, will the other provinces get left behind?'

What if they do? What if future Leinster/Munster games just become a fifty-point romp? *if*, that is, Leinster bother to put out a full-strength side. They might not.

That, he says, would be down to David Humphreys, the new IRFU performance director, to try to find ways of negating such a scenario. As Bowe says, it's brilliant to have a strong national team and one strong province, but it's very important to think about the health of the game overall and the individuals in it. Everybody thinks of Munster and the rivalry with Leinster, but it's only a good rivalry if there is a chance of two sides winning, he says.

'Look at motor racing and Formula One. There is very little interest in it now because Verstappen has been winning too easily. For the benefit of the game of rugby it's important that competitiveness and rivalry is there. It's there at the underage level, but when you talk about the senior set-up it's different.'

Then there is the coaching. In that regard, some operate on different planets compared to their opponents at Irish provincial level.

Bowe agrees. 'Look at the way Leinster let Stuart Lancaster go and they brought in a South African World Cup-winning coach, Jacques Nienaber. That's brilliant for Leinster, but it doesn't help the other provinces.'

On another topic, perhaps surprisingly, he said, 'I think of the Aviva Stadium and maybe the atmosphere is not brilliant because this new audience is there to be entertained and they have paid hefty prices for tickets. They want entertainment.

'Rugby people won't always pay those prices. Which means the game must be opened up to everybody.'

Like it or not.

It has been a glittering career and his work in TV ensures it continues. Since 2020, he has been host of Virgin Media Television's *Ireland AM*, the morning show. Even so, Bowe, like most former Irish players, laments the national team's ultimate failure at the 2023 Rugby World Cup.

They couldn't have been in a better position, he felt. But the draw dealt them a bad hand. To have so many strong nations in the same half of the draw was desperate both for them and France, and a real shame for the competition. As soon as they got to the semi-finals, everybody in the host nation and Ireland lost interest. World Rugby needs to take a serious look at that, he says.

'Ireland can't get much closer. Unfortunately, Joe Schmidt did a job on them in the quarter-final. England did the same in the 2024 Six Nations.

'The quarter-final was one that got away. When I played, if we had lost the scrum battle, the battle in the air and the line-outs against New Zealand, we would have lost by forty points. That all happened this time round, and they only lost by four points. They were very unfortunate.'

Bowe says some of the lessons he learned as a schoolboy were a suitable bedrock for life.

'Rugby and sport in general taught me a lot about friendship. About teamwork, about if you work hard together things can happen. One of the biggest things I learned from rugby was respect. Over and over again. Respecting the opposition, shaking hands with an opponent. That wasn't something we did in Gaelic football. Or in soccer. And respecting referees, too. No talking back to the referee.'

He's lucky because he doesn't miss the buzz of top-class rugby. He had a brilliant run, fourteen years of activity in the sport. Most of the time, he performed regally and was paid handsomely. You can't ask for much more.

But in the last three or four years of his rugby days, he was dogged by injuries. Losing some of that searing pace that hallmarked his game was one problem. Another was the need to warm up for an hour before a simple training session, because of his past injuries. The fun goes out of it, he concedes.

Now, he has different challenges and knows he is fortunate to be doing TV.

'It's not quite the same adrenalin rush as running out at the Aviva or scoring against England in the Six Nations. But like rugby, you are representing the people and the team. You don't want to make a cock-up.'

CHAPTER 26

And Finally...

Of all the commendable achievements of Irish rugby these past thirty years under professionalism, four stand out.

None of them has anything to do with winning trophies or titles.

The first is quintessentially Irish. How on earth did a country that fought tooth and nail against the concept of professionalism in the game and feared it might be lost in the dash to a world of money-making, end up being far and away the most successful of the four Home Unions?

Secondly, the success of the game in staying together, keeping links alive throughout the Troubles, is as praiseworthy as any act in its long history.

What rugby did, what it achieved in those dark days, proved conclusively that in the case of a simple sport, amateur even at the time, the whole is greater than the sum of its constituent parts. Furthermore, it offered society a template of how people across religious divides could mix, how they could surpass hatred through friendship and companionship.

The world of rugby was one part of Ireland that united.

The third mighty achievement, which we shall come to in a

while, is the role played in Irish rugby by unknown numbers of unknown people at club level, all roused to work for the benefit of their clubs and communities. This is a heart-warming story that represents the bedrock of the entire game in this country.

Fourthly, it would be absurd to overlook the considerable role played by an increasing number of girls and women who have come to the game in a variety of roles. Theirs has been an outstanding contribution.

Three decades, thirty years into professionalism, it is incontrovertible that Ireland have left most of their competitors in the northern hemisphere, trailing in their wake. On the surface at least, it would appear that the good ship Ireland sails serenely onwards, while her sister ships in Wales, Scotland and England list badly.

Only the French *bateau* is within sight.

The marker post of thirty years into professionalism saw much of the game still convulsed in a struggle for the ideal formula. Never mind just the northern hemisphere. Crowds at Super Rugby matches in South Africa, New Zealand and Australia were dwindling through lack of interest. People were voting with their feet at much of the fare offered.

Even in England, where the game's administrators the Rugby Football Union were once known as the 'moneybags union of world rugby', times were tight. In season 2023/24, Twickenham announced a likely financial deficit and talked of 'significant losses'.

Indeed, things had become so calamitous that RFU officials were no longer able to buy up the finest Château Lafitte or Château Margaux available at the top London auction houses. So Twickenham's renowned wine cellar, always regarded as one of the best in town, lost its lustre. Was nothing sacred?

Yet in Ireland, the transition from strict amateurism to rampant commercialisation under professionalism, seemed, well, seamless. Leinster, average gates of between 15,000 and 18,000, moved their 2024 Investec Champions Cup home semi-final against Northampton to Croke Park and saw 82,300 tickets sold in a matter of hours.

Something similar had occurred for that season's quarter-final, against French club La Rochelle in Dublin. A switch from Leinster's RDS ground to the Aviva Stadium meant an 18,000 crowd suddenly swelled to 51,000. Thousands more were disappointed to miss out.

However, you, the reader of this book, should have long ago reached the conclusion that the author is not someone who believes rugby in Ireland begins and ends at Leinster or, indeed, in the Irish dressing room at the Aviva.

Pin me down and I'll confess so many of the great moments of this journey have occurred far away from Dublin. Just rocking up in places like Donegal Town, Drogheda, Oughterard, Dingle and Westport, and making contact with some of the local rugby folk to chew the cud about this great old game, represented a delightful experience.

Yes, it rained. Of course it rained. It usually does. There is a reason the fields of this country look like someone with an enormous tin of green paint has been at work. The compensation comes with the shafts of bright sunlight that illuminate the land *après le déluge*. That is a sight to make you feel glad to be alive.

But the warmth of the welcome offered, the simple and humble wish to help and offer some views on their clubs and the game in general, marked these individuals out as special people.

In fact, most are more than just special. They are largely anonymous. They go about their tasks associated with their local clubs with a cheery expression and friendly manner. They will happily fulfil any task, whatever their title.

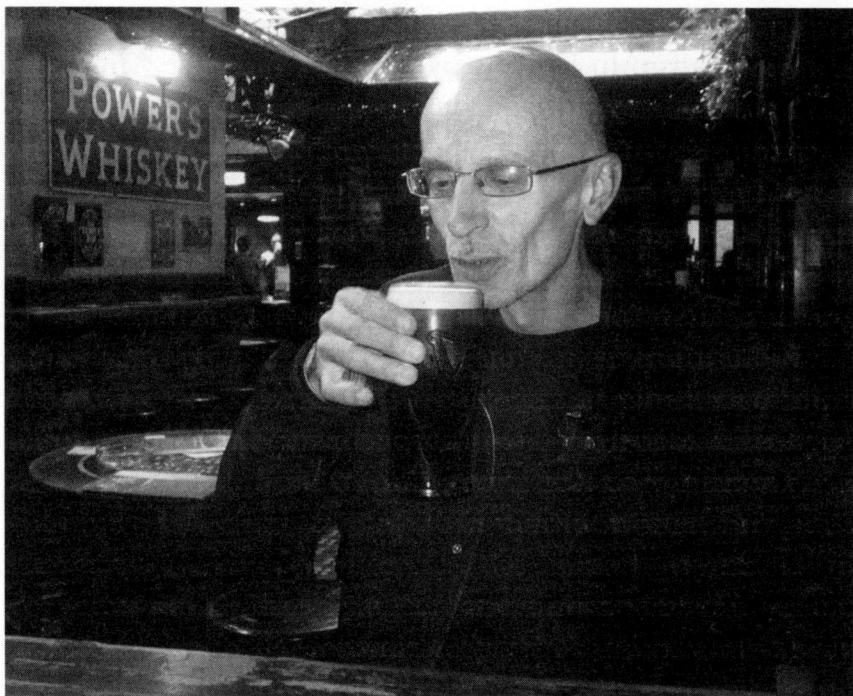

It's rugby, it's Ireland and it's a perfect pint!

You may find the first-team coach with a bucket of paint in his hand, smartening up the surroundings ahead of a new season. The club president at Inishowen can often be found making coffees and handing round plates of biscuits for everyone. It's much the same at places like Clonakilty, Omagh, Sligo, Skerries, Monkstown and assorted other clubs in all corners of Ireland.

Everyone mucks in, whatever the task. Everyone helps.

For these people have a simple desire. To strengthen their club, to see it go forward, making strides both on and off the field for the benefit of their local communities and the fostering of friendships. They put their heart and soul into their local club. But sadly, such commitment and effort is not always acknowledged by those in authority.

The greatest betrayal through the thirty years of professionalism in Irish rugby is of these people. They have become largely ignored, left to fend for themselves, and what they represent, too often overlooked. The folly of this mentality is hard to exaggerate.

Virtually to a man, or woman, these people would ignore plaudits for their work. They give copious amounts of their time yet the only reward they seek is to see their club flourish. New members, new players; these are the benefits they crave. Plus the friendships that are the hallmarks of junior clubs right across the world. They're uninterested in the spotlight, unless it is for their club. Never themselves.

Yet too many at the top of rugby in Ireland (like most other countries, it should be said) seem of a different persuasion. They are too ready to dismiss these loyal servants of the game as some kind of outsiders. Worse still, many of those in authority appear to believe that the role played by these people is largely meaningless in the bright, brash new world of professionalism.

This, of course, is the price any rugby nation pays when its governing body is in charge of both the amateur and professional wings. The demands and needs of the two, completely separate elements of the game, widen almost by the day. Alas, most of the big money sponsors gravitate towards the professional arm where doing big corporate deals, selling tickets and making as much money as possible are the priorities of the union.

I have long believed there is nothing wrong in that. What is unacceptable is when those in the world of junior clubs are overlooked and regarded as just a small, irrelevant minority. People and clubs who have nothing in common with the professional union.

Those in charge at Lansdowne Road might do well to reflect upon what happens when anything in society, whether it be a rugby union club, a small provincial town theatre or whatever ignores its base support.

We only need look at society as a whole in this year, 2025, to see the long-term cost of ignoring or, still worse, kicking away the pillars that underpinned key structures of a nation. This universal trend that has run across the Western world has seen support and respect for organisations like the state, the Church, forces of law and order, teachers and parents be allowed to erode. The cost to society already is significant.

Likewise with the denuding of junior rugby clubs across this island. They play a key role in society by offering young people friendship, companionship, a means of fitness and understanding the values associated with the sport. Most of those values are interchangeable with life.

Allow these small, in some cases tiny clubs to wither and society overall will pay a bill. It is, therefore, imperative that those at the top understand that simply offering token help without any meaningful commitment is just not good enough.

Former Ireland centre Gordon D'Arcy, a much-respected voice in Irish sports circles, calls the game's handling of junior clubs in this country 'p*** poor'. But D'Arcy is no revolutionary. All he is seeking is proper acceptance of and assistance for the lower levels of the game. Keith Wood strongly emphasised similar views.

There is much to admire in Irish rugby. Their handling of professionalism in the men's game and the structures built on through the provincial teams have been strong. Likewise, the schools system which has all the hallmarks of professionalism. It is important to remember those points.

Meanwhile, plenty of other issues arose in my conversations. For instance, will Ireland's current hegemony last forever? No, is the short answer. It never does. It may well do for a while yet. But always a foe lurks ready to strike, as England did against all expectations at Twickenham in March 2024. Defeat didn't cost Ireland the Six Nations title, but they missed a Grand Slam because of England's victory. That was a lesson for any nation in a so-called position of supremacy.

We can be sure France, with all their immensely powerful playing resources, will rise again. England, too, will surely at some point shake off their lethargy of recent times.

But in a sense, it isn't about how many Grand Slams or Six Nations trophies Ireland win in this great era. It's more about what condition will these Grand Slammers leave the game across their own country, when they finally finish?

If you missed a Grand Slam in 2024, it doesn't matter if the roof was fixed and the internal problems solved in those sunny times. By that I mean an equal spread can be found for the benefit of all involved in Irish rugby. Fail to do that and history may judge harshly those who presided over even this successful era.

Many in Irish rugby circles away from Dublin 4 believe there is too much focus on the national team and provincial sides. What about the clubs, they ask? With good reason, it would seem.

No one wishes to downplay the success of the national team, awash, as I wrote at the start, in silver cups, trophies and adulation. But equally, it would be madness to overlook the enthusiasm and contribution of the volunteers at so many junior and senior clubs. In their local environments, they have become an integral part of society, fulfilling a vital role in their communities.

Long may that continue. To offer a sporting outlet for young people of both sexes is a praiseworthy achievement. Especially when you are considering isolated communities or small towns and villages several hours away from a major city.

The sheer hard work and commitment of the people at all these clubs is admirable.

We can but hope they persevere and come through. For without them, Ireland, like every other rugby-playing nation, will be hugely reduced.

I touched a little while back in this sketch on one element of rugby football unique to this island. The Troubles, which ran for the better part of almost four decades, presented those in Irish rugby associated with the game with a considerable challenge. Not just of an intellectual kind but a physical challenge. In some cases, a mortal one.

Many innocent people who followed, enjoyed, indeed even loved this game, lost their lives in the years from the late 1960s to 1998 when the Good Friday Agreement was eventually signed. Even for those who did not succumb, these were years of deep angst, of fear and concern. Ordinary lives were uprooted, threatened.

But within what we might call the rugby code, there burned a fierce flame of determination that links between rugby clubs and men both sides of the border should not be extinguished. That flame of resistance, and hope, never went out.

In my humble opinion, this book is enriched by some tales of those who were there in those times and helped keep the flame burning. It was never easy, often complicated and sometimes dangerous. But they did it because their love for this game and for their homelands ran deep in their souls.

People were prepared to stand up to danger, to fulfil training sessions and fixtures; also to mix with their opponents whether they were from the north or south. Some, such as Nigel Carr who speaks most movingly in these pages, nearly lost their lives in their pursuit of the game.

I loved the story of Galwegians calling their contact at the Ballymena club at the height of the Troubles. Not, as someone

318

immediately thought, to call off the fixture. That wasn't on the cards at all.

What they wanted was a little financial assistance in terms of the cost of an aircraft to fly them into the north and avoid troubles on the roads. Ballymena, in the spirit of the game, readily agreed.

What is more, the party from Galwegians enjoyed themselves so much in the after-match company of the Ulstermen that they got stuck into the Guinness at the Ballymena clubhouse until the phone rang. It was the pilot of the plane waiting at Aldergrove airport warning them if they didn't come now, he'd fly home and leave them.

Finally in this summary, we come to an issue of enormous importance to the game and its future. The increasing role being played by women.

It is undeniable that rugby has changed from past times. Most clubs report a falling off in support among active players. All over Ireland (and plenty of other countries, too) playing numbers are in decline. Where some clubs fielded six or seven teams, now they are more likely to be down to two. Society has changed; other attractions, demands and responsibilities intrude upon young people's lives.

It doesn't achieve an awful lot to look simply at the downside of this, bemoaning a past era. That's like a modern-day milliner gazing forlornly at a photo of a crowd around the early 1900s. Almost everyone was wearing a hat.

That is not to minimise the problem. Some great old clubs, amateur and professional, have gone to the wall.

But in case it has escaped someone's attention, there has been an extraordinary surge of enthusiasm in a new section of the sport. Women's rugby.

All over Ireland, people told me of the burgeoning interest in the women's game. Furthermore, it is not confined solely to a humble club level. Marvellously, there now exists a Women's World Cup, a Women's Six Nations and, in a few years, a British & Irish Lions Women's tour Down Under.

At clubs great and small, famous and unknown, large numbers of girls and young women throughout Ireland are flocking to the game. Truly, this has been a fantastic development in the sport. Girls brought young to the game have forged friendships that have lasted years. The sheer pleasure of being together and playing this game with their friends has appealed to a multitude of girls and young women.

My chat with two young women at the Oughterard club outside Galway was a stirring illustration of their enthusiasm for rugby. Hannah Clarke and Karly Tierney have revelled in the qualities of the game and the opportunities it has brought them. They are not alone.

You might say this extraordinary growth in the female game is no kind of compensation for the loss of some senior men's clubs. Sorry, but I don't. To me, it is almost impossible to overstate the importance of women playing the game and supporting it in such numbers.

What is more, by their enthusiasm and growing love for the sport, the girls and young women have built a potentially huge market for sponsors to explore. The value of this to the game at large is considerable.

The sheer numbers of these girls and young women offers unions like the IRFU glorious opportunities. In some cases, the girls have almost literally saved some smaller clubs from going out of business. They turn up in healthy numbers for training sessions and matches. Off the field, too, women are playing an increasingly important role in the management and direction of these clubs. Liz Brady at Westport and Anne Scott at Inishowen, with whom I talked, are just two of numerous women doing Trojan work behind the scenes.

For sure, rugby would be an altogether poorer sport but for the infusion of passion, interest and perception brought by the women.

But who in official corridors of power truly understands this explosion of input in the women's game? Furthermore, who is exploiting it in the right way? Who will chart a future path of prosperity for the women's game?

If the task is to be left to those officials in Dublin focusing 90 per cent of their time on the men's professional game, then we risk atrophy in the women's game.

Increasingly, it seems to me, there are four elements of this game operating in Ireland: the professional men's game, the amateur men's game, women's rugby and schools/children's rugby.

To suggest the same people in the IRFU can comfortably and innovatively run all four at the same time is faintly ridiculous. It is surely time for the four to be divided up with their own officials and administrators.

It is called embracing the future.

But whatever, let's raise a glass to what Ireland have achieved in rugby terms in this professional era. Yes, as old Tom Gilligan of Sligo said, a clap on the back is only 12 inches from a kick in the arse.

But it's undeniable. There have been an awful lot more of the former than the latter for Irish rugby these last years.

And rightly so.

ACKNOWLEDGEMENTS

One group of people made this book an absolute delight to research and write.

The people of Ireland.

They were the ones who kept me at it, kept me positive, kept suggesting new ways and different people to contact. Some of them were also my fiercest critics (you know who you are!) and what you see as the final product is immensely enhanced by the great good wisdom and advice I received from all manner of people.

Wherever I was, whoever I was with, there was a warm welcome at almost every turn. As an author, you can find that wonderfully beguiling.

But of course, there was a serious book to get out, a fact which seldom escaped my mind or attention.

I detected quite an eagerness to promulgate views, to offer a candid portrait of life at their clubs with all the challenges therein. While some cauliflower-eared props of the modern day earn a King's ransom and live a life of luxury which their battered old predecessors could never have imagined prior to professionalism, some have been dealt a poor hand by the game's change of status and focus.

By no means all the clubs I visited were in pristine health. But in almost every case, there was a flame of hope which continued to burn. Those charged with these clubs' futures refused to let it go out.

Of course, the basic reality is that there would have been no book but for the efforts of my agent, David Luxton, and, once the whole process was under way, my editor at Allen & Unwin, Ed Faulkner, who made many helpful suggestions. Thank you also to Harry O'Sullivan for his due diligence in the editorial process.

Collectively, we got there in the end and my thanks to all for their differing roles. My grateful thanks, too, to Ollie Campbell for writing the foreword.

In no particular order, I would like to thank the following people I met and interviewed during my travels.

David O'Brien at Monkstown RFC, Bill Mulcahy at Skerries and Seamie Briscoe at Drogheda. In Belfast, I sat down together with J. J. McCoy and Brian McCall, the basis for an enthralling opening chapter and who both contributed more later, then individually with Willie John McBride, Nigel Carr and Trevor Ringland.

At City of Derry RFC, Gerald and Richard McCarter plus Mark McFeely all offered different views on the club and its times plus their own experiences. Gerald kindly drove me around the city and surrounding area to give me an overall picture of the scene.

I then journeyed north to Carndonagh to see how a vibrant little club, Inishowen, was faring. There, club president Anne Scott proudly showed me around and shared some personal experiences on what the club meant to her.

From there, I went to Omagh where Allan Duncan and Keith Murnaghan were valuable guides as well as welcoming hosts. I admire the extent of their achievements at that club.

Donegal Town was next where Keith Anderson entertained me regally, then to Sligo where I met Tom Gilligan and on to Westport, where Liz Brady warmly welcomed me.

After that, there was a drive to little Oughterard, where Norman Tierney, Aidan O'Flynn and Jack Clarke were

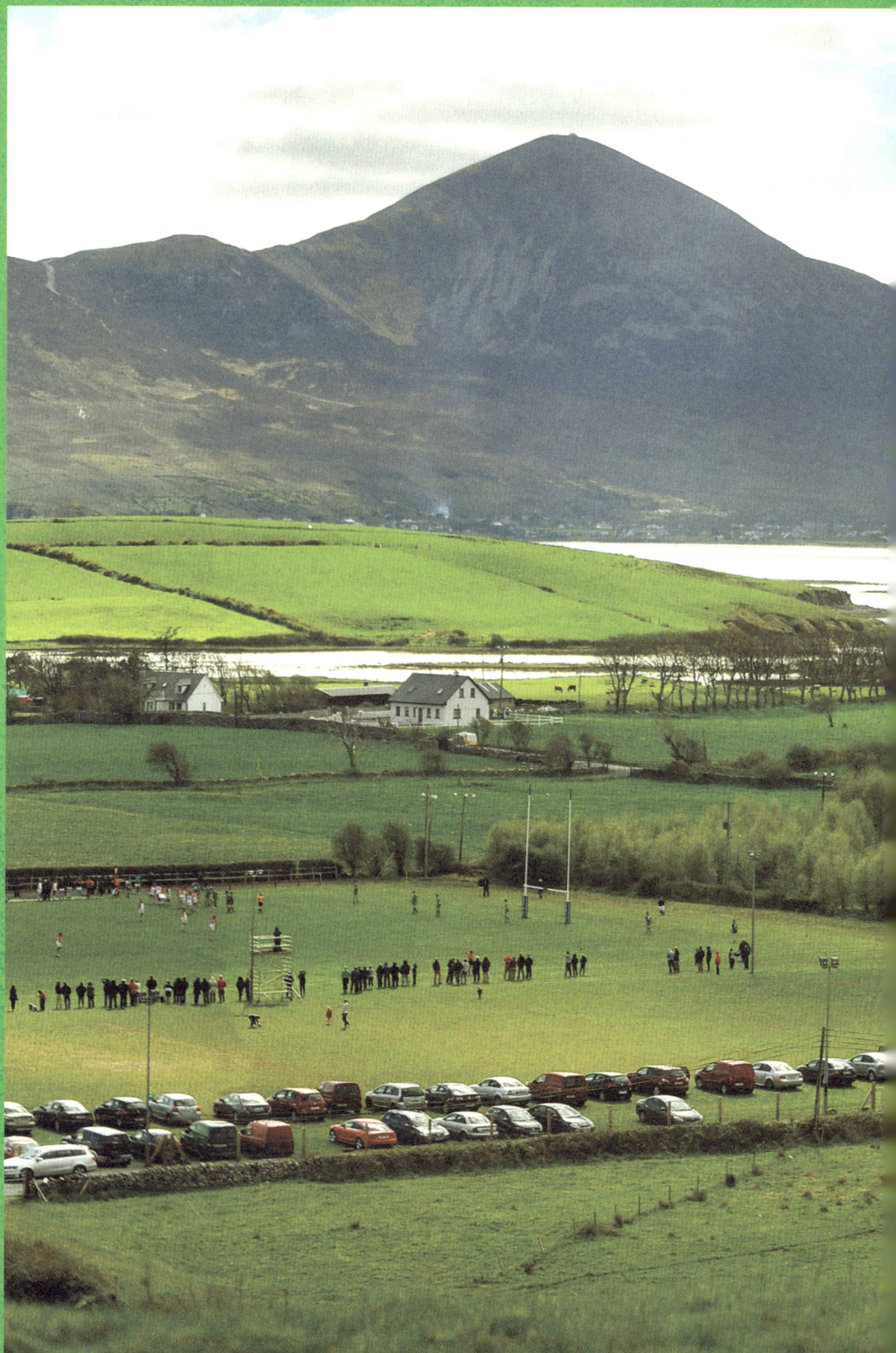

TRIUMPHS, TROPHIES AND TROUBLES

When I wrote *The Jersey* in 2018 about New Zealand rugby, I made it clear it was not the definitive book on the subject. Likewise, this book on Irish rugby. I could never make such an absurd claim. Ireland's rugby history and present has far more knowledgeable Irish writers than me to tell its story.

Rather, I wrote it, inviting the reader to join me, an outsider, on the gentle journey I took, ambling around this beautiful part of the world. If you like rugby, I'd say that's a definite advantage!

The considerable help of so many people on that journey is deeply appreciated.

Peter Bills
London.

thoroughly informative and helpful. Thanks, too, to Karly Tierney and Heather and Hannah Clarke.

Then came the long journey south-west to 'Rugbaí Chorca Dhuibhne', the club of Dingle, where Paddy Fenton proved to be a highly valued source, both at the time and afterwards.

East to Limerick, where I met the irrepressible Keith Wood at his beloved Garryowen club, as well as club official Kieran Ryan. Then to Cork and the clubs of Kinsale and Clonakilty.

I criss-crossed Ireland again to reach Dublin where I could trace the game's origins from 1854, but also Leinster's role at several levels in the modern-day game.

Gordon D'Arcy offered several highly perceptive thoughts, on both his own experiences but also the modern-day scene. Mick Dawson came to meet me at a city hotel to recount his own times as CEO during Leinster's golden era. With both of them, it was great to recharge friendships from back in the day. On the schools scene, Bobby Byrne was a valued informant.

I owe a deep gratitude to Tony Ward, who was a constant source of great help and advice and gave me some lovely anecdotes of his times playing club rugby in Ireland. Likewise, Tommy Bowe up in the north. Thanks, too, to Hugo MacNeill for his sterling efforts and to Ian Greensill for his work on the text. My thanks to one and all.

Personal friends read part of the manuscript and offered many worthy thoughts and constant encouragement. I would like to thank Rolan Knezevic, Mark Baldwin, Tim Arlott, Ian Malin, Peter Franklyn, Joe O'Connor, Martin Lindsay, Darina Clancy, Gerald Mallinick, Serge Manificat and Dave Rogers.

Also to Averil, Hannah and Katie, who played their usual sounding board roles over many long months. My grateful thanks to them and to James for his great story from his time at Monkstown.